Nginx HTTP Server
Second Edition

Make the most of your infrastructure and serve pages
faster than ever with Nginx

Clément Nedelcu

[PACKT] open source*
PUBLISHING   community experience distilled

BIRMINGHAM - MUMBAI

Nginx HTTP Server
Second Edition

First published: July 2010

Second edition: July 2013

Production Reference: 1120713

Published by Packt Publishing Ltd.
Livery Place
35 Livery Street
Birmingham B3 2PB, UK.

ISBN 978-1-78216-232-2

www.packtpub.com

Cover Image by Suresh Mogre (suresh.mogre.99@gmail.com)

Credits

Author
Clément Nedelcu

Reviewers
Michael Shadle

Alex Kapranoff

Acquisition Editor
Usha Iyer

Lead Technical Editor
Azharuddin Sheikh

Technical Editors
Vrinda Nitesh Bhosale

Athira Laji

Dominic Pereira

Project Coordinator
Rahul Dixit

Proofreader
Joel T. Johnson

Indexer
Rekha Nair

Graphics
Valentina D'Silva

Disha Haria

Production Coordinator
Prachali Bhiwandkar

Cover Work
Prachali Bhiwandkar

About the Author

Clément Nedelcu was born in France and studied in UK, French, and Chinese universities. After teaching computer science and programming in several eastern Chinese universities, he worked as a Technology Consultant in France, specializing in web and Microsoft .NET programming as well as Linux server administration. Since 2005, he has also been administering a major network of websites in his spare time. This eventually led him to discover Nginx: it made such a difference that he started his own blog about it. One thing leading to another…

I would like to express my gratitude to my wife Julie, my son Leo who was born during the writing of this book and never ceased to cheer me up; my family and my friends who have all been very supportive all along the writing stage. This book is dedicated to Martin Fjordvald for originally directing me to Nginx when my servers were about to kick the bucket. Special thanks to Cliff Wells, Maxim Dounin, and all the folks on the #nginx IRC channel on Freenode.

About the Reviewers

Michael Shadle is a self-proclaimed surgeon, when it comes to procedural PHP. He has been using PHP for over ten years along with MySQL and various Linux and BSD distributions. He has switched between many different web servers over the years and considers Nginx to be the best solution yet.

During the day he works as a senior Web Developer at Intel Corporation on a handful of public-facing websites. He enjoys using his breadth of knowledge to come up with "out of the box" solutions to solve the variety of issues that come up. During the off-hours, he has a thriving personal consulting, web development practice, and has many more personal project ideas than he can tackle at once.

He is a minimalist by heart, and believes that when architecting solutions, starting small and simple allows for a more agile approach in the long run. Michael also coined the phrase, "A simple stack is a happy stack."

Alex Kapranoff was born in a family of an electronics engineer and a programmer for old Soviet "Big Iron" computers. He started to write programs at the age of 12 and has never worked outside of the IT industry since then. After getting his Software Engineering degree with honors he had a short stint in the world of enterprise databases and Windows. Then he settled on open-source Unix-like environments for good, first FreeBSD and then Linux, working as a developer for many Russian companies from ISPs to search engines. Most of his experience has been with e-mail/messaging systems and web security. Right now he is trying his hand at a product and project management position in Yandex, one of the biggest search engines in the world.

He took his first look at Nginx working in Rambler side-by-side with Nginx's author Igor Sysoev before the initial public release of the product. Since then, Nginx has been an essential tool in his kit. He won't launch a website, no matter how complex it is, without using Nginx nowadays.

He strongly believes in the Free Software Movement, loves Perl, plain C, LISP, cooking, and fishing, and lives with a beautiful girlfriend and an old cat in Moscow, Russia.

www.PacktPub.com

Support files, eBooks, discount offers and more

You might want to visit www.PacktPub.com for support files and downloads related to your book.

Did you know that Packt offers eBook versions of every book published, with PDF and ePub files available? You can upgrade to the eBook version at www.PacktPub.com and as a print book customer, you are entitled to a discount on the eBook copy. Get in touch with us at service@packtpub.com for more details.

At www.PacktPub.com, you can also read a collection of free technical articles, sign up for a range of free newsletters and receive exclusive discounts and offers on Packt books and eBooks.

http://PacktLib.PacktPub.com

Do you need instant solutions to your IT questions? PacktLib is Packt's online digital book library. Here, you can access, read and search across Packt's entire library of books.

Why Subscribe?

- Fully searchable across every book published by Packt
- Copy and paste, print and bookmark content
- On demand and accessible via web browser

Free Access for Packt account holders

If you have an account with Packt at www.PacktPub.com, you can use this to access PacktLib today and view nine entirely free books. Simply use your login credentials for immediate access.

Table of Contents

Preface

It is a well-known fact that the market of web servers has a long-established leader: Apache. According to recent surveys, as of January 2013, over 55 percent of the World Wide Web is served by this eighteen-year old open source application. However, for the past few years, the same reports reveal the rise of a new competitor: Nginx, a lightweight HTTP server originating from Russia (pronounced *engine X*). There have been many interrogations surrounding this young web server. Why has the blogosphere become so effervescent about it? What is the reason causing so many server administrators to switch to Nginx since the beginning of 2009? Is this tiny piece of software mature enough to run my high-traffic website?

To begin with, Nginx is not as young as one might think. Originally started in 2002, the project was first carried out by a standalone developer, Igor Sysoev, for the needs of an extremely high-traffic Russian website, namely Rambler, which as of September 2008, received over 500 million HTTP requests per day. The application is now used to serve some of the most popular websites on the Web such as Facebook, Netflix, WordPress, SourceForge, and many more. Nginx has proven to be a very efficient, lightweight, yet powerful web server.

Along the chapters of this book, you will discover the many features of Nginx and progressively understand why so many administrators have decided to place their trust in this new HTTP server, often at the expense of Apache. There are many aspects in which Nginx is more efficient than its competitors are. Primarily, speed. Making use of asynchronous sockets, Nginx does not spawn processes as many times as it receives requests. One process per core suffices to handle thousands of connections, allowing for a much lighter CPU load and memory consumption. Secondly, ease of use. Configuration files are much simpler to read and tweak than with other web server solutions such as Apache. A couple of lines are enough to set up a complete virtual host configuration.

Last but not least, modularity. Not only is Nginx a completely open source project released under a BSD-like license, but it also comes with a powerful plug-in system—referred to as "modules." A large variety of modules are included with the original distribution archive, and many third-party ones can be downloaded online. Overall, Nginx combines speed, efficiency, and power, providing you the perfect ingredients for a successful web server. It appears to be the best Apache alternative as of today.

Although Nginx is available for Windows since version 0.7.52, it is common knowledge that Linux, or BSD-based distributions, are preferred for hosting production sites. During the various processes described in this book, we will therefore assume that you are hosting your website on a Linux operating system such as Debian, CentOS, or other well-known distributions.

What this book covers

Chapter 1, Downloading and Installing Nginx, guides you through the setup process, by downloading and installing Nginx as well as its prerequisites.

Chapter 2, Basic Nginx Configuration, helps you discover the fundamentals of Nginx configuration and set up the Core module.

Chapter 3, HTTP Configuration, details the HTTP Core module which contains most of the major configuration sections and directives.

Chapter 4, Module Configuration, helps you discover the many first-party modules of Nginx among which are the Rewrite and the SSI modules.

Chapter 5, PHP and Python with Nginx, explains how to set up PHP and other third-party applications (if you are interested in serving dynamic websites) to work together with Nginx via FastCGI.

Chapter 6, Apache and Nginx Together, teaches you how to set up Nginx as a reverse proxy server working together with Apache.

Chapter 7, From Apache to Nginx, provides a detailed guide to switching from Apache to Nginx.

Appendix A, Directive Index, lists and describes all configuration directives, sorted alphabetically. Module directives are also described in their respective chapters too.

Appendix B, Module Reference, lists available modules.

Appendix C, Troubleshooting, discusses the most common issues that administrators face when they configure Nginx.

What you need for this book

Nginx is a free and open source software running under various operating systems: Linux-based, Mac OS, Windows operating systems, and many more. As such, there is no real requirement in terms of software. Nevertheless, in this book, and particularly in the first chapter, we will be working in a Linux environment, so running a Linux-based operating system would be a plus. Prerequisites for compiling the application are further detailed in *Chapter 1, Downloading and Installing Nginx*.

Who this book is for

By covering both early setup stages as well as advanced topics, this book will suit web administrators interested in solutions to optimize their infrastructure; whether they are looking into replacing existing web server software or integrating a new tool cooperating with applications already up and running. If you, your visitors, and your operating system have been disappointed by Apache, this book is exactly what you need.

Conventions

In this book, you will find a number of styles of text that distinguish between different kinds of information. Here are some examples of these styles, and an explanation of their meaning.

Code words in text, database table names, folder names, filenames, file extensions, pathnames, dummy URLs, user input, and Twitter handles are shown as follows: "The process consists of appending certain switches to the `configure` script that comes with the source code."

A block of code is set as follows:

```
#user nobody;
worker_processes 1;
```

Any command-line input or output is written as follows:

```
apt-get install nginx
```

Warnings or important notes appear in a box like this.

Tips and tricks appear like this.

Reader feedback

Feedback from our readers is always welcome. Let us know what you think about this book—what you liked or may have disliked. Reader feedback is important for us to develop titles that you really get the most out of.

To send us general feedback, simply send an e-mail to feedback@packtpub.com, and mention the book title via the subject of your message.

If there is a topic that you have expertise in and you are interested in either writing or contributing to a book, see our author guide on www.packtpub.com/authors.

Customer support

Now that you are the proud owner of a Packt book, we have a number of things to help you to get the most from your purchase.

Downloading the example code

You can download the example code files for all Packt books you have purchased from your account at http://www.packtpub.com. If you purchased this book elsewhere, you can visit http://www.packtpub.com/support and register to have the files e-mailed directly to you.

Errata

Although we have taken every care to ensure the accuracy of our content, mistakes do happen. If you find a mistake in one of our books—maybe a mistake in the text or the code—we would be grateful if you would report this to us. By doing so, you can save other readers from frustration and help us improve subsequent versions of this book. If you find any errata, please report them by visiting http://www.packtpub.com/submit-errata, selecting your book, clicking on the **errata submission form** link, and entering the details of your errata. Once your errata are verified, your submission will be accepted and the errata will be uploaded on our website, or added to any list of existing errata, under the Errata section of that title. Any existing errata can be viewed by selecting your title from http://www.packtpub.com/support.

Piracy

Piracy of copyright material on the Internet is an ongoing problem across all media. At Packt, we take the protection of our copyright and licenses very seriously. If you come across any illegal copies of our works, in any form, on the Internet, please provide us with the location address or website name immediately so that we can pursue a remedy.

Please contact us at copyright@packtpub.com with a link to the suspected pirated material.

We appreciate your help in protecting our authors, and our ability to bring you valuable content.

Questions

You can contact us at questions@packtpub.com if you are having a problem with any aspect of the book, and we will do our best to address it.

1
Downloading and Installing Nginx

In this first chapter, we will proceed with the necessary steps towards establishing a functional setup of Nginx. This moment is crucial for the smooth functioning of your web server—there are some required libraries and tools for installing the web server, some parameters that you will have to decide upon when compiling the binaries, and there may also be some configuration changes to perform on your system.

This chapter covers the following:

- Downloading and installing the prerequisites for compiling the Nginx binaries
- Downloading a suitable version of the Nginx source code
- Configuring Nginx compile-time options
- Controlling the application with an `init` script
- Configuring the system to launch Nginx automatically on startup

Setting up the prerequisites

As you can see, we have chosen to download the source code of the application and compile it manually, as opposed to installing it using a package manager, such as Yum, Aptitude, or Yast. There are two reasons behind this choice. First, the package may not be available in the enabled repositories of your Linux distribution. On top of that, the rare repositories that offer to download and install Nginx automatically mostly contain outdated versions. More importantly, there is the fact that we need to configure a variety of significant compile-time options. As a result of this choice, your system will require some tools and libraries for the compilation process.

Depending on the optional modules that you select at compile time, you will perhaps need different prerequisites. We will guide you through the process of installing the most common ones, such as GCC, PCRE, zlib, and OpenSSL.

> If your operating system offers the possibility to install the Nginx package from a repository, and you are confident enough that the available version will suit all of your needs with the modules included by default, you could consider skipping this chapter altogether and simply run one the following commands. We still recommend getting the latest version and building it from source seeing as it contains the latest bug fixes and security patches. For a Debian-based operating system:
>
> ```
> apt-get install nginx
> ```
>
> For Red Hat-based operating systems:
>
> ```
> yum install nginx
> ```

GCC – GNU Compiler Collection

Nginx is a program written in C, so you will first need to install a compiler tool such as the **GNU Compiler Collection (GCC)** on your system. GCC may already be present on your system, but if that is not the case you will have to install it before going any further.

> GCC is a collection of free open source compilers for various languages—C, C++, Java, Ada, FORTRAN, and so on. It is the most commonly used compiler suite in the Linux world, and Windows versions are also available. A vast amount of processors are supported, such as x86, AMD64, PowerPC, ARM, MIPS, and more.

First, make sure it isn't already installed on your system:

```
[alex@example.com ~]$ gcc
```

If you get the following output, it means that GCC is correctly installed on your system and you can skip to the next section:

```
gcc: no input files
```

If you receive the following message, you will have to proceed with the installation of the compiler:

```
~bash: gcc: command not found
```

GCC can be installed using the default repositories of your package manager. Depending on your distribution, the package manager will vary—yum for a Red Hat-based distribution, apt for Debian and Ubuntu, yast for SuSE Linux, and so on. Here is the typical way to proceed with the download and installation of the GCC package:

```
[root@example.com ~]# yum groupinstall "Development Tools"
```

If you use apt-get:

```
[root@example.com ~]# apt-get install build-essentials
```

If you use another package manager with a different syntax, you will probably find the documentation with the man utility. Either way, your package manager should be able to download and install GCC correctly, after having solved the dependencies automatically. Note that this command will not only install GCC, it also proceeds with downloading and installing all common requirements for building applications from source, such as code headers and other compilation tools.

The PCRE library

The **Perl Compatible Regular Expression (PCRE)** library is required for compiling Nginx. The Rewrite and HTTP Core modules of Nginx use PCRE for the syntax of their regular expressions, as we will discover in later chapters. You will need to install two packages—pcre and pcre-devel. The first one provides the compiled version of the library, whereas the second one provides development headers and source for compiling projects, which are required in our case.

Here are example commands that you can run in order to install both the packages.

Using yum:

```
[root@example.com ~]# yum install pcre pcre-devel
```

Or you can install all of the PCRE-related packages:

```
[root@example.com ~]# yum install pcre*
```

If you use apt-get:

```
[root@example.com ~]# apt-get install libpcre3 libpcre3-dev
```

If these packages are already installed on your system, you will receive a message saying something like **Nothing to do**, in other words, the package manager did not install or update any component:

 Both components are already present on the system.

The zlib library

The zlib library provides developers with compression algorithms. It is required for the use of gzip compression in various modules of Nginx. Again, you can use your package manager to install this component as it is part of the default repositories. Similar to PCRE, you will need both the library and its source — zlib and zlib-devel

Using yum:

```
[root@example.com ~]# yum install zlib zlib-devel
```

Using apt-get:

```
[root@example.com ~]# apt-get install zlib1g zlib1g-dev
```

These packages install quickly and have no known dependency issues.

OpenSSL

The OpenSSL project is a collaborative effort to develop a robust, commercial-grade, full-featured, and open source toolkit implementing the Secure Sockets Layer (SSL v2/v3) and Transport Layer Security (TLS v1) protocols as well as a full-strength general purpose cryptography library. The project is managed by a worldwide community of volunteers that use the Internet to communicate, plan, and develop the OpenSSL toolkit and its related documentation. For more information, visit `http://www.openssl.org`

The OpenSSL library will be used by Nginx to serve secure web pages. We thus need to install the library and its development package. The process remains the same here—you install openssl and openssl-devel:

```
[root@example.com ~]# yum install openssl openssl-devel
```

Using apt-get:

```
[root@example.com ~]# apt-get install openssl openssl-dev
```

 Please be aware of the laws and regulations in your own country. Some countries do not allow usage of a strong cryptography. The author, publisher, and the developers of the OpenSSL and Nginx projects will not be held liable for any violations or law infringements on your part.

Now that you have installed all of the prerequisites, you are ready to download and compile the Nginx source code.

Downloading Nginx

This approach to the download process will lead us to discover the various resources at the disposal of server administrators—websites, communities, and wikis all relating to Nginx. We will also quickly discuss the different version branches available to you, and eventually select the most appropriate one for your setup.

Websites and resources

Although Nginx is a relatively new and growing project, there are already a good number of resources available on the World Wide Web (WWW) and an active community of administrators and developers.

The official website, which is at www.nginx.org, looks rather bare and does not provide a tremendous amount of information or documentation, other than links for downloading the latest versions. On the contrary, you will find a lot of interesting documentation and examples on the official wiki, wiki.nginx.org, seen below:

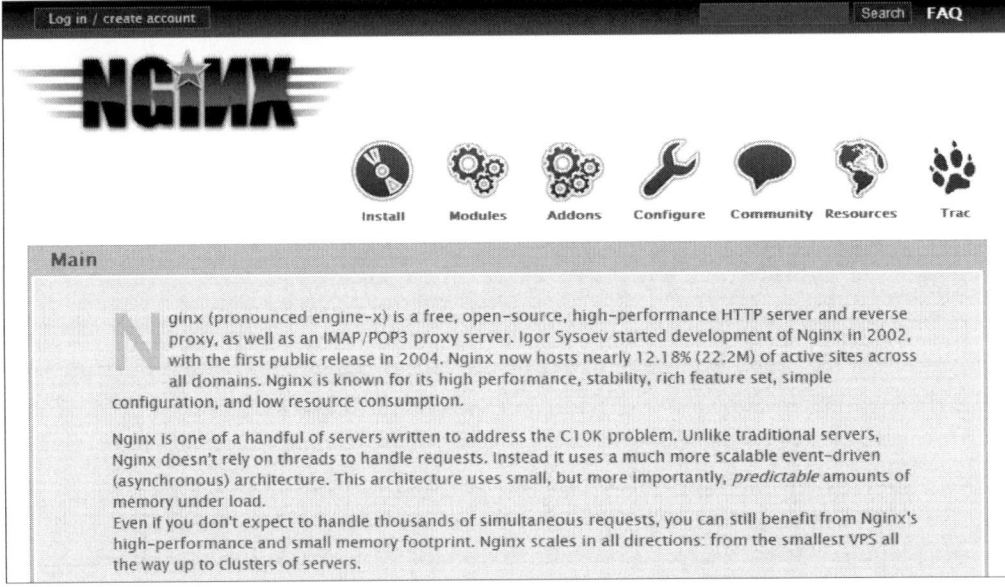

The wiki provides a large variety of documentation and configuration examples, and it may prove very useful to you in many situations. Moreover, it can be edited by its (registered) users, which is a great help towards keeping the documentation up-to-date. If you have specific questions though, you might as well use the forums—forum.nginx.org. An active community of users will answer your questions in no time. Additionally, the Nginx mailing list, which is relayed on the Nginx forum, will also prove to be an excellent resource for any question you may have. And if you need direct assistance, there is always a bunch of regulars helping each other out on the IRC channel #Nginx on irc.freenode.net.

Another interesting source of information—the **blogosphere**. A simple query on your favorite search engine should return a good amount of blog articles documenting Nginx, its configuration, and modules.

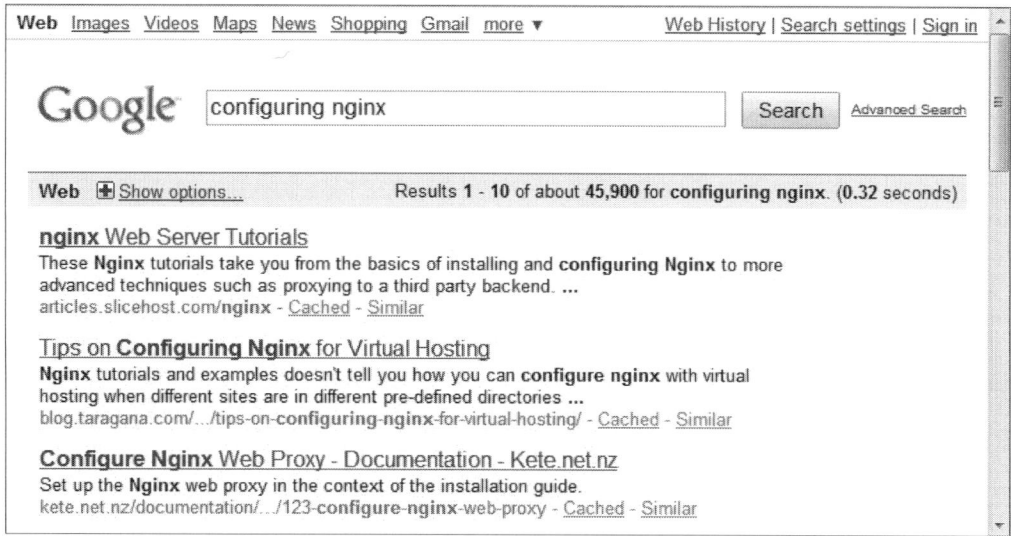

Personal websites and blogs documenting Nginx

It's now time to head over to the official website and get started with downloading the source code for compiling and installing Nginx. Before you do so, let us have a quick summary of the available versions and the features that come with them.

Version branches

Igor Sysoev, a talented Russian developer and server administrator, initiated this open source project back in 2002. Between the first release in 2004 and the current version, the market share of Nginx has been growing steadily. It now serves over 15 percent of websites on the Internet, according to a May 2013 Netcraft.com survey. The features are plenty and render the application both powerful and flexible at the same time.

There are currently three version branches on the project:

- **Stable version**: This version is usually recommended, as it is approved by both developers and users, but is usually a little behind the development version.

- **Development version**: This is the latest version available for download. Although it is generally solid enough to be installed on production servers, you may run into the occasional bug. As such, the stable version is recommended, even though you do not get to use the latest features.

- **Legacy version**: If, for some reason, you are interested in looking at the older versions, you will find several of them.

A recurrent question regarding development versions is "are they stable enough to be used on production servers?" Cliff Wells, founder and maintainer of the nginx. org wiki website and community, believes so—"I generally use and recommend the latest development version. It's only bit me once!" Early adopters rarely report critical problems. It is up to you to select the version you will be using on your server, knowing that the instructions given in this book should be valid regardless of the release as the Nginx developers have decided to maintain overall backwards compatibility in new versions. You can find more information on version changes, new additions, and bug fixes in the dedicated change log page on the official website.

Features

As of the stable version 1.2.9, Nginx offers an impressive variety of features, which, contrary to what the title of this book indicates, are not all related to serving HTTP content. Here is a list of the main features of the web branch, quoted from the official website www.nginx.org:

- Handling of static files, index files, and autoindexing; open file descriptor cache.
- Accelerated reverse proxying with caching; simple load balancing and fault tolerance.
- Accelerated support with caching of remote FastCGI servers; simple load balancing and fault tolerance.
- Modular architecture. Filters include Gzipping, byte ranges, chunked responses, XSLT, SSI, and image resizing filter. Multiple SSI inclusions within a single page can be processed in parallel if they are handled by FastCGI or proxied servers.
- SSL and TLS SNI support (TLS with Server Name Indication (SNI), required for using TLS on a server doing virtual hosting).

Nginx can also be used as a mail proxy server, although this aspect is not closely documented in the book:

- User redirection to IMAP/POP3 backend using an external HTTP authentication server
- User authentication using an external HTTP authentication server and connection redirection to an internal SMTP backend
- Authentication methods:
  - POP3: USER/PASS, APOP, AUTH LOGIN/PLAIN/CRAM-MD5
  - IMAP: LOGIN, AUTH LOGIN/PLAIN/CRAM-MD5
  - SMTP: AUTH LOGIN/PLAIN/CRAM-MD5

- SSL support
- STARTTLS and STLS support

Nginx is compatible with many computer architectures and operating systems such as Windows, Linux, Mac OS, FreeBSD, and Solaris. The application runs fine on 32- and 64-bit architectures.

Downloading and extracting

Once you have made your choice as to which version you will be using, head over to www.nginx.org and find the URL of the file you wish to download. Position yourself in your home directory, which will contain the source code to be compiled, and download the file using wget:

```
[alex@example.com ~]$ mkdir src && cd src

[alex@example.com src]$ wget http://nginx.org/download/nginx-1.2.9.tar.gz
```

We will be using version 1.2.9, the latest stable version as of April, 2013. Once downloaded, extract the archive contents in the current folder:

```
[alex@example.com src]$ tar zxf nginx-1.2.9.tar.gz
```

You have successfully downloaded and extracted Nginx. Now, the next step will be to configure the compilation process in order to obtain a binary that perfectly fits your operating system.

Configure options

There are usually three steps when building an application from source—the configuration, the compilation, and the installation. The configuration step allows you to select a number of options that will not be *editable* after the program is built, as it has a direct impact on the project binaries. Consequently, it is a very important stage that you need to follow carefully if you want to avoid surprises later, such as the lack of a specific module or files being located in a random folder.

The process consists of appending certain switches to the configure script that comes with the source code. We will discover the three types of switches that you can activate; but let us first study the easiest way to proceed.

The easy way

If, for some reason, you do not want to bother with the configuration step, such as for testing purposes or simply because you will be recompiling the application in the future, you may simply use the `configure` command with no switches. Execute the following three commands to build and install a working version of Nginx:

```
[alex@example.com nginx-1.2.9]# ./configure
```

Running this command should initiate a long procedure of verifications to ensure that your system contains all of the necessary components. If the configuration process fails, please make sure to check the prerequisites section again, as it is the most common cause of errors. For information about why the command failed, you may also refer to the `objs/autoconf.err` file, which provides a more detailed report:

```
[alex@example.com nginx-1.2.9]# make
```

The `make` command will compile the application. This step should not cause any errors as long as the configuration went fine:

```
[root@example.com nginx-1.2.9]# make install
```

This last step will copy the compiled files as well as other resources to the installation directory, by default, `/usr/local/nginx`. You may need to be logged in as root to perform this operation depending on permissions granted to the `/usr/local` directory.

Again, if you build the application without configuring it, you take the risk to miss out on a lot of features, such as the optional modules and others that we are about to discover.

Path options

When running the `configure` command, you are offered the possibility to enable some switches that let you specify the directory or file paths for a variety of elements. Please note that the options offered by the configuration switches may change according to the version you downloaded. The options listed below are valid with the stable version, `release 1.2.9`. If you use another version, run the `configure --help` command to list the available switches for your setup.

Using a switch typically consists of appending some text to the command line. For instance, using the `--conf-path` switch:

```
[alex@example.com nginx-1.2.9]# ./configure --conf-path=/etc/nginx/nginx.
conf
```

Here is an exhaustive list of the configuration switches for configuring paths:

Switch	Usage	Default Value
`--prefix=`...	The base folder in which Nginx will be installed.	`/usr/local/nginx`. Note: If you configure other switches using relative paths, they will connect to the base folder. For example: Specifying `--conf-path=conf/nginx.conf` will result in your configuration file being found at `/usr/local/nginx/conf/nginx.conf`.
`--sbin-path=`...	The path where the Nginx binary file should be installed.	`<prefix>/sbin/nginx`.
`--conf-path=`...	The path of the main configuration file.	`<prefix>/conf/nginx.conf`.
`--error-log-path=`...	The location of your error log. Error logs can be configured very accurately in the configuration files. This path only applies in case you do not specify any error logging directive in your configuration.	`<prefix>/logs/error.log`.
`--pid-path=`...	The path of the Nginx pid file. You can specify the pid file path in the configuration file. If that's not the case, the value you specify for this switch will be used.	`<prefix>/logs/nginx.pid`. Note: The pid file is a simple text file containing the process identifier. It is placed in a well-defined location so that other applications can easily find the pid of a running program.
`--lock-path=`...	The location of the lock file. Again, it can be specified in the configuration file, but if it isn't, this value will be used.	`<prefix>/logs/nginx.lock`. Note: The lock file allows other applications to determine whether or not the program is running. In the case of Nginx, it is used to make sure that the process is not started twice.

Switch	Usage	Default Value
`--with-perl_ modules_path=`...	Defines the path to the Perl modules. This switch must be defined if you want to include additional Perl modules.	
`--with-perl=`...	Path to the Perl binary file; used for executing Perl scripts. This path must be set if you want to allow execution of Perl scripts.	
`--http-log- path=`...	Defines the location of the access logs. This path is used only if the access log directive is unspecified in the configuration files.	`<prefix>/logs/access.log.`
`--http-client- body-temp-path=`...	Directory used for storing temporary files generated by client requests.	`<prefix>/client_body_temp.`
`--http-proxy- temp-path=`...	Location of the temporary files used by the proxy.	`<prefix>/proxy_temp.`
`--http-fastcgi- temp-path=`...	Location of the temporary files used by the HTTP FastCGI, uWSGI, and SCI modules.	Respectively `<prefix>/ fastcgi_temp`,
`--http-uwsgi- temp-path=`...		`<prefix>/uwsgi_temp`, and `<prefix>/scgi_temp.`
`--http-scgi- temp-path=`...		
`--builddir=`...	Location of the application build.	

Prerequisites options

Prerequisites come in the form of libraries and binaries. You should by now have them all installed on your system. Yet, even though they are present on your system, there may be occasions where the configuration script cannot locate them. The reasons might be diverse, for example, if they were installed in non-standard directories. In order to solve such problems, you are given the option to specify the path of prerequisites using the following switches. Miscellaneous prerequisite-related options are grouped together.

Compiler options

`--with-cc=...`	Specifies an alternate location for the C compiler.
`--with-cpp=...`	Specifies an alternate location for the C preprocessor.
`--with-cc-opt=...`	Defines additional options to be passed to the C compiler command line.
`--with-ld-opt=...`	Defines additional options to be passed to the C linker command line.
`--with-cpu-opt=...`	Specifies a different target processor architecture, among the following values: `pentium`, `pentiumpro`, `pentium3`, `pentium4`, `athlon`, `opteron`, `sparc32`, `sparc64`, and `ppc64`.

PCRE options

`--without-pcre`	Disables usage of the PCRE library. This setting is not recommended, as it will remove support for regular expressions, consequently disabling the Rewrite module.
`--with-pcre`	Forces usage of the PCRE library.
`--with-pcre=...`	Allows you to specify the path of the PCRE library source code.
`--with-pcre-opt=...`	Additional options for building the PCRE library.
`--with-pcre-jit=...`	Build PCRE with JIT compilation support.

MD5 options

`--with-md5=...`	Specifies the path to the MD5 library sources.
`--with-md5-opt=...`	Additional options for building the MD5 library.
`--with-md5-asm`	Uses assembler sources for the MD5 library.

SHA1 options

`--with-sha1=...`	Specifies the path to the SHA1 library sources.
`--with-sha1-opt=...`	Additional options for building the SHA1 library.
`--with-sha1-asm`	Uses assembler sources for the SHA1 library.

zlib options

`--with-zlib=...`	Specifies the path to the zlib library sources.
`--with-zlib-opt=...`	Additional options for building the zlib library.
`--with-zlib-asm=...`	Uses assembler optimizations for the following target architectures: `pentium`, `pentiumpro`.

OpenSSL options

`--with-openssl=...`	Specifies the path of the OpenSSL library sources.
`--with-openssl-opt=...`	Additional options for building the OpenSSL library.

Libatomic	
`--with-libatomic=...`	Forces usage of the `libatomic_ops` library on systems other than `x86`, `amd64`, and `sparc`. This library allows Nginx to perform atomic operations directly instead of resorting to lock files. Depending on your system, it may result in a decrease in `SEGFAULT` errors and possibly higher request serving rate.
`--with-libatomic=...`	Specifies the path of the Libatomic library sources.

Module options

Modules, which will be detailed in *Chapter 3, HTTP Configuration*, and further, need to be selected before compiling the application. Some are enabled by default and some need to be enabled manually, as you will see in the following table. Please note that an exhaustive and more detailed list of modules can be found in *Appendix B, Module Reference*.

Modules enabled by default

The following switches allow you to disable modules that are enabled by default:

Modules enabled by default	Description
`--without-http_charset_module`	Disables the Charset module for re-encoding web pages.
`--without-http_gzip_module`	Disables the Gzip compression module.
`--without-http_ssi_module`	Disables the Server Side Include module.
`--without-http_userid_module`	Disables the User ID module providing user identification via cookies.
`--without-http_access_module`	Disables the Access module allowing access configuration for IP address ranges.
`--without-http_auth_basic_module`	Disables the Basic Authentication module.
`--without-http_autoindex_module`	Disables the Automatic Index module.
`--without-http_geo_module`	Disables the Geo module allowing you to define variables depending on IP address ranges.
`--without-http_map_module`	Disables the Map module that allows you to declare map blocks.
`--without-http_referer_module`	Disables the Referer control module.
`--without-http_rewrite_module`	Disables the Rewrite module.

Modules enabled by default	Description
`--without-http_proxy_module`	Disables the Proxy module for transferring requests to other servers.
`--without-http_fastcgi_module` `--without-http_uwsgi_module` `--without-http_scgi_module`	Disables the FastCGI, uWSGI, or SCGI modules for interacting with respectively FastCGI, uWSGI, or SCGI processes.
`--without-http_memcached_module`	Disables the Memcached module for interacting with the *memcache daemon*.
`--without-http_limit_conn_module`	Disables the Limit Connections module for restricting resource usage according to defined zones.
`--without-http_limit_req_module`	Disables the Limit Requests module allowing you to limit the amount of requests per user.
`--without-http_empty_gif_module`	Disables the Empty Gif module for serving a blank GIF image from memory.
`--without-http_browser_module`	Disables the Browser module for interpreting the User Agent string.
`--without-http_upstream_ip_hash_ module`	Disables the Upstream module for configuring load-balanced architectures.
`--without-http_upstream_least_ conn_module`	Disables the Least Connections feature

Modules disabled by default

The following switches allow you to enable modules that are disabled by default:

Modules disabled by default	Description
`--with-http_ssl_module`	Enables the SSL module for serving pages using HTTPS.
`--with-http_realip_module`	Enables the Real IP module for reading the real IP address from the request header data.
`--with-http_addition_module`	Enables the Addition module which lets you append or prepend data to the response body.
`--with-http_xslt_module`	Enables the XSLT module for applying XSL transformations to XML documents.
	Note: You will need to install the `libxml2` and `libxslt` libraries on your system if you wish to compile these modules.

Modules disabled by default	Description
`--with-http_image_filter_module`	Enables the Image Filter module that lets you apply modification to images.
	Note: You will need to install the `libgd` library on your system if you wish to compile this module.
`--with-http_geoip_module`	Enables the GeoIP module for achieving geographic localization using MaxMind's GeoIP binary database.
	Note: You will need to install the `libgeoip` library on your system if you wish to compile this module.
`--with-http_sub_module`	Enables the Substitution module for replacing text in web pages.
`--with-http_dav_module`	Enables the WebDAV module (Distributed Authoring and Versioning via Web).
`--with-http_flv_module`	Enables the FLV module for special handling of `.flv` (Flash video) files.
`--with-http_mp4_module`	Enables the MP4 module for special handling of `.mp4` video files.
`--with-http_gzip_static_module`	Enables the Gzip Static module for sending pre-compressed files.
`--with-http_random_index_module`	Enables the Random Index module for picking a random file as the directory index.
`--with-http_secure_link_module`	Enables the Secure Link module to check the presence of a keyword in the URL.
`--with-http_stub_status_module`	Enables the Stub Status module, which generates a server statistics and information page.
`--with-google_perftools_module`	Enables the Google Performance Tools module.
`--with-http_degradation_module`	Enables the Degradation module that controls the behavior of your server depending on current resource usage.
`--with-http_perl_module`	Enables the Perl module allowing you to insert Perl code directly into your Nginx configuration files, and to make Perl calls from SSI.

Miscellaneous options

Other options are available in the configuration script, for example, regarding the mail server proxy feature or event management.

Mail server proxy options

`--with-mail`	Enables mail server proxy module. Supports POP3, IMAP4, SMTP. It is disabled by default.
`--with-mail_ssl_module`	Enables SSL support for the mail server proxy. It is disabled by default.
`--without-mail_pop3_module`	Disables the POP3 module for the mail server proxy. It is enabled by default when the mail server proxy module is enabled.
`--without-mail_imap_module`	Disables the IMAP4 module for the mail server proxy. It is enabled by default when the mail server proxy module is enabled.
`--without-mail_smtp_module`	Disables the SMTP module for the mail server proxy. It is enabled by default when the mail server proxy module is enabled.

Event management:

Allows you to select the event notification system for the Nginx sequencer. For advanced users only.

`--with-rtsig_module`	Enables the `rtsig` module to use `rtsig` as event notification mechanism.
`--with-select_module`	Enables the select module to use select as event notification mechanism. By default, this module is enabled unless a better method is found on the system — kqueue, epoll, rtsig, or poll.
`--without-select_module`	Disables the select module.
`--with-poll_module`	Enables the poll module to use poll as event notification mechanism. By default, this module is enabled if available, unless a better method is found on the system — kqueue, epoll, or rtsig.
`--without-poll_module`	Disables the poll module.

User and group options

`--user=...`	Default user account for starting the Nginx worker processes. This setting is used only if you omit to specify the user directive in the configuration file.
`--group=...`	Default user group for starting the Nginx worker processes. This setting is used only if you omit to specify the group directive in the configuration file.

Other options

--with-ipv6	Enables IPv6 support.
--without-http	Disables the HTTP server.
--without-http-cache	Disables HTTP caching features.
--add-module=PATH	Adds a third-party module to the compile process by specifying its path. This switch can be repeated indefinitely if you wish to compile multiple modules.
--with-debug	Enables additional debugging information to be logged.
--with-file-aio	Enables support for Asynchronous IO disk operations.

Configuration examples

Here are a few examples of configuration commands that may be used for various cases. In these examples, the path switches were omitted as they are specific to each system and leaving the default values may simply function correctly.

 Be aware that these configurations do not include additional third-party modules. Please refer to *Chapter 5*, *PHP and Python with Nginx*, for more information about installing add-ons.

About the prefix switch

During the configuration, you should take particular care over the --prefix switch. Many of the future configuration directives (that we will approach in further chapters) will be based on the path you select at this point. While it is not a definitive problem since absolute paths can still be employed, you should know that the prefix cannot be changed once the binaries have been compiled.

There is also another issue that you may run into if you plan to keep up with the times and update Nginx as new versions are released. The default prefix (if you do not override the setting by using the --prefix switch) is /usr/local/nginx. This is a path that does not include the version number. Consequently, when you upgrade Nginx, if you do not specify a different prefix, the new install files will override the previous ones, which among other problems, could potentially erase your currently running binaries.

It is thus recommended to use a different prefix for each version you will be using:

```
./configure --prefix=/usr/local/nginx-1.2.9
```

Additionally, to make future changes simpler, you may create a symbolic link /usr/local/nginx pointing to /usr/local/nginx-1.2.9. Once you upgrade, you can update the link to make it point to /usr/local/nginx-newer.version. This will allow the init script to always make use of the latest installed version of Nginx.

Regular HTTP and HTTPS servers

The first example describes a situation where the most important features and modules for serving HTTP and HTTPS content are enabled, and the mail-related options are disabled:

```
./configure --user=www-data --group=www-data --with-http_ssl_module
--with-http_realip_module
```

As you can see, the command is rather simple and most switches were left out. The reason being is that the default configuration is rather efficient and most of the important modules are enabled. You will only need to include the http_ssl module for serving HTTPS content, and optionally, the "real IP" module for retrieving your visitors' IP addresses in case you are running Nginx as backend server.

All modules enabled

The next situation: the entire package. All modules are enabled and it is up to you whether you want to use them or not at runtime:

```
./configure --user=www-data --group=www-data --with-http_ssl_module
--with-http_realip_module --with-http_addition_module --with-http_xslt_
module --with-http_image_filter_module --with-http_geoip_module --with-
http_sub_module --with-http_dav_module --with-http_flv_module --with-
http_mp4_module --with-http_gzip_static_module --with-http_random_index_
module --with-http_secure_link_module --with-http_stub_status_module
--with-http_perl_module --with-http_degradation_module
```

This configuration opens up a wide range of possible configuration options. *Chapters 3, HTTP Configuration*, to *Chapter 6, Apache and Nginx Together*, provide more detailed information on module configuration.

With this setup, all optional modules are enabled, thus requiring additional libraries to be installed—libgeoip for the Geo IP module, libgd for the Image Filter module, libxml2, and libxslt for the XSLT module. You may install those prerequisites using your system package manager such as running yum install libxml2 or apt-get install libxml2.

Mail server proxy

This last build configuration is somewhat special as it is dedicated to enabling mail server proxy features—a darker and less documented side of Nginx. The related features and modules are all enabled:

```
./configure --user=www-data --group=www-data --with-mail --with-mail_ssl_
module
```

If you wish to completely disable the HTTP serving features and only dedicate Nginx to mail proxying, you may add the `--without-http` switch.

 Note that in the commands listed above, the user and group used for running the Nginx worker processes will be www-data, which implies that this user and group must exist on your system.

Build configuration issues

In some cases, the `configure` command may fail—after a long list of checks, you may receive a few error messages on your terminal. In most (if not all) cases, these errors are related to missing prerequisites or unspecified paths.

In such cases, proceed with the following verifications carefully to make sure you have all it takes to compile the application, and optionally consult the `objs/autoconf.err` file for more details about the compilation problem. This file is generated during the configure process and will tell you exactly where the process failed.

Make sure you installed the prerequisites

There are basically four main prerequisites: GCC, PCRE, zlib, and OpenSSL. The last three are libraries that must be installed in two packages: the library itself and its development sources. Make sure you have installed both for each of them. Please refer to the prerequisites section at the beginning of this chapter. Note that other prerequisites, such as LibXML2 or LibXSLT, might be required for enabling extra modules (for example, in the case of the HTTP XSLT module).

If you are positive that all of the prerequisites were installed correctly, perhaps the issue comes from the fact that the `configure` script is unable to locate the prerequisite files. In that case, make sure that you include the switches related to file paths, as described earlier.

For example, the following switch allows you to specify the location of the OpenSSL library files:

```
./configure [...] --with-openssl=/usr/lib64
```

The OpenSSL library file will be looked for in the specified folder.

Directories exist and are writable

Always remember to check the obvious; everyone makes even the simplest of mistakes sooner or later. Make sure the directory you placed the Nginx files in has *read and write* permissions for the user running the configuration and compilation scripts. Also ensure that all paths specified in the `configure` script switches are existing, valid paths.

Compiling and installing

The configuration process is of utmost importance—it generates a `makefile` for the application depending on the selected switches and performs a long list of requirement checks on your system. Once the `configure` script is successfully executed, you can proceed with compiling Nginx.

Compiling the project equates to executing the `make` command in the project source directory:

```
[alex@example.com nginx-1.2.9]$ make
```

A successful build should result in a final message appearing: `make[1]: leaving directory` followed by the project source path.

Again, problems might occur at compile time. Most of these problems can originate in missing prerequisites or invalid paths specified. If this occurs, run the `configure` script again and triple-check the switches and all of the prerequisite options. It may also occur that you downloaded a too recent version of the prerequisites that might not be backwards compatible. In such cases, the best option is to visit the official website of the missing component and download an older version.

If the compilation process was successful, you are ready for the next step: installing the application. The following command must be executed with root privileges:

```
[root@example.com nginx-1.2.9]# make install
```

The make install command executes the install section of the makefile. In other words, it performs a few simple operations, such as copying binaries and configuration files to the specified install folder. It also creates directories for storing log and HTML files if these do not already exist. The make install step is not generally a source of problems, unless your system encounters some exceptional error, such as a lack of storage space or memory.

 You might require root privileges for installing the application in the /usr/local/ folder, depending on the folder permissions.

Controlling the Nginx service

At this stage, you should have successfully built and installed Nginx. The default location for the output files is /usr/local/nginx, so we will be basing future examples on this.

Daemons and services

The next step is obviously to execute Nginx. However, before doing so, it's important to understand the nature of this application. There are two types of computer applications—those that require immediate user input, thus running on the *foreground*, and those that do not, thus running in the *background*. Nginx is of the latter type, often referred to as **daemon**. Daemon names usually come with a trailing "d" and a couple of examples can be mentioned here—httpd the HTTP server daemon, named the name server daemon, or crond the task scheduler—although, as you will notice, it is not the case for Nginx. When started from the command line, a daemon immediately returns the prompt, and in most cases, does not even bother outputting data to the terminal.

Consequently, when starting Nginx you will not see any text appear on the screen and the prompt will return immediately. While this might seem startling, it is on the contrary a good sign. It means the daemon was started correctly and the configuration did not contain any errors.

User and group

It is of utmost importance to understand the process architecture of Nginx and particularly the user and groups its various processes run under. A very common source of troubles when setting up Nginx is invalid file access permissions—due to a user or group misconfiguration, you often end up getting **403 Forbidden** HTTP errors because Nginx cannot access the requested files.

There are two levels of processes with possibly different permission sets:

- The **Nginx master process**, which should be started as root. In most Unix-like systems, processes started with the root account are allowed to open TCP sockets on any port, whereas other users can only open listening sockets on a port above 1024. If you do not start Nginx as root, standard ports such as 80 or 443 will not be accessible. Additionally, the user directive that allows you to specify a different user and group for the worker processes will not be taken into consideration.

- The **Nginx worker processes**, which are automatically spawned by the master process under the account you specified in the configuration file with the user directive (detailed in *Chapter 2, Basic Nginx Configuration*). The configuration setting takes precedence over the configure switch you may have entered at compile time. If you did not specify any of those, the worker processes will be started as user nobody, and group nobody (or nogroup depending on your OS).

Nginx command-line switches

The Nginx binary accepts command-line arguments for performing various operations, among which is controlling the background processes. To get the full list of commands, you may invoke the help screen using the following commands:

```
[alex@example.com ~]$ cd /usr/local/nginx/sbin
[alex@example.com sbin]$ ./nginx -h
```

The next few sections will describe the purpose of these switches. Some allow you to control the daemon, some let you perform various operations on the application configuration.

Starting and stopping the daemon

You can start Nginx by running the Nginx binary without any switches. If the daemon is already running, a message will show up indicating that a socket is already listening on the specified port:

```
[emerg]: bind() to 0.0.0.0:80 failed (98: Address already in use) […]
[emerg]: still could not bind().
```

Beyond this point, you may control the daemon by stopping it, restarting it, or simply reloading its configuration. Controlling is done by sending signals to the process using the `nginx -s` command.

Command	Description
`nginx -s stop`	Stops the daemon immediately (using the TERM signal)
`nginx -s quit`	Stops the daemon gracefully (using the QUIT signal)
`nginx -s reopen`	Reopens the log files
`nginx -s reload`	Reloads the configuration

Note that when starting the daemon, stopping it, or performing any of the preceding operations, the configuration file is first *parsed* and verified. If the configuration is invalid, whatever command you have submitted will fail, even when trying to stop the daemon. In other words, in some cases you will not be able to even stop Nginx if the configuration file is invalid.

An alternate way to terminate the process, in desperate cases only, is to use the `kill` or `killall` commands with root privileges:

```
[root@example.com ~]# killall nginx
```

Testing the configuration

As you can imagine, this tiny bit of detail might become an important issue if you constantly tweak your configuration. The slightest mistake in any of the configuration files can result in a loss of control over the service—you are then unable to stop it via regular `init control` commands, and obviously, it will refuse to start again.

In consequence, the following command will be useful to you in many occasions. It allows you to check the syntax, validity, and integrity of your configuration:

```
[alex@example.com ~]$ /usr/local/nginx/sbin/nginx -t
```

The `-t` switch stands for *test configuration*. Nginx will parse the configuration anew and let you know whether it is valid or not. A valid configuration file does not necessarily mean Nginx will start though as there might be additional problems such as socket issues, invalid paths, or incorrect access permissions.

Obviously, manipulating your configuration files while your server is in production is a dangerous thing to do and should be avoided at all costs. The best practice, in this case, is to place your new configuration into a separate temporary file and run the test on that file. Nginx makes it possible by offering the `-c` switch:

```
[alex@example.com sbin]$ ./nginx -t -c /home/alex/test.conf
```

This command will parse `/home/alex/test.conf` and make sure it is a valid Nginx configuration file. When you are done, after making sure that your new file is valid, proceed to replacing your current configuration file and reload the server configuration:

```
[alex@example.com sbin]$ cp -i /home/alex/test.conf /usr/local/nginx/
conf/nginx.conf
cp: erase 'nginx.conf' ? yes
[alex@example.com sbin]$ ./nginx -s reload
```

Other switches

Another switch that might come in handy in many situations is -v. Not only does it tell you the current Nginx build version, but more importantly it also reminds you about the arguments that you used during the configuration step—in other words, the command switches that you passed to the `configure` script before compilation.

```
[alex@example.com sbin]$ ./nginx -V
nginx version: nginx/1.2.9
built by gcc 4.4.6 20120305 (Red Hat 4.4.6-4) (GCC)
TLS SNI support enabled
configure arguments: --with-http_ssl_module
```

In this case, Nginx was configured with the `--with-http_ssl_module` switch only.

Why is this so important? Well, if you ever try to use a module that was not included with the `configure` script during the pre-compilation process, the directive enabling the module will result in a configuration error. Your first reaction will be to wonder where the syntax error comes from. Your second reaction will be to wonder if you even built the module in the first place! Running `nginx -V` will answer this question.

Additionally, the -g option lets you specify additional configuration directives in case they were not included in the configuration file:

```
[alex@example.com sbin]$ ./nginx -g "timer_resolution 200ms";
```

Adding Nginx as a system service

In this section, we will create a script that will transform the Nginx daemon into an actual system service. This will result in mainly two outcomes—the daemon will be controllable using standard commands, and more importantly, it will automatically be launched on system startup and stopped on system shutdown.

System V scripts

Most Linux-based operating systems to date use a System-V style *init daemon*. In other words, their startup process is managed by a daemon called `init`, which functions in a way that is inherited from the old **System V** Unix-based operating system.

This daemon functions on the principle of *runlevels*, which represent the state of the computer. Here is a table representing the various runlevels and their signification:

Runlevel	State
0	System is halted
1	Single-user mode (rescue mode)
2	Multiuser mode, without NFS support
3	Full multiuser mode
4	Not used
5	Graphical interface mode
6	System reboot

You can manually initiate a runlevel transition: use the `telinit 0` command to shut down your computer or `telinit 6` to reboot it.

For each runlevel transition, a set of services are executed. This is the key concept to understand here: when your computer is stopped, its runlevel is 0. When you turn it on, there will be a transition from runlevel 0 to the default computer startup runlevel. The default startup runlevel is defined by your own system configuration (in the `/etc/inittab` file) and the default value depends on the distribution you are using: Debian and Ubuntu use runlevel 2, Red Hat and Fedora use runlevel 3 or 5, CentOS and Gentoo use runlevel 3, and so on, as the list is long.

So let us summarize. When you start your computer running CentOS, it operates a transition from runlevel 0 to runlevel 3. That transition consists of starting all services that are scheduled for runlevel 3. The question is — how to schedule a service to be started at a specific runlevel?

/etc/rc.d					
Name	Ext		Size	Changed	Rights	Owner
..				12/29/2009 4:36:09 PM	rwxr-xr-x	root
init.d				10/18/2009 3:31:43 PM	rwxr-xr-x	root
rc0.d				1/1/2010 6:55:49 PM	rwxr-xr-x	root
rc1.d				1/1/2010 6:55:49 PM	rwxr-xr-x	root
rc2.d				1/1/2010 6:55:49 PM	rwxr-xr-x	root
rc3.d				1/1/2010 6:55:49 PM	rwxr-xr-x	root
rc4.d				1/1/2010 6:55:49 PM	rwxr-xr-x	root
rc5.d				1/1/2010 6:55:49 PM	rwxr-xr-x	root
rc6.d				1/1/2010 6:55:49 PM	rwxr-xr-x	root

For each runlevel, there is a directory containing scripts to be executed. If you enter these directories (rc0.d, rc1.d, to rc6.d) you will not find actual files, but rather symbolic links referring to scripts located in the init.d directory. Service startup scripts will indeed be placed in init.d, and links will be created by tools placing them in the proper directories.

What is an init script?

An init script, also known as service startup script or even *sysv script*, is a shell script respecting a certain standard. The script will control a daemon application by responding to commands such as start, stop, and others, which are triggered at two levels. Firstly, when the computer starts, if the service is scheduled to be started for the system runlevel, the init daemon will run the script with the start argument. The other possibility for you is to manually execute the script by calling it from the shell:

```
[root@example.com ~]# service httpd start
```

Or if your system does not come with the service command:

```
[root@example.com ~]# /etc/init.d/httpd start
```

The script must accept at least the start and stop commands as they will be used by the system to respectively start up and shut down the service. However, for enlarging your field of action as a system administrator, it is often interesting to provide further options, such as a reload argument to reload the service configuration or a restart argument to stop and start the service again.

Note that since service httpd start and /etc/init.d/httpd start essentially do the same thing, with the exception that the second command will work on all operating systems, we will make no further mention of the service command and will exclusively use the /etc/init.d/ method.

Init script for Debian-based distributions

We will thus create a shell script for starting and stopping our Nginx daemon and also restarting and reloading it. The purpose here is not to discuss Linux shell script programming, so we will merely provide the source code of an existing init script, along with some comments to help you understand it.

Due to differences in the format of the init scripts from one distribution to another, we will here discover two separate scripts: this first one is meant for Debian-based distributions such as Debian, Ubuntu, Knoppix, and so forth.

First, create a file called `nginx` with the text editor of your choice, and save it in the `/etc/init.d/` directory (on some systems, `/etc/init.d/` is actually a symbolic link to `/etc/rc.d/init.d/`). In the file you just created, copy the following script carefully. Make sure that you change the paths to make them correspond to your actual setup.

You will need root permissions to save the script into the `init.d` directory.

> The complete `init` script for Debian-based distributions can be found in the code bundle.

Init script for Red Hat-based distributions

Due to the system tools, shell programming functions, and specific formatting that it requires, the script described above is only compatible with Debian-based distributions. If your server is operated by a Red Hat-based distribution such as CentOS, Fedora, and many more, you will need an entirely different script.

> The complete `init` script for Red Hat-based distributions can be found in the code bundle.

Installing the script

Placing the file in the `init.d` directory does not complete our work. There are additional steps that will be required for enabling the service. First of all, you need to make the script executable. So far, it is only a piece of text that the system refuses to run. Granting executable permissions on the script is done with the `chmod` command:

```
[root@example.com ~]# chmod +x /etc/init.d/nginx
```

Note that if you created the file as the root user, you will need to be logged in as root to change the file permissions.

At this point, you should already be able to start the service using `service nginx start` or `/etc/init.d/nginx start`, as well as stopping, restarting, or reloading the service.

The last step here will be to make it so the script is automatically started at the proper runlevels. Unfortunately, doing this entirely depends on what operating system you are using. We will cover the two most popular families—Debian, Ubuntu, or other Debian-based distributions and Red Hat/Fedora/CentOS, or other Red Hat-derived systems.

Debian-based distributions

For the former, a simple command will enable the init script for the system runlevel:

```
[root@example.com ~]# update-rc.d -f nginx defaults
```

This command will create links in the default system runlevel folders. For the reboot and shutdown runlevels, the script will be executed with the stop argument; for all other runlevels, the script will be executed with start. You can now restart your system and see your Nginx service being launched during the boot sequence.

Red Hat-based distributions

For the Red Hat-based systems family, the command differs, but you get an additional tool for managing system startup. Adding the service can be done via the following command:

```
[root@example.com ~]# chkconfig nginx on
```

Once that is done, you can then verify the runlevels for the service:

```
[root@example.com ~]# chkconfig --list nginx
Nginx   0:off   1:off   2:on   3:off   4:on   5:on   6:off
```

Another tool will be useful to you for managing system services, namely, ntsysv. It lists all services scheduled to be executed on system startup and allows you to enable or disable them at will:

[`ntsysv` requires root privileges to be executed.]

Note that prior to using `ntsysv`, you must first run the `chkconfig nginx on` command, otherwise nginx will not appear in the list of services.

[**Downloading the example code**

You can download the example code files for all Packt books you have purchased from your account at `http://www.packtpub.com`. If you purchased this book elsewhere, you can visit `http://www.packtpub.com/support` and register to have the files e-mailed directly to you]

Summary

This chapter covered a number of critical steps. We first made sure that your system contained all required components for compiling Nginx. We then proceeded to select the proper version branch for your usage—will you be using the stable version or a more advanced yet potentially unstable one? After downloading the source and configuring the compilation process by enabling or disabling features and modules such as SSL, GeoIP, and more, we compiled the application and installed it on the system in the directory of your choice. We created an *init script* and modified the system boot sequence to schedule for the service to be started.

From this point on, Nginx is installed on your server and automatically starts with the system. Your web server is functional, though it does not yet answer the most basic functionality—serving a website. The first step towards hosting a website will be to establish a configuration file. The next chapter will cover the basic configuration of Nginx and will teach you how to optimize performance based on the expected audience and system resources.

Basic Nginx Configuration

2

In this chapter, we will begin to establish an appropriate configuration for the web server. For this purpose, we first need to approach the topic of syntax used in the configuration files. Then we need to understand the various directives that will let you optimize your web server for different traffic patterns and hardware setups. Finally, we will create some test pages to make sure that everything has been done correctly and that the configuration is valid. We will only approach the basic configuration directives here. The following chapters will detail more advanced topics such as HTTP module configuration and usage, creating virtual hosts, and more.

This chapter covers the following topics:

- Presentation of the configuration syntax
- Basic configuration directives
- Establishing an appropriate configuration for your profile
- Serving a test website
- Testing and maintaining your web server

Configuration file syntax

A configuration file is generally a text file that is edited by the administrator and parsed by a program. By specifying a set of values, you define the behavior of the program. In Linux-based operating systems, a large share of applications rely on vast, complex configuration files, which often turn out to be a nightmare to manage. Apache, Qmail, and Bind — all these names bring up bad memories. The fact is that all of these applications use their own configuration file with different syntaxes and styles. PHP works with a Windows-style `.ini` file, *sendmail* uses the *M4 macro-processor* to compile configuration files, *Zabbix* pulls its configuration from a MySQL database, and so on. There is, unfortunately, no well-established standard, and the same applies to Nginx — you will be required to study a new syntax with its own particularities and its own vocabulary.

On the other hand (and this is one of its advantages), configuring Nginx turns out to be rather simple—at least in comparison to Apache or other mainstream web servers. There are only a few mechanisms that need to be mastered—directives, blocks, and the overall logical structure. Most of the actual configuration process will consist of writing values for directives.

Configuration Directives

The Nginx configuration file can be described as a list of directives organized in a logical structure. The entire behavior of the application is defined by the values that you give to those directives.

By default, Nginx makes use of one main configuration file. The path of this file was defined in the steps described in *Chapter 1, Downloading and Installing Nginx* under the *Build configuration* section. If you did not edit the configuration file path and prefix options, it should be located at /usr/local/nginx/conf/nginx.conf. Now let's take a quick peek at the first few lines of this initial setup:

```
nginx.conf
1    #user   nobody;
2    worker_processes  1;
3    #error_log  logs/error.log;
4    #error_log  logs/error.log  notice;
5    #error_log  logs/error.log  info;
6    #pid        logs/nginx.pid;
7
8    events {
9        worker_connections  1024;
10   }
11
12   http {
13       include       mime.types;
14       default_type  application/octet-stream;
```

A closer look at the first two lines:

```
#user nobody;
worker_processes 1;
```

As you can probably make out from the # character, the first line is a **comment**. In other words, a piece of text that is not interpreted and has no value whatsoever. Its sole purpose is to be read by whoever opens the file, or to temporarily disable parts of an existing configuration section. You may use the # character at the beginning of a line or following a directive.

The second line is an actual statement — a **directive**. The first bit (`worker_processes`) represents a setting key to which you append one or more values. In this case, the value is 1, indicating that Nginx should function with a single worker process (more information about this particular directive is given in further sections).

 Directives always end with a semicolon (`;`).

Each directive has a unique meaning and defines a particular feature of the application. It may also have a particular syntax. For example, the `worker_process` directive only accepts one numeric value, whereas the `user` directive lets you specify up to two character strings — one for the *user account* (the Nginx worker processes should run as) and a second for the *user group*.

Nginx works in a modular way, and as such, each module comes with a specific set of directives. The most fundamental directives are part of the Nginx Core module and will be detailed in this chapter. As for other directives brought in by other modules, they will be explored in the later chapters.

Organization and inclusions

In the preceding screenshot, you may have noticed a particular directive — **include**.

```
include mime.types;
```

As the name suggests, this directive will perform an inclusion of the specified file. In other words, the contents of the file will be inserted at this exact location. Here is a practical example that will help you understand:

nginx.conf:

```
user nginx nginx;
worker_processes 4;
include other_settings.conf;
```

other_settings.conf:

```
error_log logs/error.log;
pid logs/nginx.pid;
```

The final result, as interpreted by Nginx, is as follows:

```
user nginx nginx;
worker_processes 4;
error_log logs/error.log;
pid logs/nginx.pid;
```

Inclusions are processed recursively. In this case, you have the possibility to use the `include` directive again in the `other_settings.conf` file in order to include yet another file.

In the initial configuration setup, there are two files at use—`nginx.conf` and `mime.types`. However, in the case of a more advanced configuration, there may be five or more files, as described in the following table:

Standard name	Description
`nginx.conf`	Base configuration of the application.
`mime.types`	A list of file extensions and their associated MIME types.
`fastcgi.conf`	FastCGI-related configuration.
`proxy.conf`	Proxy-related configuration.
`sites.conf`	Configuration of the websites served by Nginx, also known as virtual hosts. It's recommended to create separate files for each domain.

These filenames were defined conventionally, nothing actually prevents you from regrouping your FastCGI and proxy settings into a common file named `proxy_and_fastcgi_config.conf`.

Note that the `include` directive supports *filename globbing*. In other words, filenames referenced with the * wildcard, where * may match zero, one, or more consecutive characters:

```
include sites/*.conf;
```

This will include all files with a name that ends with `.conf` in the `sites` folder. This mechanism allows you to create a separate file for each of your websites and include them all at once.

Be careful when including a file—if the specified file does not exist, the configuration checks will fail, and Nginx will not start:

```
[alex@example sbin]# ./nginx -t
[emerg]: open() "/usr/local/nginx/conf/dummyfile.conf" failed (2: No such file or directory) in /usr/local/nginx/conf/nginx.conf:48
```

The previous statement is not true for inclusions with wildcards. Moreover, if you insert `include dummy*.conf` in your configuration and test it (whether there is any file matching this pattern on your system or not), here is what should happen:

```
[alex@example sbin]# ./nginx -t
the configuration file /usr/local/nginx/conf/nginx.conf syntax is ok
configuration file /usr/local/nginx/conf/nginx.conf test is successful
```

Directive blocks

Directives are brought in by modules—if you activate a new module, a specific set of directives becomes available. Modules may also enable **directive blocks**, which allow for a logical construction of the configuration:

```
events {
    worker_connections 1024;
}
```

The `events` block that you can find in the default configuration file is brought in by the *Events module*. The directives that the module enables can only be used within that block—in the `preceding` example, `worker_connections` will only make sense in the context of the `events` block. There is one important exception though—some directives may be placed at the root of the configuration file because they have a global effect on the server. The root of the configuration file is also known as the **main** block.

Note that in some cases, blocks can be nested into each other, following a specific logic:

```
http {
    server {
        listen 80;
        server_name example.com;
        access_log /var/log/nginx/example.com.log;
        location ^~ /admin/ {
            index index.php;
        }
    }
}
```

This example shows how to configure Nginx to serve a website, as you can tell from the `http` block (as opposed to, say, `imap`, if you want to make use of the mail server proxy features).

Within the `http` block, you may declare one or more server blocks. A `server` block allows you to configure a virtual host. The `server` block, in this example, contains some configuration that applies to all requests with a `Host` HTTP header exactly matching `example.com`.

Within this `server` block, you may insert one or more `location` blocks. These allow you to enable settings only when the requested URI matches the specified path. More information is provided in the *The Location block* section of *Chapter 3, HTTP Configuration*.

Last but not least, configuration is inherited within children blocks. The `access_log` directive (defined at the `server` block level in this example) specifies that all HTTP requests for this server should be logged into a text file. This is still true within the `location` child block, although you have the possibility of disabling it by reusing the `access_log` directive:

```
[...]
    location ^~ /admin/ {
        index index.php;
        access_log off;
    }
[...]
```

In this case, logging will be enabled everywhere on the website, except for the `/admin/` location path. The value set for the `access_log` directive at the `server` block level is overridden by the one at the `location` block level.

Advanced language rules

There are a number of important observations regarding the Nginx configuration file syntax. These will help you understand certain syntax rules that may seem confusing if you have never worked with Nginx before.

Directives accept specific syntaxes

You may indeed stumble upon complex syntaxes that can be confusing at first sight:

```
rewrite ^/(.*)\.(png|jpg|gif)$ /image.php? file=$1&format=$2 last;
```

Syntaxes are directive-specific. While the `listen` directive may only accept a port number to open a listening socket, the `location` block or the `rewrite` directive support complex expressions in order to match particular patterns. Syntaxes will be explained along with directives in their respective chapters.

Later on, we will approach a module (the *Rewrite* module) which allows for a much more advanced logical structure through the `if`, `set`, `break`, and `return` directives and the use of variables. With all of these new elements, configuration files will begin to look like programming scripts. Anyhow, the more modules we discover, the richer the syntax becomes.

Diminutives in directive values

Finally, you may use the following diminutives for specifying a file size in the context of a directive value:

- k or K: Kilobytes
- m or M: Megabytes

As a result, the following two syntaxes are correct and equal:

```
client_max_body_size 2M;
client_max_body_size 2048k;
```

Additionally, when specifying a time value, you may use the following shortcuts:

- ms: Milliseconds
- s: Seconds
- m: Minutes
- h: Hours
- d: Days
- w: Weeks
- M: Months (30 days)
- y: Years (365 days)

This becomes especially useful in the case of directives accepting a period of time as a value:

```
client_body_timeout 3m;
client_body_timeout 180s;
client_body_timeout 180;
```

Note that the default time unit is seconds; the last two lines above thus result in an identical behavior. It is also possible to combine two values with different units:

```
client_body_timeout 1m30s;
client_body_timeout '1m 30s 500ms';
```

The latter variant is enclosed in quotes since values are separated by spaces.

Variables

Modules also provide variables that can be used in the definition of directive values. For example, the Nginx HTTP Core module defines the `$nginx_version` variable. Variables in Nginx always start with "$"—the dollar sign. When setting the `log_format` directive, you may include all kinds of variables in the format string:

```
[...]
location ^~ /admin/ {
    access_log logs/main.log;
    log_format main '$pid - $nginx_version - $remote_addr';
}
[...]
```

Note that some directives do not allow you to use variables:

```
error_log logs/error-$nginx_version.log;
```

The preceding directive is valid, syntax-wise. However, it simply generates a file named `error-$nginx_version.log`, without parsing the variable.

String values

Character strings that you use as directive values can be written in three forms. First, you may enter the value without quotes:

root /home/example.com/www;

However, if you want to use a particular character, such as a blank space (" "), a semicolon (;), or curly brace ({ and }), you will need to either prefix said character with a backslash (\), or enclose the entire value in single or double quotes:

root '/home/example.com/my web pages';

Nginx makes no difference whether you use single or double quotes. Note that variables inserted in strings within quotes will be expanded normally, unless you prefix the $ character with a backslash (\).

Base module directives

In this section, we will take a closer look at the base modules. We are particularly interested in answering two questions: what are base modules? and what directives are made available?

What are base modules?

The base modules offer directives that allow you to define parameters of the basic functionality of Nginx. They cannot be disabled at compile time, and as a result, the directives and blocks they offer are always available. Three base modules are distinguished:

- **Core module**: Essential features and directives such as process management and security

- **Events module**: Lets you configure the inner mechanisms of the networking capabilities

- **Configuration module**: Enables the inclusion mechanism

These modules offer a large range of directives; we will be detailing them individually with their syntaxes and default values.

Nginx process architecture

Before we start detailing the basic configuration directives, it's necessary to understand the process architecture, that is, how Nginx works behind the scenes. Although the application comes as a simple binary file (lightweight background process), the way it functions at runtime can be relatively complex.

At the very moment of starting Nginx, one unique process exists in memory — the **Master Process**. It is launched with the current user and group permissions — usually root/root if the service is launched at boot time by an `init` script. The master process itself does not process any client request, instead, it spawns processes that do — the **Worker Processes**, which are affected to a customizable user and group.

From the configuration file, you are able to define the amount of worker processes, the maximum connections per worker process, the user and group the worker processes are running under, and more:

Core module directives

The following is the list of directives made available by the Core module. Most of these directives must be placed at the root of the configuration file and can only be used once. However, some of them are valid in multiple contexts. If that is the case, the following is the list of valid contexts under the directive name:

Name and context	Syntax and description
daemon	Accepted values: on or off
	Syntax: daemon on;
	Default value: on
	Enables or disables daemon mode. If you disable it, the program will not be started in the background; it will stay in the foreground when launched from the shell. This may come in handy for debugging, in situations where you need to know what causes Nginx to crash, and when.
debug_points	Accepted values: stop or abort
	Syntax: debug_points stop;
	Default value: None
	Activates debug points in Nginx. Use stop to interrupt the application when a debug point comes about in order to attach a debugger. Use abort to abort the debug point and create a core dump file.
	To disable this option, simply do not use the directive.

Name and context	Syntax and description

`env`	Syntax:
	
	 `env MY_VARIABLE;`
	 `env MY_VARIABLE=my_value;`
	
	 Lets you (re)define environment variables.

`error_log`
 	
 Context: `main,` `http, server,` and `location`
	Syntax:
	
	 `error_log /file/path level;`
	 Default value: `logs/error.log error`.
	
	 Where level is one of the following values: `debug`, `info`, `notice`, `warn`, `error`, and `crit` (from most to least detailed: debug provides frequent log entries, `crit` only reports critical errors).
	
	 Enables error logging at different levels: Application, HTTP server, virtual host, and virtual host directory.
	
	 By redirecting the log output to `/dev/null`, you can disable error logging. Use the following directive at the root of the configuration file:
	
	 `error_log /dev/null crit;`

`lock_file`	Syntax: File path `lock_file logs/nginx.lock;` Default value: Defined at compile time Use a lock file for mutual exclusion. This is disabled by default, unless you enabled it at compile time. On most operating systems the locks are implemented using atomic operations, so this directive is ignored anyway.
`log_not_found` Context: `main,` `http, server,` and `location`	Accepted values: `on` or `off` `log_not_found on;` Default value: `on` Enables or disables logging of **404 not found** HTTP errors. If your logs get filled with 404 errors due to missing `favicon.ico` or `robots.txt` files, you might want to turn this off.
`master_process`	Accepted values: `on` or `off` `master_process on;` Default value: `on` If enabled, Nginx will start multiple processes: a main process (the master process) and worker processes. If disabled, Nginx works with a unique process. This directive should be used for testing purposes only as it disables the master process — clients thus cannot connect to your server.

Name and context	Syntax and description
pcre_jit	Accepted values: on or off
	`pcre_jit on;`
	Enables or disables Just-In-Time compilation for regular expressions (PCRE from version 8.20 and above) which may speed up their processing significantly. For this to work, the PCRE libraries on your system must be specifically built with the `--enable-jit` configuration argument. When configuring your Nginx build, you must also add the `--with-pcre-jit` argument.
pid	Syntax: File path
	`pid logs/nginx.pid;`
	Default value: Defined at compile time.
	Path of the pid file for the Nginx daemon. The default value can be configured at compile time. Make sure to enable this directive and set its value properly, since the pid file may be used by the Nginx init script depending on your operating system.
ssl_engine	Syntax: Character string
	`ssl_engine enginename;`
	Default value: None
	Where `enginename` is the name of an available hardware SSL accelerator on your system. To check for available hardware SSL accelerators, run this command from the shell:
	`openssl engine -t`
thread_stack_ size	Syntax: Numeric (size)
	`thread_stack_size 1m;`
	Default value: None
	Defines the size of the thread stack; please refer to the `worker_ threads` directive below.
timer_ resolution	Syntax: Numeric (time)
	`timer_resolution 100ms;`
	Default value: None
	Controls the interval between system calls to `gettimeofday()` to synchronize the internal clock. If this value is not specified, the clock is refreshed after each kernel event notification.

Name and context	Syntax and description

`user`	Syntax:
	
	`user username groupname;`
	`user username;`
	
	Default value: Defined at compile time. If still undefined, the user and group of the Nginx master process are used.
	
	Lets you define the user account, and optionally the user group used for starting the Nginx worker processes. For security reasons, you should make sure to specify a user and group with limited privileges. For example, create a new user and group dedicated to Nginx, and remember to apply proper permissions on the files that will be served.

`worker_threads`	Syntax: Numeric `worker_threads 8;` Default value: None Defines the amount of threads per worker process. Warning! Threads are disabled by default. The author stated that "the code is currently broken."

`worker_cpu_ affinity`	Syntax:
	
	`worker_cpu_affinity 1000 0100 0010 0001;`
	`worker_cpu_affinity 10 10 01 01;`
	`worker_cpu_affinity;`
	
	Default value: None
	
	This directive works in conjunction with `worker_processes`. It lets you affect worker processes to CPU cores.
	
	There are as many series of digit blocks as worker processes; there are as many digits in a block as your CPU has cores.
	
	If you configure Nginx to use three worker processes, there are three blocks of digits. For a dual-core CPU, each block has two digits:
	
	`worker_cpu_affinity 01 01 10;`
	
	The first block (01) indicates that the first worker process should be affected to the second core.
	
	The second block (01) indicates that the second worker process should be affected to the second core.
	
	The third block (10) indicates that the third worker process should be affected to the first core.
	
	Note that affinity is only recommended for multi-core CPUs, not for processors with hyper-treading or similar technologies.

Name and context	Syntax and description
`worker_priority`	Syntax: Numeric `worker_priority 0;` Default value: 0 Defines the priority of the worker processes, from `-20` (highest) to `19` (lowest). The default value is 0. Note that kernel processes run at priority level `-5`, so it's not recommended that you set the priority to `-5` or less.
`worker_processes`	Syntax: Numeric, or auto `worker_processes 4;` Default value: 1 Defines the amount of worker processes. Nginx offers to separate the treatment of requests into multiple processes. The default value is 1, but it's recommended to increase this value if your CPU has more than one core. Besides, if a process gets blocked due to slow I/O operations, incoming requests can be delegated to the other worker processes. Alternatively, you may use the `auto` value which will let Nginx select an appropriate value for this directive. By default, it is the amount of CPU cores detected on the system.
`worker_rlimit_core`	Syntax: Numeric (size) `worker_rlimit_core 100m;` Default value: None Defines the size of core files per worker process.
`worker_rlimit_nofile`	Syntax: Numeric `worker_rlimit_nofile 10000;` Default value: None Defines the amount of files a worker process may use simultaneously.
`worker_rlimit_sigpending`	Syntax: Numeric `worker_rlimit_sigpending 10000;` Default value: None Defines the amount of signals that can be queued per user (user ID of the calling process). If the queue is full, signals are ignored past this limit.

Name and context	Syntax and description
working_ directory	Syntax: Directory path `working_directory /usr/local/nginx/;` Default value: The prefix switch defined at compile time. Working directory used for worker processes, it is only used to define the location of core files. The worker process user account (`user` directive) must have write permissions on this folder in order to be able to write core files.
worker_aio_ requests	Syntax: Numeric `worker_aio_requests 10000;` If you are using `aio` with the `epoll` connection processing method, this directive sets the maximum number of outstanding asynchronous I/O operations for a single worker process.

Events module

The Events module comes with directives that allow you to configure network mechanisms. Some of the parameters have an important impact on the application's performance.

All of the directives listed in the following table must be placed in the `events` block, which is located at the root of the configuration file:

```
user nginx nginx;
master_process on;
worker_processes 4;
events {
  worker_connections 1024;
  use epoll;
}
[...]
```

These directives cannot be placed elsewhere (if you do so, the configuration test will fail).

Directive name	Syntax and description
`accept_mutex`	Accepted values: on or off `accept_mutex on;` Default value: on Enables or disables the use of an accept mutex (mutual exclusion) to open listening sockets.
`accept_mutex_delay`	Syntax: Numeric (time) `accept_mutex_delay 500ms;` Default value: `500 milliseconds` Defines the amount of time a worker process should wait before trying to acquire the resource again. This value is not used if the `accept_mutex` directive is set to off.
`connections`	Replaced by `worker_connections`. This directive is now deprecated.

`debug_connection`	Syntax: IP address or CIDR block.
	
	`debug_connection 172.63.155.21;`
	`debug_connection 172.63.155.0/24;`
	
	Default value: None.
	
	Writes detailed logs for clients matching this IP address or address block. The debug information is stored in the file specified with the `error_log` directive, enabled with the debug level.
	
	Note: Nginx must be compiled with the `--debug` switch in order to enable this feature.

`multi_accept`	Syntax: on or off `multi_accept off;` Default value: off Defines whether or not Nginx should accept all incoming connections at once from the listening queue.

Directive name	Syntax and description
use	Accepted values: `/dev/poll`, `epoll`, `eventport`, `kqueue`, `rtsig`, or `select`
	`use kqueue;`
	Default value: Defined at compile time
	Selects the event model among the available ones (the ones that you enabled at compile time), though Nginx automatically selects the most appropriate one.
	The supported models are:
	• `select`: The default and standard module, it is used if the OS does not support a more efficient one (it's the only available method under Windows). This method is not recommended for servers that expect to be under high load.
	• `poll`: It is automatically preferred over `select`, but is not available on all systems.
	• `kqueue`: An efficient method for FreeBSD 4.1+, OpenBSD 2.9+, NetBSD 2.0, and MacOS X operating systems.
	• `epoll`: An efficient method for Linux 2.6+ based operating systems.
	• `rtsig`: Real-time signals, available as of Linux 2.2.19, but unsuited for high-traffic profiles as default system settings only allow 1,024 queued signals.
	• `/dev/poll`: An efficient method for Solaris 7 11/99+, HP/UX 11.22+, IRIX 6.5.15+, and Tru64 UNIX 5.1A+ operating systems.
	• `eventport`: An efficient method for Solaris 10, though a security patch is required.
worker_connections	Syntax: Numeric
	`worker_connections 1024;`
	Default value: None
	Defines the amount of connections that a worker process may treat simultaneously.

Configuration module

The Nginx Configuration module is a simple module enabling file inclusions with the `include` directive, as previously described in the *Organization and inclusions* section. The directive can be inserted anywhere in the configuration file and accepts a single parameter—the file's path.

```
include /file/path.conf;
include sites/*.conf;
```

> Note that if you do not specify an absolute path, the file path is relative to the configuration directory. By default, `include sites/example.conf` will include the following file: `/usr/local/nginx/conf/sites/example.conf`

A configuration for your profile

Following this long list of directives from the base modules, we can begin to envision a first configuration adapted to your profile in terms of targeted traffic and, more importantly, to your hardware. In this section, we will first take a closer look at the default configuration file to understand the implications of each setting.

Understanding the default configuration

There is a reason why Nginx stands apart from other web servers—it's extremely lightweight, optimized, and to put it simply, it's fast. As such, the default configuration is efficient, and in many cases, you will not need to apply radical changes to the initial setup.

We will study the default configuration by opening up the main configuration file `nginx.conf`, although you will find this file to be almost empty. The reason lies in the fact that when a directive does not appear in the configuration file, the default value is employed. We will thus consider the default values here as well as the directives found in the original setup:

```
user root root;
worker_processes 1;
worker_priority 0;
error_log logs/error.log error;
log_not_found on;
events {
```

```
    accept_mutex on;
    accept_mutex_delay 500ms;
    multi_accept off;
    worker_connections 1024;
}
```

While this configuration may work out of the box, there are some issues you need to address right away.

Necessary adjustments

We will review some of the configuration directives that need to be changed immediately and the possible values you may set:

- `user root root;`

    This directive specifies that the worker processes will be started as root. It is dangerous for security as it grants full permissions over the filesystem. You need to create a new user account on your system and make use of it here. Recommended value (granted that a `www-data` user account and group exist on the system): `user www-data www-data;`

- `worker_processes 1;`

    With this setting, only one worker process will be started, which implies that all requests will be processed by a unique execution flow (the current version of Nginx is not multi-threaded, by choice). This also implies that the execution is delegated to only one core of your CPU. It is highly recommended to increase this value; you should have at least one process per CPU core. Recommended value (granted your server is powered by a quad-core CPU): `worker_processes 4;`

- `worker_priority 0;`

    By default, the worker processes are started with a regular priority. If your system performs other tasks simultaneously, you might want to grant a higher priority to the Nginx worker processes. In this case, you should decrease the value — the smaller the value, the higher the priority. Values range from `-20` (highest priority) to `19` (lowest priority). There is no recommended value here as it completely depends on your situation. However, you should not set it under `-5` as it is the default priority for kernel processes.

- `log_not_found on;`

  This directive specifies whether Nginx should log `404 errors` or not. While these errors may, of course, provide useful information about missing resources, a lot of them may be generated by web browsers trying to reach the *favicon* (the conventional `/favicon.ico` of a website) or robots trying to access the indexing instructions (`robots.txt`). Set this to `off` if you want to ensure your log files don't get cluttered by "Error 404" entries, but keep in mind that this could deprive you from potentially important information about other pages that visitors failed to reach. Note that this directive is part of the HTTP Core module. Refer to the next chapter for more information.

- `worker_connections 1024;`

  This setting, combined with the amount of worker processes, allows you to define the total amount of connections accepted by the server simultaneously. If you enable four worker processes, each accepting 1,024 connections, your server will treat a total of 4,096 simultaneous connections. You need to adjust this setting to match your hardware: the more RAM and CPU power your server relies on, the more connections you can accept concurrently.

Adapting to your hardware

We will now establish three different setups—a standard one to be used by a regular website with decent hardware, a low-traffic setup intended to optimize performance on modest hardware, and finally an adequate setup for production servers in high-traffic situations.

It is always difficult to classify computer power. Firstly, each situation comes with its own resources. If you work in a large company, talking about a *powerful computer* will not have the same meaning as in the case of standalone website administrators who need to resort to third-party web hosting providers. Secondly, computers get more powerful every year: faster CPUs, cheaper RAM, and the rise of new technologies (SSDs). Consequently, the specifications given below are here for reference and need to be adjusted to your own situation and to your era. The recommended values for the directives are directly based on the specifications—one worker process per CPU core, maximum connections depending on the RAM, and so on.

Low-traffic setup	Standard setup	High-traffic setup
CPU: Dual-core	CPU: Quad-core	CPU: 8-core
RAM: 2 GB	RAM: 4 GB	RAM: 12 GB
Requests: ~ 1/s	Requests: ~ 50/s	Requests: ~1000/s
Recommended values		

```
worker_processes 2;
worker_rlimit_nofile
1024;
worker_priority -5;
worker_cpu_affinity
01 10;
events {
  multi_accept on;
  work
er_connections 128;
}
```

```
worker_processes 4;
worker_rlimit_nofile
8192;
worker_priority 0;
worker_cpu_affinity
0001 0010 0100 1000;
events {
  multi_accept off;
  work
er_connections
1024;
}
```

```
worker_processes
8;
worker_priority 0;
worker_rlimit_
nofile 16384;
events {
  multi_accept
off;
worker_connections
8192;
}
```

There are two adjustments that have a critical effect on the performance, namely, the amount of worker processes and the connection limit. The first one, if set improperly, may clutter particular cores of your CPU and leave other ones unused or underused. Make sure the `worker_processes` match the quantity of cores in your CPU.

The second one, if set too low, could result in connections being refused; if set too high, could overflow the RAM and cause a system-wide crash. Unfortunately, there is no simple equation to calculate the value of the `worker_connections` directive; you will need to base it on expected traffic estimations.

Testing your server

The base configuration of your server is now established. In the following chapters, we will advance to the `http modules` and how to create virtual hosts. But for now, let's make sure that our setup is correct and suitable for production.

Creating a test server

In order to perform simple tests, such as connecting to the server with a web browser, we need to set up a website for Nginx to serve. A test page comes with the default package in the `html` folder (`/usr/local/nginx/html/index.html`) and the original `nginx.conf` is configured to serve this page. Here is the section that we are interested in for now:

```
http {
    include         mime.types;
    default_type    application/octet-stream;
    sendfile            on;
    keepalive_timeout   65;
    server {
        listen          80;
        server_name     localhost;
        location / {
            root    html;
            index   index.html index.htm;
        }
        error_page    500 502 503 504   /50x.html;
        location = /50x.html {
            root    html;
        }
    }
}
```

As you can already tell, this segment configures Nginx to serve a website:

- By opening a listening socket on port 80
- Accessible at the address: `http://localhost/`
- The index page is `index.html`

For more details about these directives, please refer to *Chapter 3, HTTP Configuration* and go to the *HTTP module configuration* section. Anyhow, fire up your favorite web browser and visit `http://localhost/`:

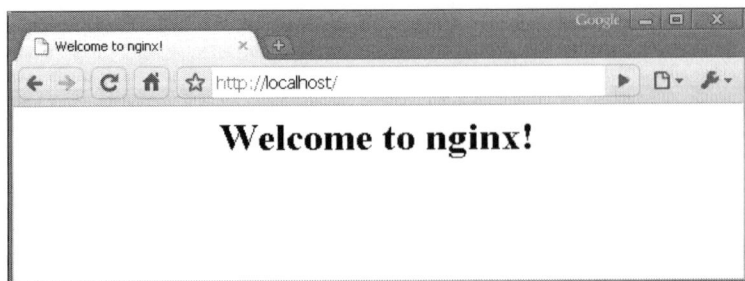

You should be greeted with a welcome message; if you aren't, then check the configuration again and make sure you reloaded Nginx in order to apply the changes.

Performance tests

Having configured the basic functioning and the architecture of your Nginx setup, you may already want to proceed with running some tests. The methodology here is experimental — run the tests, edit the configuration, reload the server, run the tests again, edit the configuration again, and so on. Ideally, you should avoid running the testing tool on the same computer that is used to run Nginx as it may cause the results to be biased.

> One could question the pertinence of running performance tests at this stage. On one hand, virtual hosts and modules are not fully configured yet and your website might use FastCGI applications (PHP, Python, and so on). On the other hand, we are testing the raw performance of the server without additional components (for example, to make sure that it fully makes use of all CPU cores). Besides, it's always better to come up with a polished configuration before the server is put into production.

We have retained three tools to evaluate the server performance here. All three applications were specifically designed for load tests on web servers and have different approaches due to their origin:

- `httperf`: A relatively well-known open source utility developed by HP, for Linux operating systems only
- `Autobench`: Perl wrapper for `httperf` improving the testing mechanisms and generating detailed reports
- `OpenWebLoad`: Smaller scale open source load testing application that supports both Windows and Linux platforms

The principle behind each of these tools is to generate a massive amount of HTTP requests in order to clutter the server and study the results.

Httperf

`Httperf` is a simple command-line tool that can be downloaded from its official website: `http://www.hpl.hp.com/research/linux/httperf/` (it might also be available in the default repositories of your operating system). The source comes as a `tar.gz` archive and needs to be compiled using the standard method: `./configure`, `make`, and `make install`.

Once installed, you may execute the following command:

```
[alex@example ~]$ httperf --server 192.168.1.10 --port 80 --uri /index.
html --rate 300 --num-conn 30000 --num-call 1 --timeout 5
```

Replace the values in the preceding command with your own:

- `--server`: The website hostname you wish to test
- `--uri`: The path of the file that will be downloaded
- `--rate`: How many requests should be sent every second
- `--num-conn`: The total amount of connections
- `--num-call`: How many requests should be sent per connection
- `--timeout`: Quantity of seconds elapsed before a request is considered lost

In this example, `httperf` will download `http://192.168.1.10/index.html` repeatedly, 300 times per second, resulting in a total of 30,000 requests.

```
alex@example: /home/alex                                                _□×
Maximum connect burst length: 6298

Total: connections 21767 requests 21710 replies 21710 test-duration 14.692 s

Connection rate: 1481.6 conn/s (0.7 ms/conn, <=1022 concurrent connections)
Connection time [ms]: min 1.4 avg 563.4 max 3922.6 median 197.5 stddev 988.4
Connection time [ms]: connect 397.6
Connection length [replies/conn]: 1.000

Request rate: 1477.7 req/s (0.7 ms/req)
Request size [B]: 72.0

Reply rate [replies/s]: min 1942.8 avg 2077.3 max 2211.8 stddev 190.2 (2 samples)
Reply time [ms]: response 165.7 transfer 0.0
Reply size [B]: header 215.0 content 151.0 footer 0.0 (total 366.0)
Reply status: 1xx=0 2xx=21702 3xx=0 4xx=0 5xx=8

CPU time [s]: user 0.22 system 8.88 (user 1.5% system 60.5% total 62.0%)
Net I/O: 633.5 KB/s (5.2*10^6 bps)

Errors: total 78290 client-timo 57 socket-timo 0 connrefused 0 connreset 0
Errors: fd-unavail 78233 addrunavail 0 ftab-full 0 other 0
```

The results indicate the response times and the amount of successful requests. If the success ratio is 100 percent or the response time near 0 ms, increase the request rate and run the test again until the server shows signs of weakness. Once the results begin to look a little less perfect, tweak the appropriate configuration directives and run the test again.

Autobench

Autobench is a Perl script that makes use of `httperf` more efficiently—it runs continuous tests and automatically increases request rates until your server gets saturated. One of the interesting features of Autobench is that it generates a `.tsv` report that you can open with various applications to generate graphs. You may download the source code from the author's personal website: `http://www.xenoclast.org/autobench/`. Once again, extract the files from the archive, run `make` then `make install`.

Although it supports testing of multiple hosts at once, we will only be using the single host test for more simplicity. The command we will execute resembles the `httperf` one:

```
[alex@example ~]$ autobench --single_host --host1 192.168.1.10 --uri1 /
index.html --quiet --low_rate 20 --high_rate 200 --rate_step 20 --num_
call 10 --num_conn 5000 --timeout 5 --file results.tsv
```

The switches can be configured as follows:

- `--host1`: The website host name you wish to test
- `--uri1`: The path of the file that will be downloaded
- `--quiet`: Does not display `httperf` information on the screen
- `--low_rate`: Connections per second at the beginning of the test
- `--high_rate`: Connections per second at the end of the test
- `--rate_step`: The number of connections to increase the rate by after each test
- `--num_call`: How many requests should be sent per connection
- `--num_conn`: Total amount of connections
- `--timeout`: The number of seconds elapsed before a request is considered lost
- `--file`: Export results as specified (`.tsv` file)

Once the test terminates, you end up with a `.tsv` file that you can import in applications such as Microsoft Excel. Here is a graph generated from results on a test server (note that the report file contains up to 10 series of statistics):

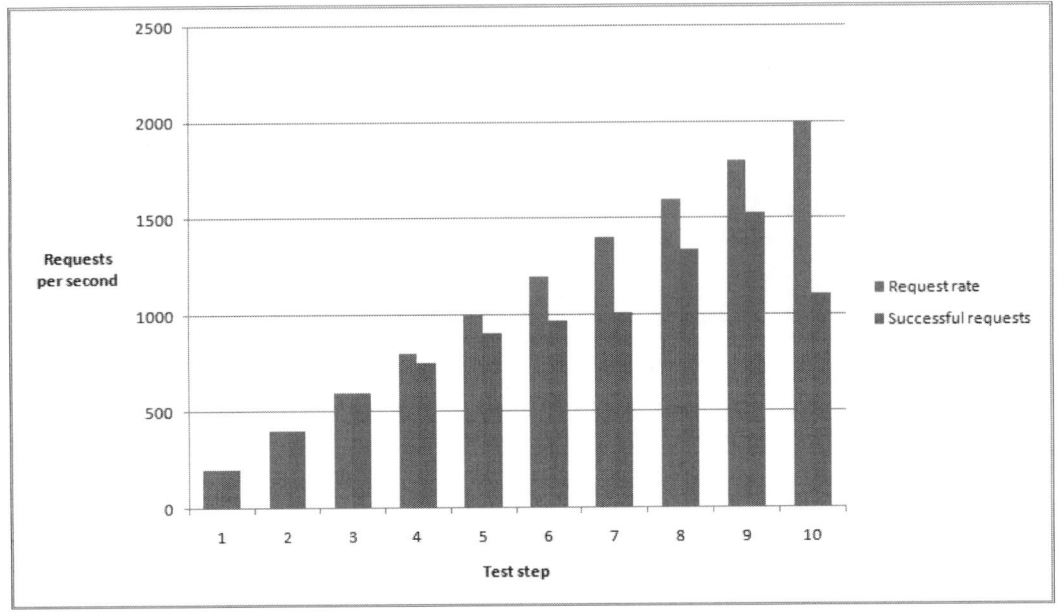

As you can tell from the graph, this test server supports up to 600 requests per second without a loss. Past this limit, some connections get dropped as Nginx cannot handle the load. It stills gets up to over 1,500 successful requests per second at step 9.

OpenWebLoad

OpenWebLoad is a free open source application. It is available for both Linux and Windows platforms and was developed in the early 2000s, back in the days of Web 1.0. A different approach is offered here. Instead of throwing loads of requests at the server and seeing how many are handled correctly, it will simply send as many requests as possible using a variable amount of connections and report to you every second.

You may download it from its official website: `http://openwebload.sourceforge.net`. Extract the source from the `.tar.gz` archive, run `./configure`, `make`, and `make install`.

Its usage is simpler than the previous two utilities:

```
[alex@example ~]$ openload example.com/index.html 10
```

The first argument is the URL of the website you want to test. The second one is the amount of connections that should be opened.

```
C:\WINDOWS\system32\cmd.exe
C:\>openload.exe example.com/index.html 10
URL: http://example.com:80/index.html
Clients: 10
MaTps 210.37, Tps 210.37, Resp Time 0.046, Err 0%, Count 211
MaTps 211.51, Tps 221.78, Resp Time 0.045, Err 0%, Count 433
MaTps 212.69, Tps 223.33, Resp Time 0.045, Err 0%, Count 657
MaTps 213.38, Tps 219.56, Resp Time 0.046, Err 0%, Count 877
MaTps 214.63, Tps 225.87, Resp Time 0.044, Err 0%, Count 1104
MaTps 215.20, Tps 220.34, Resp Time 0.045, Err 0%, Count 1325
Total TPS: 216.40
Avg. Response time:  0.045 sec.
Max Response time:   0.097 sec
Total Requests:      1325
Total Errors:        0

C:\>
```

A new result line is produced every second. Requests are sent continuously until you press the *Enter* key, following that a result summary is displayed. Here is how to decipher the output:

- **Tps** (transactions per second): A transaction corresponds to a completed request (back and forth)
- **MaTps**: Average Tps over the last 20 seconds
- **Resp Time**: Average response time for the elapsed second
- **Err** (error rate): Errors occur when the server returns a response that is not the expected HTTP 200 OK
- **Count**: Total transaction count

You can fiddle with the amount of simultaneous connections and see how your server performs in order to establish a balanced configuration for your setup. Three tests were run here with a different amount of connections. The results speak for themselves:

	Test 1	Test 2	Test 3
Simultaneous connections	1	20	1000
Transactions per second (Tps)	67.54	205.87	185.07
Average response time	14 ms	91 ms	596 ms

Too few connections result in a low Tps rate however, the response times are optimal. Too many connections produce a relatively high Tps, but the response times are critically high. You thus need to find a happy medium.

Upgrading Nginx gracefully

There are many situations where you need to replace the Nginx binary, for example, when you compile a new version and wish to put it in production or simply after having enabled new modules and rebuilt the application. What most administrators would do in this situation is stop the server, copy the new binary over the old one, and start Nginx again. While this is not considered to be a problem for most websites, there may be some cases where uptime is critical and connection losses should be avoided at all costs. Fortunately, Nginx embeds a mechanism allowing you to switch binaries with uninterrupted uptime—zero percent request loss is guaranteed if you follow these steps carefully:

1. Replace the old Nginx binary (by default, `/usr/local/nginx/sbin/nginx`) with the new one.

2. Find the pid of the Nginx master process, for example, with `ps x | grep nginx | grep master` or by looking at the value found in the pid file.

3. Send a `USR2` (12) signal to the master process—`kill -USR2 ***`, replacing `***` with the pid found in step 2. This will initiate the upgrade by renaming the old `.pid` file and running the new binary.

4. Send a `WINCH` (28) signal to the old master process—`kill -WINCH ***`, replacing `***` with the pid found in step 2. This will engage a graceful shutdown of the old worker processes.

5. Make sure that all of the old worker processes are terminated, and then send a `QUIT` signal to the old master process—`kill -QUIT ***`, replacing `***` with the pid found in step 2.

Congratulations! You have successfully upgraded Nginx and have not lost a single connection.

Summary

This chapter provided a first approach of the configuration architecture by studying the syntax and the core module directives that have an impact on the overall server performance. We then went through a series of adjustments in order to fit your own profile, followed by performance tests that have probably led you to fine-tune some more.

This is just the beginning though. Practically everything that we will be doing from now on is to establish configuration sections. The next chapter will detail more advanced directives by further exploring the module system and the exciting possibilities that are offered to you.

3 HTTP Configuration

At this stage, we have a working Nginx setup—not only is it installed on the system and launched automatically on startup, but it's also organized and optimized with the help of basic directives. It's now time to go one step further into the configuration by discovering the HTTP Core module. This module constitutes the essential component of the HTTP configuration—it allows you to set up websites to be served, also referred to as *virtual hosts*.

This chapter will cover:

- An introduction to the HTTP Core module
- The http / server / location structure
- HTTP Core module directives, thematically
- HTTP Core module variables
- The in-depths of the location block

HTTP Core module

The HTTP Core module is the component that contains all of the fundamental blocks, directives, and variables of the HTTP server. It's enabled by default when you configure the build (as described in *Chapter 1*, *Downloading and Installing Nginx*), but as it turns out, it's actually optional—you can decide not to include it in your custom build. Doing so will completely disable all HTTP functionalities, and all of the other HTTP modules will not be compiled. Though obviously if you purchased this book, it's highly likely that you are interested in the web serving capacities of Nginx, so you will have this enabled.

This module is the largest of all standard Nginx modules—it provides an impressive amount of directives and variables. In order to understand all of these new elements and how they come into play, we first need to understand the logical organization introduced by the three main blocks—http, server, and location.

Structure blocks

In the previous chapter, we discovered the Core module by studying the default Nginx configuration file which includes a sequence of directives and values, with no apparent organization. Then came the Events module, which introduced the first block (`events`). This block would be the only placeholder for all of the directives brought in by the Events module.

As it turns out, the HTTP module introduces three new logical blocks:

- `http`: This block is inserted at the root of the configuration file. It allows you to start defining directives and blocks from all modules related to the HTTP facet of Nginx. Although there is no real purpose in doing so, the block can be inserted multiple times, in which case the directive values inserted in the last block will override the previous ones.

- `server`: This block allows you to *declare a website*. In other words, a specific website (identified by one or more hostnames, for example, `www.mywebsite.com`) becomes acknowledged by Nginx and receives its own configuration. This block can only be used within the `http` block.

- `location`: Lets you define a group of settings to be applied to a particular location on a website. The next part of this section provides more details about the `location` block. This block can be used within a `server` block or nested within another `location` block.

The following diagram summarizes the final structure by providing a couple of basic examples corresponding to actual situations:

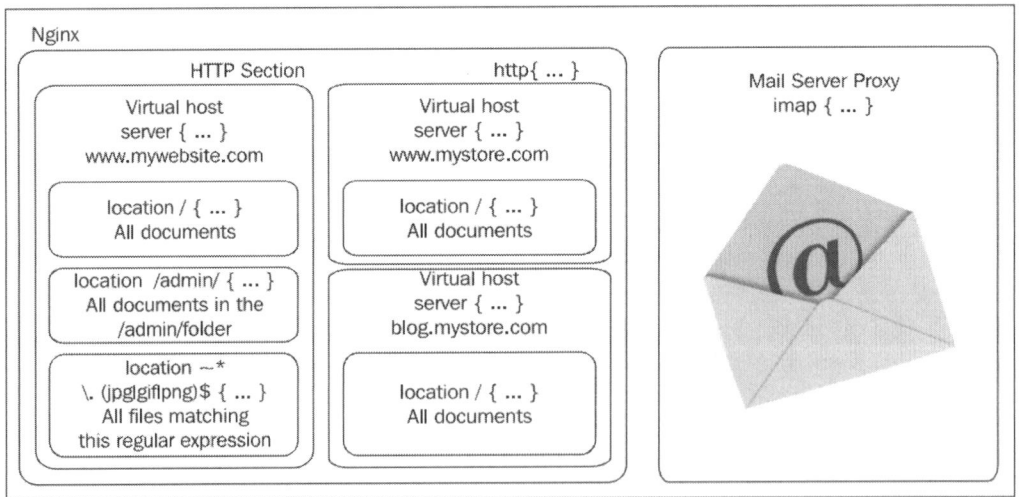

The HTTP section, defined by the **http** block, encompasses the entire web-related configuration. It may contain one or more **server** blocks, defining the domains and sub-domains that you are hosting. For each of these websites, you have the possibility to define **location** blocks that let you apply additional settings to a particular request URI or request URIs matching a pattern.

Remember that the principle of setting inheritance applies here. If you define a setting at the `http` block level (for example, `gzip on` to enable gzip compression), the setting will preserve its value in the potentially incorporated `server` and `location` blocks:

```
http {
    # Enable gzip compression at the http block level
    gzip on;

    server {
        server_name localhost;
         listen 80;

        # At this stage, gzip still set to on

        location /downloads/ {
            gzip off;
    #       This directive only applies to documents found
    #       in /downloads/
         }
    }
}
```

Module directives

At each of the three levels, directives can be inserted in order to affect the behavior of the web server. The following is the list of all directives that are introduced by the main HTTP module, grouped by thematic. For each directive, an indication regarding the context is given. Some cannot be used at certain levels. For instance, it would make no sense to insert a `server_name` directive inside a `location` block. In that extent, the table indicates the possible levels where each directive is allowed—the `http` block, the `server` block, the `location` block, and additionally the `if` block, later introduced by the *Rewrite module*.

 Note that this documentation is valid as of stable version 1.2.9. Future updates may alter the syntax of some directives or provide new features that are not discussed here.

Socket and host configuration

This set of directives will allow you to configure your virtual hosts. In practice, this materializes by creating `server` blocks that you identify either by a hostname or by an IP address and port combination. In addition, some directives will let you fine-tune your network settings by configuring TCP socket options.

listen

Context: `server`

Specifies the IP address and/or the port to be used by the listening socket that will serve the website. Sites are generally served on port 80 (the default value) via HTTP, or 443 via HTTPS.

Syntax: `listen [address] [:port] [additional options];`

Additional options:

- `default_server`: Specifies that this `server` block is to be used as the default website for any request received at the specified IP address and port
- `ssl`: Specifies that the website should be served using SSL
- Other options are related to the *bind* and *listen* system calls: `backlog=num`, `rcvbuf=size`, `sndbuf=size`, `accept_filter=filter`, `deferred`, `setfib=number`, and `bind`

Examples:

```
listen 192.168.1.1:80;
listen 127.0.0.1;
listen 80 default;
listen [:::a8c9:1234]:80; # IPv6 addresses must be put between square
brackets
listen 443 ssl;
```

This directive also allows Unix sockets:

```
listen unix:/tmp/nginx.sock;
```

server_name

Context: `server`

Assigns one or more hostnames to the `server` block. When Nginx receives an HTTP request, it matches the `Host` header of the request against all of the `server` blocks. The first `server` block to match this hostname is selected.

Plan B: If no `server` block matches the desired host, Nginx selects the first `server` block that matches the parameters of the `listen` directive (such as `listen *:80` would be a catch-all for all requests received on port `80`), giving priority to the first block that has the default option enabled on the `listen` directive.

Note that this directive accepts wildcards as well as regular expressions (in which case, the hostname should start with the ~ character).

Syntax: `server_name hostname1 [hostname2...]` ;

Examples:

```
server_name www.website.com;
server_name www.website.com website.com;
server_name *.website.com;
server_name .website.com; # combines both *.website.com and website.
com
server_name *.website.*;
server_name ~^\.example\.com$;
```

Note that you may use an empty string as the directive value in order to catch all of the requests that do not come with a `Host` header, but only after at least one regular name (or "_" for a dummy hostname):

```
server_name website.com "";
server_name _ "";
```

server_name_in_redirect

Context: `http, server, location`

This directive applies the case of internal redirects (for more information about internal redirects, check the *Rewrite Module* section below). If set to `on`, Nginx will use the first hostname specified in the `server_name` directive. If set to `off`, Nginx will use the value of the `Host` header from the HTTP request.

Syntax: `on` or `off`

Default value: `off`

server_names_hash_max_size

Context: `http`

Nginx uses hash tables for various data collections in order to speed up the processing of requests. This directive defines the maximum size of the server names hash table. The default value should fit with most configurations. If this needs to be changed, Nginx will automatically tell you on startup, or when you reload its configuration.

Syntax: Numeric value

Default value: `512`

server_names_hash_bucket_size

Context: `http`

Sets the bucket size for server names hash tables. Similarly, you should only change this value if Nginx tells you to.

Syntax: Numeric value

Default value: `32` (or `64`, or `128`, depending on your processor cache specifications).

port_in_redirect

Context: `http`, `server`, `location`

In the case of a redirect, this directive defines whether or not Nginx should append the port number to the redirection URL.

Syntax: `on` or `off`

Default value: `on`

tcp_nodelay

Context: `http`, `server`, `location`

Enables or disables the `TCP_NODELAY` socket option for keep-alive connections only. Quoting the Linux documentation on sockets programming:

> *"TCP_NODELAY is for a specific purpose; to disable the Nagle buffering algorithm. It should only be set for applications that send frequent small bursts of information without getting an immediate response, where timely delivery of data is required (the canonical example is mouse movements)."*

Syntax: on or off

Default value: on

tcp_nopush

Context: http, server, location

Enables or disables the TCP_NOPUSH (FreeBSD) or TCP_CORK (Linux) socket option. Note that this option only applies if the sendfile directive is enabled. If tcp_nopush is set to on, Nginx will attempt to transmit the entire HTTP response headers in a single TCP packet.

Syntax: on or off

Default value: off

sendfile

Context: http, server, location

If this directive is enabled, Nginx will use the sendfile kernel call to handle file transmission. If disabled, Nginx will handle the file transfer by itself. Depending on the physical location of the file being transmitted (such as NFS), this option may affect the server performance.

Syntax: on or off

Default value: off

sendfile_max_chunk

Context: http, server

This directive defines a maximum size of data to be used for each call to sendfile (read above).

Syntax: Numeric value (size)

Default value: 0

send_lowat

Context: `http, server`

An option allowing you to make use of the `SO_SNDLOWAT` flag for TCP sockets under FreeBSD only. This value defines the minimum number of bytes in the buffer for output operations.

Syntax: Numeric value (size)

Default value: `0`

reset_timedout_connection

Context: `http, server, location`

When a client connection times out, its associated information may remain in memory depending on the state it was on. Enabling this directive will erase all memory associated to the connection after it times out.

Syntax: `on` or `off`

Default value: `off`

Paths and documents

This section describes directives that configure the documents that should be served for each website such as the document root, the site index, error pages, and so on.

root

Context: `http, server, location, if`. Variables are accepted.

Defines the document root, containing the files you wish to serve to your visitors.

Syntax: Directory path

Default value: `html`

```
root /home/website.com/public_html;
```

alias

Context: `location`. Variables are accepted.

`alias` is a directive that you place in a `location` block only. It assigns a different path for Nginx to retrieve documents for a specific request. As an example, consider the following configuration:

```
http {
    server {
        server_name localhost;
        root /var/www/website.com/html;
        location /admin/ {
          alias /var/www/locked/;
        }
    }
}
```

When a request for `http://localhost/` is received, files are served from the `/var/www/website.com/html/` folder. However, if Nginx receives a request for `http://localhost/admin/`, the path used to retrieve the files is `/home/website.com/locked/`. Moreover, the value of the document `root` directive (root) is not altered. This procedure is invisible in the eyes of dynamic scripts.

Syntax: Directory (do not forget the trailing /) or file path

error_page

Context: `http`, `server`, `location`, `if`. Variables are accepted.

Allows you to affect URIs to HTTP response code and optionally to substitute the code with another.

Syntax: `error_page code1 [code2...] [=replacement code] [=@block | URI]`

Examples :

```
error_page 404 /not_found.html;
error_page 500 501 502 503 504 /server_error.html;
error_page 403 http://website.com/;
error_page 404 @notfound; # jump to a named location block
error_page 404 =200 /index.html; # in case of 404 error, redirect to
index.html with a 200 OK response code
```

if_modified_since

Context: `http, server, location`

Defines how Nginx handles the `If-Modified-Since` HTTP header. This header is mostly used by search engine spiders (such as Google web crawling bots). The robot indicates the date and time of the last pass. If the requested file was not modified since that time the server simply returns a `304 Not Modified` response code with no body.

This directive accepts the following three values:

- `off`: Ignores the `If-Modified-Since` header.
- `exact`: Returns `304 Not Modified` if the date and time specified in the HTTP header are an exact match with the actual requested file modification date. If the file modification date is anterior or ulterior, the file is served normally (`200 OK` response).
- `before`: Returns `304 Not Modified` if the date and time specified in the HTTP header is anterior or equal to the requested file modification date.

Syntax: `if_modified_since off | exact | before`

Default value: `exact`

index

Context: `http, server, location`. Variables are accepted.

Defines the default page that Nginx will serve if no filename is specified in the request (in other words, the index page). You may specify multiple filenames and the first file to be found will be served. If none of the specified files are found, Nginx will either attempt to generate an automatic index of the files, if the `autoindex` directive is enabled (check the `HTTP Autoindex` module) or return a `403 Forbidden` error page. Optionally, you may insert an absolute filename (such as `/page.html`, based from the document root directory) but only as the last argument of the directive.

Syntax: `index file1 [file2...] [absolute_file];`

Default value: `index.html`

```
index index.php index.html index.htm;
index index.php index2.php /catchall.php;
```

recursive_error_pages

Context: http, server, location

Sometimes an error page itself served by the error_page directive may trigger an error, in this case the error_page directive is used again (recursively). This directive enables or disables recursive error pages.

Syntax: on or off

Default value: off

try_files

Context: server, location. Variables are accepted.

Attempts to serve the specified files (arguments 1 to N-1), if none of these files exist, jumps to the respective named location block (last argument) or serves the specified URI.

Syntax: Multiple file paths, followed by a named location block or a URI

Example:

```
location / {
    try_files $uri $uri.html $uri.php $uri.xml @proxy;
}
# the following is a "named location block"
location @proxy {
    proxy_pass 127.0.0.1:8080;
}
```

In this example, Nginx tries to serve files normally. If the request URI does not correspond to any existing file, Nginx appends .html to the URI and tries to serve the file again. If it still fails, it tries with .php, then .xml. Eventually, if all of these possibilities fail, another location block (@proxy) handles the request.

 You may also specify $uri/ in the list of values in order to test for the existence of a directory with that name.

Client requests

This section documents the way that Nginx will handle client requests. Among other things, you are allowed to configure the keep-alive mechanism behavior and possibly logging client requests into files.

keepalive_requests

Context: `http, server, location`

Maximum amount of requests served over a single keep-alive connection.

Syntax: Numeric value

Default value: `100`

keepalive_timeout

Context: `http, server, location`

This directive defines the amount of seconds the server will wait before closing a keep-alive connection. The second (optional) parameter is transmitted as the value of the `Keep-Alive: timeout=` HTTP response header. The intended effect is to let the client browser close the connection itself after this period has elapsed. Note that some browsers ignore this setting. Internet Explorer, for instance, automatically closes the connection after around 60 seconds.

Syntax: `keepalive_timeout time1 [time2];`

Default value: `75`

```
keepalive_timeout 75;
keepalive_timeout 75 60;
```

keepalive_disable

Context: `http, server, location`

This option allows you to disable the `keepalive` functionality for the browser families of your choice.

Syntax: `keepalive_disable browser1 browser2;`

Default value: `msie6`

send_timeout

Context: `http, server, location`

The amount of time after which Nginx closes an inactive connection. A connection becomes inactive the moment a client stops transmitting data.

Syntax: Time value (in seconds)

Default value: `60`

client_body_in_file_only

Context: `http`, `server`, `location`

If this directive is enabled, the body of incoming HTTP requests will be stored into actual files on the disk. The *client body* corresponds to the client HTTP request raw data, minus the headers (in other words, the content transmitted in POST requests). Files are stored as plain text documents.

This directive accepts three values:

- `off`: Do not store the request body in a file
- `clean`: Store the request body in a file and remove the file after a request is processed
- `on`: Store the request body in a file, but do not remove the file after the request is processed (not recommended unless for debugging purposes)

Syntax: `client_body_in_file_only on | clean | off`

Default value: `off`

client_body_in_single_buffer

Context: `http`, `server`, `location`

Defines whether or not Nginx should store the request body in a single buffer in memory.

Syntax: `on` or `off`

Default value: `off`

client_body_buffer_size

Context: `http`, `server`, `location`

Specifies the size of the buffer holding the body of client requests. If this size is exceeded, the body (or at least part of it) will be written to the disk. Note that if the `client_body_in_file_only` directive is enabled, request bodies are always stored to a file on the disk, regardless of their size (whether they fit in the buffer or not).

Syntax: Size value

Default value: `8k` or `16k` (2 memory pages) depending on your computer architecture

client_body_temp_path

Context: `http`, `server`, `location`

Allows you to define the path of the directory that will store the client request body files. An additional option lets you separate those files into a folder hierarchy over up to three levels.

Syntax: `client_body_temp_path path [level1] [level2] [level3]`

Default value: `client_body_temp`

```
client_body_temp_path /tmp/nginx_rbf;
client_body_temp_path temp 2; # Nginx will create 2-digit folders to
hold request body files
client_body_temp_path temp 1 2 4; # Nginx will create 3 levels of
folders (first level: 1 digit, second level: 2 digits, third level: 4
digits)
```

client_body_timeout

Context: `http`, `server`, `location`

Defines the inactivity timeout while reading a client request body. A connection becomes inactive the moment the client stops transmitting data. If the delay is reached, Nginx returns a `408 Request timeout` HTTP error.

Syntax: Time value (in seconds)

Default value: `60`

client_header_buffer_size

Context: `http`, `server`, `location`

This directive allows you to define the size of the buffer that Nginx allocates to request headers. Usually, `1k` is enough. However, in some cases, the headers contain large chunks of cookie data or the request URI is lengthy. If that is the case, then Nginx allocates one or more larger buffers (the size of larger buffers is defined by the `large_client_header_buffers` directive).

Syntax: Size value

Default value: `1k`

client_header_timeout

Context: `http`, `server`, `location`

Defines the inactivity timeout while reading a client request header. A connection becomes inactive the moment the client stops transmitting data. If the delay is reached, Nginx returns a `408 Request timeout` HTTP error.

Syntax: Time value (in seconds)

Default value: `60`

client_max_body_size

Context: `http`, `server`, `location`

It is the maximum size of a client request body. If this size is exceeded, Nginx returns a `413 Request entity too large` HTTP error. This setting is particularly important if you are going to allow users to upload files to your server over HTTP.

Syntax: Size value

Default value: `1m`

large_client_header_buffers

Context: `http`, `server`, `location`

Defines the amount and size of larger buffers to be used for storing client requests, in case the default buffer (`client_header_buffer_size`) was insufficient. Each line of the header must fit in the size of a single buffer. If the request URI line is greater than the size of a single buffer, Nginx returns the `414 Request URI too large` error. If another header line exceeds the size of a single buffer, Nginx returns a `400 Bad request` error.

Syntax: `large_client_header_buffers amount size`

Default value: 4*8 kilobytes

lingering_time

Context: http, server, location

This directive applies to client requests with a request body. As soon as the amount of uploaded data exceeds max_client_body_size, Nginx immediately sends a 413 Request entity too large HTTP error response. However, most browsers continue uploading data regardless of that notification. This directive defines the amount of time Nginx should wait after sending this error response before closing the connection.

Syntax: Numeric value (time)

Default value: 30 seconds

lingering_timeout

Context: http, server, location

This directive defines the amount of time that Nginx should wait between two read operations before closing the client connection.

Syntax: Numeric value (time)

Default value: 5 seconds

lingering_close

Context: http, server, location

Controls the way Nginx closes client connections. Set this to off to immediately close connections after all of the request data has been received. The default value (on) allows to wait and process additional data if necessary. If set to always, Nginx will always wait to close the connection. The amount of waiting time is defined by the lingering_timeout directive.

Syntax: on, off, or always

Default value: on

ignore_invalid_headers

Context: http, server

If this directive is disabled, Nginx returns a 400 Bad Request HTTP error in case request headers are malformed.

Syntax: on or off

Default value: on

chunked_transfer_encoding

Context: http, server, location

Enables or disables chunked transfer encoding for HTTP 1.1 requests.

Syntax: on or off

Default value: on

max_ranges

Context: http, server, location

Defines how many byte ranges Nginx will accept to serve when a client requests partial content from a file. If you do not specify a value, there is no limit. If you set this to 0, the byte range functionality is disabled.

Syntax: Size value

MIME types

Nginx offers two particular directives that will help you configure MIME types: types and default_type, which defines the default MIME types for documents. This will affect the *Content-Type* HTTP header sent within responses. Read on.

types

Context: http, server, location

This directive allows you to establish correlations between MIME types and file extensions. It's actually a block accepting a particular syntax:

```
types {
  mimetype1   extension1;
  mimetype2   extension2 [extension3...];
  [...]
}
```

When Nginx serves a file, it checks the file extension in order to determine the MIME type. The MIME type is then sent as the value of the Content-Type HTTP header in the response. This header may affect the way browsers handle files. For example, if the MIME type of the file you are requesting is `application/pdf`, your browser may, for instance, attempt to render the file using a plugin associated to that MIME type instead of merely downloading it.

Nginx includes a basic set of MIME types as a standalone file (`mime.types`) to be included with the `include` directive:

```
include mime.types;
```

This file already covers the most important file extensions so you will probably not need to edit it. If the extension of the served file is not found within the listed types, the default type is used, as defined by the `default_type` directive (read below).

Note that you may override the list of types by re-declaring the `types` block. A useful example would be to force all files in a folder to be downloaded instead of being displayed:

```
http {
    include mime.types;
    [...]
    location /downloads/ {
        # removes all MIME types
        types { }
        default_type application/octet-stream;
    }
    [...]
}
```

Note that some browsers ignore MIME types and may still display files if their filename ends with a known extension, such as `.html` or `.txt`.

 To control the way files are handled by the browser of your visitors in a more certain and definitive manner, you should make use of the `Content-Disposition` HTTP header via the `add_header` directive — detailed in the HTTP Headers module (*Chapter 4, Module Configuration*).

The default values, if the `mime.types` file is not included, are:

```
types {
    text/html html;
    image/gif gif;
    image/jpeg jpg;
}
```

default_type

Context: `http, server, location`

Defines the default MIME type. When Nginx serves a file, the file extension is matched against the known types declared within the `types` block in order to return the proper MIME type as value of the `Content-Type` HTTP response header. If the extension doesn't match any of the known MIME types, the value of the `default_type` directive is used.

Syntax: MIME type

Default value: `text/plain`

types_hash_max_size

Context: `http, server, location`

Defines the maximum size of an entry in the MIME types hash table.

Syntax: Numeric value.

Default value: `4 k` or `8 k` (1 line of CPU cache)

Limits and restrictions

This set of directives will allow you to add restrictions that apply when a client attempts to access a particular location or document on your server. Note that you will find additional directives for restricting access in the next chapter.

limit_except

Context: `location`

This directive allows you to prevent the use of all HTTP methods, except the ones that you explicitly allow. Within a `location` block, you may want to restrict the use of some HTTP methods, such as forbidding clients from sending POST requests. You need to define two elements—first, the methods that are not forbidden (the allowed methods; all others will be forbidden), and second, the audience that is affected by the restriction:

```
location /admin/ {
    limit_except GET {
      allow 192.168.1.0/24;
      deny all;
    }
}
```

This example applies a restriction to the /admin/ location—all visitors are only allowed to use the GET method. Visitors that have a local IP address, as specified with the allow directive (detailed in the HTTP Access module), are not affected by this restriction. If a visitor uses a forbidden method, Nginx will return in a 403 Forbidden HTTP error. Note that the GET method implies the HEAD method (if you allow GET, both GET and HEAD are allowed).

The syntax is particular:

```
limit_except METHOD1 [METHOD2...] {
    allow | deny | auth_basic | auth_basic_user_file | proxy_pass |
perl;
}
```

The directives that you are allowed to insert within the block are documented in their respective module section in *Chapter 4, Module Configuration*.

limit_rate

Context: http, server, location, if

Allows you to limit the transfer rate of individual client connections. The rate is expressed in bytes per second:

```
limit_rate 500k;
```

This will limit connection transfer rates to 500 kilobytes per second. If a client opens two connections, the client will be allowed 2 * 500 kilobytes.

Syntax: Size value

Default value: No limit

limit_rate_after

Context: http, server, location, if

Defines the amount of data transferred before the limit_rate directive takes effect.

```
limit_rate 10m;
```

Nginx will send the first 10 megabytes at maximum speed. Past this size, the transfer rate is limited by the value specified with the limit_rate directive (see above). Similar to the limit_rate directive, this setting only applies to a single connection.

Syntax: Size value

Default: None

satisfy

Context: `location`

The `satisfy` directive defines whether clients require all access conditions to be valid (satisfy all) or at least one (satisfy any).

```
location /admin/ {
    allow 192.168.1.0/24;
    deny all;
    auth_basic "Authentication required";
    auth_basic_user_file conf/htpasswd;
}
```

In the previous example, there are two conditions for clients to be able to access the resource:

- Through the `allow` and `deny` directives (HTTP Access module), we only allow clients that have a local IP address, all other clients are denied access
- Through the `auth_basic` and `auth_basic_user_file` directives (HTTP Auth Basic module), we only allow clients that provide a valid username and password

With `satisfy all`, the client must satisfy both conditions in order to gain access to the resource. With `satisfy any`, if the client satisfies either condition, they are granted access.

Syntax: `satisfy any | all`

Default value: `all`

internal

Context: `location`

This directive specifies that the `location` block is internal. In other words, the specified resource cannot be accessed by external requests.

```
server {
    [...]
    server_name .website.com;
    location /admin/ {
        internal;
    }
}
```

With the previous configuration, clients will not be able to browse `http://website.com/admin/`. Such requests will be met with `404 Not Found` errors. The only way to access the resource is via internal redirects (check the *Rewrite module* section for more information on internal redirects).

File processing and caching

It's important for your websites to be built upon solid foundations. File access and caching is a critical aspect of web serving. In this perspective, Nginx lets you perform precise tweaking with the use of the following directives.

disable_symlinks

This directive allows you to control the way Nginx handles symbolic links when they are to be served. By default (directive value is `off`) symbolic links are allowed and Nginx follows them. You may decide to disable the following of symbolic links under different conditions by specifying one of these values:

- `on`: If any part of the requested URI is a symbolic link, access to it is denied and Nginx returns a `403 HTTP` error page.

- `if_not_owner`: Similar to the above, but access is denied only if the link and the object it points to have different owners.

- The optional parameter `from=` allows you to specify a part of the URL that will not be checked for symbolic links. For example, `disable_symlinks on from=$document_root` will tell Nginx to normally follow symbolic links in the URI up to the `$document_root` folder. If a symbolic link is found in the URI parts after that, access to the requested file will be denied.

directio

Context: `http`, `server`, `location`

If this directive is enabled, files with a size greater than the specified value will be read with the Direct I/O system mechanism. This allows Nginx to read data from the storage device and place it directly in memory with no intermediary caching process involved.

Syntax: Size value, or off

Default value: `off`

directio_alignment

Context: `http, server, location`

Sets byte alignment when using `directio`. Set this value to `4k` if you use XFS under Linux.

Syntax: Size value

Default value: 512

open_file_cache

Context: `http, server, location`

This directive allows you to enable the cache which stores information about open files. It does not actually store file contents itself but only information such as:

- File descriptors (file size, modification time, and so on).
- The existence of files and directories.
- File errors, such as Permission denied, File not found, and so on. Note that this can be disabled with the `open_file_cache_errors` directive.

This directive accepts two arguments:

- `max=X`, where `X` is the amount of entries that the cache can store. If this amount is reached, older entries will be deleted in order to leave room for newer entries.
- Optionally `inactive=Y`, where `Y` is the amount of seconds that a cache entry should be stored. By default, Nginx will wait 60 seconds before clearing a cache entry. If the cache entry is accessed, the timer is reset. If the cache entry is accessed more than the value defined by `open_file_cache_min_uses`, the cache entry will not be cleared (until Nginx runs out of space and decides to clear out older entries).

Syntax: `open_file_cache max=X [inactive=Y] | off`

Default value: `off`

Example:

```
open_file_cache max=5000 inactive=180;
```

open_file_cache_errors

Context: `http`, `server`, `location`

Enables or disables the caching of file errors with the `open_file_cache` directive (read above).

Syntax: `on` or `off`

Default value: `off`

open_file_cache_min_uses

Context: `http`, `server`, `location`

By default, entries in the `open_file_cache` are cleared after a period of inactivity (60 seconds, by default). If there is activity though, you can prevent Nginx from removing the cache entry. This directive defines the amount of time an entry must be accessed in order to be eligible for protection.

```
open_file_cache_min_uses 3;
```

If the cache entry is accessed more than three times, it becomes permanently active and is not removed until Nginx decides to clear out older entries to free up some space.

Syntax: Numeric value

Default value: `1`

open_file_cache_valid

Context: `http`, `server`, `location`

The open file cache mechanism is important, but cached information quickly becomes obsolete especially in the case of a fast-moving filesystem. In that perspective, information needs to be re-verified after a short period of time. This directive specifies the amount of seconds that Nginx will wait before revalidating a cache entry.

Syntax: Time value (in seconds)

Default value: `60`

read_ahead

Context: http, server, location

Defines the amount of bytes to pre-read from files. Under Linux-based operating systems, setting this directive to a value above 0 will enable reading ahead, but the actual value you specify has no effect. Set this to 0 to disable pre-reading.

Syntax: Size value

Default value: 0

Other directives

The following directives relate to various aspects of the web server — logging, URI composition, DNS, and so on.

log_not_found

Context: http, server, location

Enables or disables logging of 404 Not Found HTTP errors. If your logs get filled with 404 errors due to missing favicon.ico or robots.txt files, you might want to turn this off.

Syntax: on or off

Default value: on

log_subrequest

Context: http, server, location

Enables or disables logging of sub-requests triggered by internal redirects (see the *Rewrite module* section) or SSI requests (see the *Server Side Includes* module section).

Syntax: on or off

Default value: off

merge_slashes

Context: `http`, `server`, `location`

Enabling this directive will have the effect of merging multiple consecutive slashes in a URI. It turns out to be particularly useful in situations resembling the following:

```
server {
    [...]
    server_name website.com;
    location /documents/ {
        type { }
        default_type text/plain;
    }
}
```

By default, if the client attempts to access `http://website.com//documents/` (note the `//` in the middle of the URI), Nginx will return a `404 Not found` HTTP error. If you enable this directive, the two slashes will be merged into one and the location pattern will be matched.

Syntax: `on` or `off`

Default value: `off`

msie_padding

Context: `http`, `server`, `location`

This directive functions with the Microsoft Internet Explorer (MSIE) and Google Chrome browser families. In the case of error pages (with error code 400 or higher), if the length of the response body is less than 512 bytes, these browsers will display their own error page, sometimes at the expense of a more informative page provided by the server. If you enable this option, the body of responses with a status code of 400 or higher will be padded to 512 bytes.

Syntax: `on` or `off`

Default value: `off`

msie_refresh

Context: `http, server, location`

It is another MSIE-specific directive that will take effect in the case of HTTP response codes `301 Moved permanently` and `302 Moved temporarily`. When enabled, Nginx sends clients running an MSIE browser a response body containing a refresh meta tag (`<meta http-equiv="Refresh"`...`>`) in order to redirect the browser to the new location of the requested resource.

Syntax: `on` or `off`

Default value: `off`

resolver

Context: `http, server, location`

Specifies the name servers that should be employed by Nginx to resolve hostnames to IP addresses and vice-versa. DNS query results are cached for some time, either by respecting the TTL provided by the DNS server, or by specifying a time value to the valid argument.

Syntax: IP addresses, `valid=Time value`

Default value: None (system default)

```
resolver 127.0.0.1; # use local DNS
resolver 8.8.8.8 8.8.4.4 valid=1h; # use Google DNS and cache results
for 1 hour
```

resolver_timeout

Context: `http, server, location`

Timeout for a hostname resolution query.

Syntax: Time value (in seconds)

Default value: 30

server_tokens

Context: `http, server, location`

This directive allows you to define whether or not Nginx should inform the clients of the running version number. There are two situations where Nginx indicates its version number:

- In the server header of HTTP responses (such as `nginx/1.2.9`). If you set `server_tokens` to `off`, the server header will only indicate `Nginx`.
- On error pages, Nginx indicates the version number in the footer. If you set `server_tokens` to `off`, the footer of error pages will only indicate `Nginx`.

If you are running an older version of Nginx and do not plan to update it, it might be a good idea to hide your version number for security reasons.

Syntax: `on` or `off`

Default value: `on`

underscores_in_headers

Context: `http, server`

Allows or disallows underscores in custom HTTP header names. If this directive is set to `on`, the following example header is considered valid by `Nginx: test_header: value`.

Syntax: `on` or `off`

Default value: `off`

variables_hash_max_size

Context: `http`

This directive defines the maximum size of the variables hash tables. If your server configuration uses a total of more than 512 variables, you will have to increase this value.

Syntax: Numeric value

Default value: `512`

variables_hash_bucket_size

Context: `http`

This directive allows you to set the bucket size for the variables hash tables.

Syntax: Numeric value

Default value: `64` (or `32`, or `128`, depending on your processor cache specifications)

post_action

Context: `http`, `server`, `location`, `if`

Defines a post-completion action, a URI that will be called by Nginx after the request has been completed.

Syntax: URI or named `location` block.

Example:

```
location /payment/ {
    post_action /scripts/done.php;
}
```

Module variables

The HTTP Core module introduces a large set of variables that you can use within the value of directives. Be careful though, as only a handful of directives accept variables in the definition of their value. If you insert a variable in the value of a directive that does not accept variables, no error is reported; instead the variable name appears as raw text.

There are three different kinds of variables that you will come across. The first set represents the values transmitted in the headers of the client request. The second set corresponds to the headers of the response sent to the client. Finally, the third set comprises variables that are completely generated by Nginx.

Request headers

Nginx lets you access the client request headers under the form of variables that you will be able to employ later on in the configuration:

Variable	Description
$http_host	Value of the *Host* HTTP header, a string indicating the hostname that the client is trying to reach.
$http_user_agent	Value of the *User-Agent* HTTP header, a string indicating the web browser of the client.
$http_referer	Value of the *Referer* HTTP header, a string indicating the URL of the previous page from which the client comes.
$http_via	Value of the *Via* HTTP header, which informs us about possible proxies used by the client.
$http_x_forwarded_for	Value of the *X-Forwarded-For* HTTP header, which shows the actual IP address of the client if the client is behind a proxy.
$http_cookie	Value of the *Cookie* HTTP header, which contains the cookie data sent by the client.
$http_...	Additional headers sent by the client can be retrieved using $http_ followed by the header name in lowercase and with dashes (-) replaced by underscores (_).

Response headers

In a similar fashion, you are allowed to access the HTTP headers of the response that was sent to the client. These variables are not available at all times—they will only carry a value after the response is sent, for instance, at the time of writing messages in the logs.

Variable	Description
$sent_http_content_type	Value of the *Content-Type* HTTP header, indicating the MIME type of the resource being transmitted.
$sent_http_content_length	Value of the *Content-Length* HTTP header informing the client of the response body length.
$sent_http_location	Value of the *Location* HTTP header, which indicates that the location of the desired resource is different than the one specified in the original request.
$sent_http_last_modified	Value of the *Last-Modified* HTTP header corresponding to the modification date of the requested resource.

Variable	Description
`$sent_http_connection`	Value of the *Connection* HTTP header, defining whether the connection will be kept alive or closed.
`$sent_http_keep_alive`	Value of the *Keep-Alive* HTTP header that defines the amount of time a connection will be kept alive.
`$sent_http_transfer_encoding`	Value of the *Transfer-Encoding* HTTP header, giving information about the response body encoding method (such as compress, gzip).
`$sent_http_cache_control`	Value of the *Cache-Control* HTTP header, telling us whether the client browser should cache the resource or not.
`$sent_http_...`	Additional headers sent to the client can be retrieved using `$sent_http_` followed by the header name, in lowercase and with dashes (-) replaced by underscores (_).

Nginx generated

Apart from the HTTP headers, Nginx provides a large amount of variables concerning the request, the way it was and will be handled, as well as settings in use with the current configuration.

Variable	Description
`$arg_XXX`	Allows you to access the query string (GET parameters), where XXX is the name of the parameter you want to utilize.
`$args`	All of the arguments of the query string combined together.
`$binary_remote_addr`	IP address of the client as binary data (4 bytes).
`$body_bytes_sent`	Amount of bytes sent in the body of the response.
`$connection_requests`	Amount of requests already served by the current connection.
`$content_length`	Equates to the *Content-Length* HTTP header.
`$content_type`	Equates to the *Content-Type* HTTP header.
`$cookie_XXX`	Allows you to access cookie data where XXX is the name of the parameter you want to utilize.
`$document_root`	Returns the value of the `root` directive for the current request.
`$document_uri`	Returns the current URI of the request. It may differ from the original request URI if internal redirects were performed. It is identical to the `$uri` variable.

Variable	Description
$host	This variable equates to the *Host* HTTP header of the request. Nginx itself gives this variable a value for cases where the *Host* header is not provided in the original request.
$hostname	Returns the system hostname of the server computer
$https	Set to on for HTTPS connections, empty otherwise.
$is_args	If the $args variable is defined, $is_args equates to ?. If $args is empty, $is_args is empty as well. You may use this variable for constructing an URI that optionally comes with a query string, such as index.phpis_argsargs. If there is any query string argument in the request, $is_args is set to ?, making this a valid URI.
$limit_rate	Returns the per-connection transfer rate limit, as defined by the limit_rate directive. You are allowed to edit this variable by using set (directive from the Rewrite module): `set $limit_rate 128k;`
$nginx_version	Returns the version of Nginx you are running.
$pid	Returns the Nginx process identifier.
$query_string	Identical to $args.
$remote_addr	Returns the IP address of the client.
$remote_port	Returns the port of the client socket.
$remote_user	Returns the client username if they used authentication.
$realpath_root	Returns the document root in the client request, with symbolic links resolved into the actual path.
$request_body	Returns the body of the client request, or - if the body is empty.
$request_body_file	If the request body was saved (see the client_body_in_file_only directive) this variable indicates the path of the temporary file.
$request_completion	Returns OK if the request is completed, an empty string otherwise.
$request_filename	Returns the full filename served in the current request.
$request_method	Indicates the HTTP method used in the request, such as GET or POST.
$request_uri	Corresponds to the original URI of the request, remains unmodified all along the process (unlike $document_uri/$uri).
$scheme	Returns either http or https, depending on the request.

Variable	Description
`$server_addr`	Returns the IP address of the server. Be aware as each use of the variable requires a system call, which could potentially affect overall performance in the case of high-traffic setups.
`$server_name`	Indicates the value of the `server_name` directive that was used while processing the request.
`$server_port`	Indicates the port of the server socket that received the request data.
`$server_protocol`	Returns the protocol and version, usually `HTTP/1.0` or `HTTP/1.1`.
`$tcpinfo_rtt`, `$tcpinfo_rttvar`, `$tcpinfo_snd_cwnd`, `$tcpinfo_rcv_space`	If your operating system supports the `TCP_INFO` socket option, these variables will be populated with information on the current client TCP connection.
`$time_iso8601`, `$time_local`	Provides the current time respectively in ISO 8601 and local formats for use with the `access_log` directive.
`$uri`	Identical to `$document_uri`.

The Location block

We have established that Nginx offers you the possibility to fine-tune your configuration down to three levels—at the *protocol* level (`http` block), the server level (`server` block), and the requested URI level (`location` block). Let us now detail the latter.

Location modifier

Nginx allows you to `define` location blocks by specifying a pattern that will be matched against the requested document URI.

```
server {
    server_name website.com;
    location /admin/ {
    # The configuration you place here only applies to
    # http://website.com/admin/
    }
}
```

Instead of a simple folder name, you can indeed insert complex patterns. The syntax of the `location` block is:

```
location [=|~|~*|^~|@] pattern { ... }
```

The first optional argument is a symbol called **location modifier** that will define the way Nginx matches the specified pattern and also defines the very nature of the pattern (simple string or regular expression). The following paragraphs detail the different modifiers and their behavior.

The = modifier

The requested document URI must match the specified pattern exactly. The pattern here is limited to a simple literal string; you cannot use a regular expression:

```
server {
    server_name website.com;
    location = /abcd {
    [...]
    }
}
```

The configuration in the `location` block:

- Applies to `http://website.com/abcd` (exact match)
- Applies to `http://website.com/ABCD` (it is case-sensitive if your operating system uses a case-sensitive filesystem)
- Applies to `http://website.com/abcd?param1&param2` (regardless of query string arguments)
- Does not apply to `http://website.com/abcd/` (trailing slash)
- Does not apply to `http://website.com/abcde` (extra characters after the specified pattern)

No modifier

The requested document URI must begin with the specified pattern. You may not use regular expressions:

```
server {
    server_name website.com;
    location /abcd {
    [...]
    }
}
```

The configuration in the `location` block:

- Applies to `http://website.com/abcd` (exact match)
- Applies to `http://website.com/ABCD` (it is case-sensitive if your operating system uses a case-sensitive filesystem)
- Applies to `http://website.com/abcd?param1&param2` (regardless of query string arguments)
- Applies to `http://website.com/abcd/` (trailing slash)
- Applies to `http://website.com/abcde` (extra characters after the specified pattern)

The ~ modifier

The requested URI must be a case-sensitive match to the specified regular expression:

```
server {
    server_name website.com;
    location ~ ^/abcd$ {
    [...]
    }
}
```

The `^/abcd$` regular expression used in this example specifies that the pattern must begin (`^`) with /, be followed by `abc`, and finish (`$`) with `d`. Consequently, the configuration in the `location` block:

- Applies to `http://website.com/abcd` (exact match)
- Does not apply to `http://website.com/ABCD` (case-sensitive)
- Applies to `http://website.com/abcd?param1&param2` (regardless of query string arguments)
- Does not apply to `http://website.com/abcd/` (trailing slash) due to the specified regular expression
- Does not apply to `http://website.com/abcde` (extra characters) due to the specified regular expression

> With operating systems such as Microsoft Windows, ~ and ~* are both case-insensitive, as the OS uses a case-insensitive filesystem.

The ~* modifier

The requested URI must be a case-insensitive match to the specified regular expression:

```
server {
    server_name website.com;
    location ~* ^/abcd$ {
    [...]
    }
}
```

The regular expression used in the example is similar to the previous one. Consequently, the configuration in the `location` block:

- Applies to `http://website.com/abcd` (exact match)
- Applies to `http://website.com/ABCD` (case-insensitive)
- Applies to `http://website.com/abcd?param1&param2` (regardless of query string arguments)
- Does not apply to `http://website.com/abcd/` (trailing slash) due to the specified regular expression
- Does not apply to `http://website.com/abcde` (extra characters) due to the specified regular expression

The ^~ modifier

Similar to the no-symbol behavior, the location URI must begin with the specified pattern. The difference is that if the pattern is matched, Nginx stops searching for other patterns (read the section below about search order and priority).

The @ modifier

Defines a named `location` block. These blocks cannot be accessed by the client, but only by internal requests generated by other directives, such as `try_files` or `error_page`.

Search order and priority

Since it's possible to define multiple `location` blocks with different patterns, you need to understand that when Nginx receives a request, it searches for the `location` block that best matches the requested URI:

```
server {
    server_name website.com;
    location /files/ {
```

```
# applies to any request starting with "/files/"
# for example /files/doc.txt, /files/, /files/temp/
}
location = /files/ {
# applies to the exact request to "/files/"
# and as such does not apply to /files/doc.txt
# but only /files/
}
}
```

When a client visits `http://website.com/files/doc.txt`, the first `location` block applies. However, when they visit `http://website.com/files/`, the second block applies (even though the first one matches) because it has priority over the first one (it is an exact match).

The order you established in the configuration file (placing the `/files/` block before the `= /files/` block) is irrelevant. Nginx will search for matching patterns in a specific order:

1. `location` blocks with the = modifier: If the specified string exactly matches the requested URI, Nginx retains the `location` block.

2. `location` blocks with no modifier: If the specified string exactly matches the requested URI, Nginx retains the `location` block.

3. `location` blocks with the ^~ modifier: If the specified string matches the beginning of the requested URI, Nginx retains the `location` block.

4. `location` blocks with ~ or ~* modifier: If the regular expression matches the requested URI, Nginx retains the `location` block.

5. `location` blocks with no modifier: If the specified string matches the beginning of the requested URI, Nginx retains the `location` block.

In that extent, the ^~ modifier begins to make sense, and we can envision cases where it becomes useful.

Case 1:

```
server {
    server_name website.com;
    location /doc {
    [...] # requests beginning with "/doc"
    }
    location ~* ^/document$ {
    [...] # requests exactly matching "/document"
    }
}
```

You might wonder: when a client requests `http://website.com/document`, which of these two `location` blocks applies? Indeed, both blocks match this request. Again, the answer does not lie in the order in which the blocks appear in the configuration files. In this case, the second `location` block will apply as the ~* modifier has priority over the other.

Case 2:

```
server {
    server_name website.com;
    location /document {
    [...] # requests beginning with "/document"
    }
    location ~* ^/document$ {
    [...] # requests exactly matching "/document"
    }
}
```

The question remains the same—what happens when a client sends a request to download `http://website.com/document`? There is a trick here. The string specified in the first block now exactly matches the requested URI. As a result, Nginx prefers it over the regular expression.

Case 3:

```
server {
    server_name website.com;
    location ^~ /doc {
    [...] # requests beginning with "/doc"
    }
    location ~* ^/document$ {
    [...] # requests exactly matching "/document"
    }
}
```

This last case makes use of the ^~ modifier. Which block applies when a client visits `http://website.com/document`? The answer is the first block. The reason being that ^~ has priority over ~*. As a result, any request with a URI beginning with / doc will be affected to the first block, even if the request URI matches the regular expression defined in the second block.

Summary

All along this chapter we studied key concepts of the Nginx HTTP configuration. First, we learned about creating virtual hosts by declaring `server` blocks. Then we discovered the directives and variables of the HTTP Core module that can be inserted within those blocks and eventually understood the mechanisms governing the `location` block.

The job is done—your server now actually serves websites. We are going to take it one step further by discovering the modules that truly form the power of Nginx. The next chapter will deal with advanced topics, such as the Rewrite and SSI modules, as well as additional components of the HTTP server.

4
Module Configuration

The true richness of Nginx lies within its modules. The entire application is built on a modular system, and each module can be enabled or disabled at compile time. Some bring up simple functionality such as the *Autoindex* module that generates a listing of the files in a directory. Some will transform your perception of a web server (such as the Rewrite module). Developers are also invited to create their own modules. A quick overview of the third-party module system can be found at the end of this chapter.

This chapter covers:

- The Rewrite module, which does more than just rewriting URIs
- The SSI module, a server-side scripting language
- Additional modules enabled in the default Nginx build
- Optional modules that must be enabled at compile time
- A quick note on third-party modules

Rewrite module

This module, in particular, brings much more functionality to Nginx than a simple set of directives. It defines a whole new level of request processing that will be explained all along this section.

Initially, the purpose of this module (as the name suggests) is to perform URL rewriting. This mechanism allows you to get rid of *ugly* URLs containing multiple parameters, for instance, `http://example.com/article. php?id=1234&comment=32` — such URLs being particularly uninformative and meaningless for a regular visitor. Instead, links to your website will contain useful information that indicate the nature of the page you are about to visit. The URL given in the example becomes `http://website.com/article-1234-32-US-economy-strengthens.html`. This solution is not only more interesting for your visitors, but also for search engines — URL rewriting is a key element to **Search Engine Optimization (SEO)**.

The principle behind this mechanism is simple — it consists of rewriting the URI of the client request after it is received, before serving the file. Once rewritten, the URI is matched against `location` blocks in order to find the configuration that should be applied to the request. The technique is further detailed in the coming sections.

Reminder on regular expressions

First and foremost, this module requires a certain understanding of *regular expressions*, also known as *regexes* or *regexps*. Indeed, URL rewriting is performed by the `rewrite` directive, which accepts a pattern followed by the replacement URI.

It is a vast topic — entire books are dedicated to explaining the ins and outs. However, the simplified approach that we are about to examine should be more than sufficient to make the most of the mechanism.

Purpose

The first question we must answer is: What's the purpose of regular expressions? To put it simply, the main purpose is to verify that a string matches a pattern. The said pattern is written in a particular language that allows defining extremely complex and accurate rules.

String	Pattern	Matches?	Explanation
hello	^hello$	Yes	The string begins by character h (^h), followed by e, l, l, and then finishes by o (o$).
hell	^hello$	No	The string begins by character h (^h), followed by e, l, l but does not finish by o.
Hello	^hello$	Depends	If the engine performing the match is case-sensitive, the string doesn't match the pattern.

This concept becomes a lot more interesting when complex patterns are employed, such as one that validate an e-mail addresses: `^[A-Z0-9._%+-]+@[A-Z0-9.-]+\.[A-Z]{2,4}$`. Validating the well-forming of an e-mail address programmatically would require a great deal of code, while all of the work can be done with a single regular expression pattern matching.

PCRE syntax

The syntax that Nginx employs originates from the Perl Compatible Regular Expression (**PCRE**) library, which (if you remember *Chapter 2, Basic Nginx Configuration*) is a pre-requisite for making your own build (unless you disable modules that make use of it). It's the most commonly used form of regular expression, and nearly everything you learn here remains valid for other language variations.

In its simplest form, a pattern is composed of one character, for example, x. We can match strings against this pattern. Does `example` match the pattern x? Yes, `example` contains the character x. It can be more than one specific character — the pattern `[a-z]` matches any character between a and z, or even a combination of letters and digits: `[a-z0-9]`. In consequence, the pattern `hell[a-z0-9]` validates the following strings: `hello` and `hell4`, but not `hell` or `hell!`.

You probably noticed that we employed the characters `[` and `]`. These are called **metacharacters** and have a special effect on the pattern. There are a total of 11 metacharacters, and all play a different role. If you want to actually create a pattern containing one of these characters, you need to escape them with the `\` character.

Metacharacter	Description
^ Beginning	The entity after this character must be found at the beginning.
	Example pattern: `^h`
	Matching strings: `hello`, `h`, `hh`
	Non-matching strings: `character`, `ssh`
$ End	The entity before this character must be found at the end.
	Example pattern: `e$`
	Matching strings: `sample`, `e`, `file`
	Non-matching strings: `extra`, `shell`
. Any	Matches any character.
	Example pattern: `hell`
	Matching strings: `hello`, `hellx`, `hell5`, `hell!`
	Non-matching strings: `hell`, `helo`

Metacharacter	Description
[ ] Set	Matches any character within the specified set. Syntax: `[a-z]` for a range, `[abcd]` for a set, and `[a-z0-9]` for two ranges. Note that if you want to include the – character in a range, you need to insert it right after the `[` or just before the `]`. Example pattern: `hell[a-y123-]` Matching strings: `hello, hell1, hell2, hell3, hell-` Non-matching strings: `hellz, hell4, heloo, he-llo`
[^] Negate set	Matches any character that is not within the specified set. Example pattern: `hell[^a-np-z0-9]` Matching strings: `hello, hell;` Non-matching strings: `hella, hell5`
| Alternation	Matches the entity placed either before or after the `|`. Example pattern: `hello|welcome` Matching strings: `hello, welcome, helloes, awelcome` Non-matching strings: `hell, ellow, owelcom`
( ) Grouping	Groups a set of entities, often to be used in conjunction with `|`. Example pattern: `^(hello|hi) there$` Matching strings: `hello there, hi there.` Non-matching strings: `hey there, ahoy there`
\\ Escape	Allows you to escape special characters. Example pattern: `Hello\.` Matching strings: `Hello., Hello. How are you?, Hi! Hello...` Non-matching strings: `Hello, Hello, how are you?`

Quantifiers

So far, you are able to express simple patterns with a limited number of characters. Quantifiers allow you to extend the amount of accepted entities:

Quantifier	Description
* 0 or more times	The entity preceding * must be found 0 or more times. Example pattern: `he*llo` Matching strings: `hllo, hello, heeeello` Non-matching strings: `hallo, ello`

Quantifier	Description
+ 1 or more times	The entity preceding + must be found 1 or more times. Example pattern: `he+llo` Matching strings: `hello`, `heeeello` Non-matching strings: `hllo`, `helo`
? 0 or 1 time	The entity preceding ? must be found 0 or 1 time. Example pattern: `he?llo` Matching strings: `hello`, `hllo` Non-matching strings: `heello`, `heeeello`
{x} x times	The entity preceding {x} must be found x times. Example pattern: `he{3}llo` Matching strings: `heeello`, `oh heeello there!` Non-matching strings: `hello`, `heello`, `heeeello`
{x, } At least x times	The entity preceding {x, } must be found at least x times. Example pattern: `he{3,}llo` Matching strings: `heeello`, `heeeeeello` Non-matching strings: `hllo`, `hello`, `heello`
{x,y} x to y times	The entity preceding {x,y} must be found between x and y times. Example pattern: `he{2,4}llo` Matching strings: `heello`, `heeello`, `heeeello` Non-matching strings: `hello`, `heeeeello`

As you probably noticed, the { and } characters in the regular expressions conflict with the block delimiter of the Nginx configuration file syntax language. If you want to write a regular expression pattern that includes curly brackets, you need to place the pattern between quotes (single or double quotes):

```
rewrite hel{2,}o /hello.php; # invalid
rewrite "hel{2,}o" /hello.php; # valid
rewrite 'hel{2,}o' /hello.php; # valid
```

Captures

One last feature of the regular expression mechanism is the ability to capture sub-expressions. Whatever text is placed between parentheses ( ) is captured and can be used after the matching process.

Here are a couple of examples to illustrate the principle:

Pattern	String	Captured
`^(hello|hi) (sir|mister)$`	hello sir	$1 = hello
		$2 = sir
`^(hello (sir))$`	hello sir	$1 = hello sir
		$2 = sir
`^(.*)$`	nginx rocks	$1 = nginx rocks
`^(.{1,3})([0-9]{1,4})([?!]{1,2})$`	abc1234!?	$1 = abc
		$2 = 1234
		$3 = !?
Named captures are also supported:	/admin/doc	$folder = admin
`^/(?<folder>[^/]*)/(?<file>.*)$`		$file = doc

When you use a regular expression in Nginx, for example, in the context of a location block, the buffers that you capture can be employed in later directives:

```
server {
    server_name website.com;
    location ~* ^/(downloads|files)/(.*)$ {
        add_header Capture1 $1;
        add_header Capture2 $2;
    }
}
```

In the preceding example, the `location` block will match the request URI against a regular expression. A couple of URIs that would apply here: `/downloads/file.txt`, `/files/archive.zip`, or even `/files/docs/report.doc`. Two parts are captured: `$1` will contain either `downloads` or `files` and `$2` will contain whatever comes after `/downloads/` or `/files/`. Note that the `add_header` directive (syntax: `add_header header_name header_value`, see the *HTTP headers module* section) is employed here to append arbitrary headers to the client response for the sole purpose of demonstration.

Internal requests

Nginx differentiates external and internal requests. External requests directly originate from the client; the URI is then matched against possible `location` blocks:

```
server {
    server_name website.com;
    location = /document.html {
```

```
        deny all; # example directive
    }
}
```

A client request to `http://website.com/document.html` would directly fall into the above `location` block.

Opposite to this, internal requests are triggered by Nginx via specific directives. In default Nginx modules, there are several directives capable of producing internal requests: `error_page`, `index`, `rewrite`, `try_files`, `add_before_body`, `add_after_body` (from the Addition module), the `include` SSI command, and more.

There are two different kinds of internal requests:

- **Internal redirects** Nginx redirects the client requests internally. The URI is changed, and the request may therefore match another `location` block and become eligible for different settings. The most common case of internal redirects is when using the Rewrite directive, which allows you to rewrite the request URI.

- **Sub-requests**: Additional requests that are triggered internally to generate content that is complementary to the main request. A simple example would be with the Addition module. The `add_after_body` directive allows you to specify a URI that will be processed after the original one, the resulting content being appended to the body of the original request. The SSI module also makes use of sub-requests to insert content with the `include` command.

error_page

Detailed in the module directives of the Nginx HTTP Core module, `error_page` allows you to define the server behavior when a specific error code occurs. The simplest form is to affect a URI to an error code:

```
server {
    server_name website.com;
    error_page 403 /errors/forbidden.html;
    error_page 404 /errors/not_found.html;
}
```

When a client attempts to access a URI that triggers one of these errors, Nginx is supposed to serve the page corresponding to the error code. In fact, it does not just send the client the error page—it actually initiates a completely new request based on the new URI.

Consequently, you can end up falling back on a different configuration, like in the following example:

```
server {
    server_name website.com;
    root /var/www/vhosts/website.com/httpdocs/;
    error_page 404 /errors/404.html;
    location /errors/ {
        alias /var/www/common/errors/;
        internal;
    }
}
```

When a client attempts to load a document that does not exist, they will initially receive a 404 error. We employed the error_page directive to specify that 404 errors should create an internal redirect to /errors/404.html. As a result, a new request is generated by Nginx with the URI /errors/404.html. This URI falls under the location /errors/ block so the configuration applies.

> Logs can prove to be particularly useful when working with redirects and URL rewrites. Be aware that information on internal redirects will show up in the logs only if you set the error_log directive to debug. You can also get it to show up at the notice level, under the condition that you specify rewrite_log on; wherever you need it.

A raw, but trimmed, excerpt from the debug log summarizes the mechanism:

```
->http request line: "GET /page.html HTTP/1.1"
->http uri: "/page.html"
->test location: "/errors/"
->using configuration ""
->http filename: "/var/www/vhosts/website.com/httpdocs/page.html"
-> open() "/var/www/vhosts/website.com/httpdocs/page.html" failed (2:
No such file or directory), client: 127.0.0.1, server: website.com,
request: "GET /page.html HTTP/1.1", host:"website.com"
->http finalize request: 404, "/page.html?" 1
->http special response: 404, "/page.html?"
->internal redirect: "/errors/404.html?"
->test location: "/errors/"
->using configuration "/errors/"
->http filename: "/var/www/common/errors/404.html"
->http finalize request: 0, "/errors/404.html?" 1
```

Note that the use of the `internal` directive in the `location` block forbids clients from accessing the `/errors/` directory. This location can only be accessed from an internal redirect.

The mechanism is the same for the `index` directive (detailed further on in the Index module) — if no file path is provided in the client request, Nginx will attempt to serve the specified index page by triggering an internal redirect.

Rewrite

While the previous directive `error_page` is not actually part of the Rewrite module, detailing its functionality provides a solid introduction to the way Nginx handles requests.

Similar to how the `error_page` directive redirects to another location, rewriting the URI with the `rewrite` directive generates an internal redirect:

```
server {
    server_name website.com;
    root /var/www/vhosts/website.com/httpdocs/;
    location /storage/ {
        internal;
        alias /var/www/storage/;
    }
    location /documents/ {
        rewrite ^/documents/(.*)$ /storage/$1;
    }
}
```

A client query to `http://website.com/documents/file.txt` initially matches the second `location` block (`location /documents/`). However, the block contains a rewrite instruction that transforms the URI from `/documents/file.txt` to `/storage/file.txt`. The URI transformation reinitializes the process — the new URI is matched against the `location` blocks. This time, the first `location` block (`location /storage/`) matches the URI (`/storage/file.txt`).

Again, a quick peek at the debug log confirms the mechanism:

```
->http request line: "GET /documents/file.txt HTTP/1.1"
->http uri: "/documents/file.txt"
->test location: "/storage/"
->test location: "/documents/"
->using configuration "/documents/"
->http script regex: "^/documents/(.*)$"
```

```
->"^/documents/(.*)$" matches "/documents/file.txt", client:
127.0.0.1, server: website.com, request: "GET /documents/file.txt
HTTP/1.1", host: "website.com"
->rewritten data: "/storage/file.txt", args: "", client: 127.0.0.1,
server: website.com, request: "GET /documents/file.txt HTTP/1.1",
host: "website.com"
->test location: "/storage/"
->using configuration "/storage/"
->http filename: "/var/www/storage/file.txt"
->HTTP/1.1 200 OK
->http output filter "/storage/test.txt?"
```

Infinite loops

With all of the different syntaxes and directives, you may easily get confused.
Worse—you might get Nginx confused. This happens, for instance, when your
rewrite rules are redundant and cause internal redirects to loop infinitely:

```
server {
    server_name website.com;
    location /documents/ {
        rewrite ^(.*)$ /documents/$1;
    }
}
```

You thought you were doing well, but this configuration actually triggers internal
redirects /documents/anything to /documents//documents/anything. Moreover,
since the location patterns are re-evaluated after an internal redirect, /documents//
documents/anything becomes /documents//documents//documents/anything.

Here is the corresponding excerpt from the debug log:

```
->test location: "/documents/"
->using configuration "/documents/"
->rewritten data: "/documents//documents/file.txt", [...]
->test location: "/documents/"
->using configuration "/documents/"
->rewritten data: "/documents//documents//documents/file.txt" [...]
->test location: "/documents/"
->using configuration "/documents/"
->rewritten data: -
>"/documents//documents//documents//documents/file.txt" [...]
->[...]
```

You probably wonder if this goes on indefinitely — the answer is no. The amount of cycles is restricted to 10. You are only allowed 10 internal redirects. Anything past this limit and Nginx will produce a `500 Internal Server Error`.

Server Side Includes (SSI)

A potential source of sub-requests is the **Server Side Include (SSI)** module. The purpose of SSI is for the server to parse documents before sending the response to the client in a somewhat similar fashion to PHP or other preprocessors.

Within a regular HTML file (for example), you have the possibility to insert tags corresponding to commands interpreted by Nginx:

```
<html>
<head>
  <!--# include file="header.html" -->
</head>
<body>
  <!--# include file="body.html" -->
</body>
</html>
```

Nginx processes these two commands; in this case, it reads the contents of `head.html` and `body.html` and inserts them into the document source, which is then sent to the client.

Several commands are at your disposal; they are detailed in the SSI module section in this chapter. The one we are interested in for now is the `include` command — including a file into another file:

```
<!--# include virtual="/footer.php?id=123" -->
```

The specified file is not just opened and read from a static location. Instead, a whole subrequest is processed by Nginx, and the body of the response is inserted instead of the `include` tag.

Conditional structure

The Rewrite module introduces a new set of directives and blocks, among which is the `if` conditional structure:

```
server {
    if ($request_method = POST) {
      [...]
    }
}
```

This gives you the possibility to apply a configuration according to the specified condition. If the condition is true, the configuration is applied; otherwise, it isn't.

The following table describes the different syntaxes accepted when forming a condition:

Operator	Description
None	The condition is true if the specified variable or data is not equal to an empty string or a string starting with character 0:

	``
	if ($string) {
	    [...]
	}
	``

=, !=	The condition is true if the argument preceding the = symbol is equal to the argument following it. The following example can be read as "if the request_method is equal to POST, then apply the configuration":

	``
	if ($request_method = POST) {
	    [...]
	}
	``

	The != operator does the opposite: "if the request method is different than GET, then apply the configuration":

	``
	if ($request_method != GET) {
	    [...]
	}
	``

~, ~*, !~, !~*	The condition is true if the argument preceding the ~ symbol matches the regular expression pattern placed after it:

	``
	if ($request_filename ~ "\.txt$") {
	    [...]
	}
	``

	~ is case-sensitive, ~* is case-insensitive. Use the ! symbol to negate the matching:

	``
	if ($request_filename !~* "\.php$") {
	    [...]
	}
	``

	Note that you can insert capture buffers in the regular expression:

	``
	if ($uri ~ "^/search/(.*)$") {
	    set $query $1;
	    rewrite ^ http://google.com/search?q=$query;
	}
	``

Operator	Description

`-f, !-f`	Tests the existence of the specified file:
	
	```if (-f $request_filename) {```
	``` [...] # if the file exists```
	```}```
	```Use !-f to test the non-existence of the file:```
	```if (!-f $request_filename) {```
	``` [...] # if the file does not exist```
	```}```

`-d, !-d`	Similar to the `-f` operator, for testing the existence of a directory.
`-e, !-e`	Similar to the `-f` operator, for testing the existence of a file, directory, or symbolic link.
`-x, !-x`	Similar to the `-f` operator, for testing if a file exists and is executable.

As of version 1.2.9, there is no `else`- or `else if`-like instruction. However, other directives allowing you to control the flow sequencing are available.

You might wonder: what are the advantages of using a `location` block over an `if` block? Indeed, in the following example, both seem to have the same effect:

```
if ($uri ~ /search/) {
    [...]
}
location ~ /search/ {
    [...]
}
```

As a matter of fact, the main difference lies within the directives that can be employed within either block—some can be inserted in an `if` block and some can't; on the contrary, almost all directives are authorized within a `location` block, as you probably noticed in the directive listings. In general, it's best to only insert directives from the Rewrite module within an `if` block, as other directives were not originally intended for such usage.

Directives

The Rewrite module provides you with a set of directives that do more than just rewriting a URI. The following table describes these directives along with the context in which they can be employed:

Directive	Description

`rewrite`
 	
Context: `server,`
`location, if`
	As discussed previously, the `rewrite` directive allows you to rewrite the URI of the current request, thus resetting the treatment of the said request.

	Syntax: `rewrite regexp replacement [flag];`
	Where `regexp` is the regular expression the URI should match in order for the replacement to apply.
	Flag may take one of the following values:
	• `last`: The current rewrite rule should be the last to be applied. After its application, the new URI is processed by Nginx and a `location` block is searched for. However, further rewrite instructions will be disregarded.
	• `break`: The current rewrite rule is applied, but Nginx does not initiate a new request for the modified URI (does not restart the search for matching `location` blocks). All further rewrite directives are ignored.
	• `redirect`: Returns a `302 Moved temporarily` HTTP response, with the replacement URI set as value of the `location` header.
	• `permanent`: Returns a `301 Moved permanently` HTTP response, with the replacement URI set as the value of the `location` header.
	• If you specify a URI beginning with `http://` as the replacement URI, Nginx will automatically use the `redirect` flag.

Directive	Description
	• Note that the request URI processed by the directive is a relative URI: It does not contain the hostname and protocol. For a request such as `http://website.com/documents/page.html`, the request URI is `/documents/page.html`.
	• Is decoded: The URI corresponding to a request such as `http://website.com/my%20page.html` would be `/my page.html`.
	• Does not contain arguments: For a request such as `http://website.com/page.php?id=1&p=2`, the URI would be `/page.php`. When rewriting the URI, you don't need to consider including the arguments in the replacement URI— Nginx does it for you. If you wish for Nginx to not include the arguments in the rewritten URI, then insert a ? at the end of the replacement URI: `rewrite ^/search/(.*)$ /search.php?q=$1?`.

	• Examples:
	 ```rewrite ^/search/(.*)$ /search.php?q=$1;```
	 ```rewrite ^/search/(.*)$ /search.php?q=$1?;```
	 ```rewrite ^ http://website.com;```
	 ```rewrite ^ http://website.com permanent;```

`break`
 	
Context: `server,`
`location, if`
	The `break` directive is used to prevent further rewrite directives. Past this point, the URI is fixed and cannot be altered.
	
	Example:
	```if (-f $uri) {```
	``` break; # break if the file exists```
	```}```
	```if ($uri ~ ^/search/(.*)$) {```
	``` set $query $1;```
	``` rewrite ^ /search.php?q=$query?;```
	```}```
	
	This example rewrites `/search/anything`-like queries to `/search.php?q=anything`. However, if the requested file exists (such as `/search/index.html`), the break instruction prevents Nginx from rewriting the URI.

Directive	Description
`return` Context: `server,` `location, if`	Interrupts the request treatment process and returns the specified HTTP status code or specified text. Syntax: `return code	text;`  Where code is picked among the following status codes: `204`, `400`, `402` to `406`, `408`, `410`, `411`, `413`, `416`, and `500` to `504`. In addition, you may use the Nginx-specific code `444` in order to return a HTTP `200 OK` status code with no further header or body data. You may also specify the raw text that will be returned to the user as response body. Example: ``` if ($uri ~ ^/admin/) { return 403; # the instruction below is NOT executed # as Nginx already completed the request rewrite ^ http://website.com; } ```

`set`
 	
Context: `server,`
`location, if`
	Initializes or redefines a variable. Note that some variables cannot be redefined, for example, you are not allowed to alter `$uri`.
	
	Syntax: `set $variable value;`
	
	Examples:
	
	``
	set $var1 "some text";
	if ($var1 ~ ^(.*) (.*)$) {
	    set $var2 $1$2; #concatenation
	    rewrite ^ http://website.com/$var2;
	}
	``

`uninitialized_`
`variable_warn`
 	
Context: `http,`
`server,`
`location, if`
	If set to on, Nginx will issue log messages when the configuration employs a variable that has not yet been initialized.
	
	Syntax: on or off
	
	`uninitialized_variable_warn on;`

`rewrite_log`
 	
Context: `http,`
`server,`
`location, if`
	If set to on, Nginx will issue log messages for every operation performed by the rewrite engine at the `notice` error level (see `error_log` directive).
	
	Syntax: on or off
	
	Default value: `off`
	
	`rewrite_log off;`

Common rewrite rules

Here is a set of rewrite rules that satisfy basic needs for dynamic websites that wish to beautify their page links thanks to the URL rewriting mechanism. You will obviously need to adjust these rules according to your particular situation as every website is different.

Performing a search

This rewrite rule is intended for search queries. Search keywords are included in the URL.

Input URI	`http://website.com/search/some-search-keywords`
Rewritten URI	`http://website.com/search.php?q=some-search-keywords`
Rewrite rule	`rewrite ^/search/(.*)$ /search.php?q=$1?;`

User profile page

Most dynamic websites that allow visitors to register, offer a profile view page. URLs of this form can be employed, containing both the user ID and the username.

Input URI	`http://website.com/user/31/James`
Rewritten URI	`http://website.com/user.php?id=31&name=James`
Rewrite rule	`rewrite ^/user/([0-9]+)/(.+)$ /user.php?id=$1&name=$2?;`

Multiple parameters

Some websites may use different syntaxes for the argument string, for example, by separating non-named arguments with slashes.

Input URI	`http://website.com/index.php/param1/param2/param3`
Rewritten URI	`http://website.com/index.php?p1=param1&p2=param2&p3=param3`
Rewrite rule	`rewrite ^/index.php/(.*)/(.*)/(.*)$ /index.php?p1=$1&p2=$2&p3=$3?;`

Wikipedia-like

Many websites have now adopted the URL style introduced by Wikipedia: a prefix folder, followed by an article name.

Input URI	`http:// website.com/wiki/Some_keyword`
Rewritten URI	`http://website.com/wiki/index.php?title=Some_keyword`
Rewrite rule	`rewrite ^/wiki/(.*)$ /wiki/index.php?title=$1?;`

News website article

This URL structure is often employed by news websites as URLs contain indications of the articles' contents. It is formed of an article identifier, followed by a slash, then a list of keywords. The keywords can usually be ignored and not included in the rewritten URI.

Input URI	`http://website.com/33526/us-economy-strengthens`
Rewritten URI	`http://website.com/article.php?id=33526`
Rewrite rule	`rewrite ^/([0-9]+)/.*$ /article.php?id=$1?;`

Discussion board

Modern bulletin boards now use *pretty URLs* for the most part. This example shows how to create a *topic view* URL with two parameters—the topic identifier and the starting post. Once again, keywords are ignored:

Input URI	`http://website.com/topic-1234-50-some-keywords.html`
Rewritten URI	`http://website.com/viewtopic.php?topic=1234&start=50`
Rewrite rule	`rewrite ^/topic-([0-9]+)-([0-9]+)-(.*)\.html$ /viewtopic.php?topic=$1&start=$2?;`

SSI module

SSI, for Server Side Includes, is actually a sort of server-side programming language interpreted by Nginx. Its name is based on the fact that the most used functionality of the language is the `include` command. Back in the 1990s, such languages were employed in order to render web pages dynamic, from simple static `.html` files with client-side scripts to complex pages with server-processed compositions. Within the HTML source code, webmasters could now insert server-interpreted directives, which would then lead the way to more advanced pre-processors such as PHP or ASP.

The most famous illustration of SSI is the *quote of the day*. In order to insert a new quote every day at the top of each page of their website, webmasters would have to edit out the HTML source of every page, replacing the former quote manually. With Server Side Includes, a single command suffices to simplify the task:

```
<html>
<head><title>My web page</title></head>
<body>
  <h1>Quote of the day: <!--# include file="quote.txt" -->
  </h1>
</body>
</html>
```

All you would have to do to insert a new quote is to edit the contents of the `quote.txt` file. Automatically, all pages would show the updated quote. As of today, most of the major web servers (Apache, IIS, Lighttpd, and so on) support Server Side Includes.

Module directives and variables

Having directives inserted within the actual content of files that Nginx serves raises one major issue—what files should Nginx parse for SSI commands? It would be a waste of resources to parse binary files such as images (`.gif`, `.jpg`, `.png`) or other kinds of media. You need to make sure to configure Nginx correctly with the directives introduced by this module:

Directive	Description
`ssi` Context: `http, server, location, if`	Enables parsing files for SSI commands. Nginx only parses files corresponding to MIME types selected with the `ssi_types` directive. Syntax: `on` or `off` Default value: `off` `ssi on;`

`ssi_types`
 	
Context: `http, server, location`
	Defines the MIME file types that should be eligible for SSI parsing. The `text/html` type is always included.
	
	Syntax:
	`ssi_types type1 [type2] [type3...];`
	`ssi_types *;`
	
	Default value: `text/html`
	
	`ssi_types text/plain;`

Directive	Description

`ssi_silent_errors`
 	
Context: `http, server,`
`location`
	Some SSI commands may generate errors; when that is the case, Nginx outputs a message at the location of the command—an error occurred while processing the directive. Enabling this option silences Nginx and the message does not appear.

	Syntax: on or off
	Default value: off
	`ssi_silent_errors off;`

`ssi_value_length`
 	
Context: `http, server,`
`location`
	SSI commands have arguments that accept a value (for example, `<!--# include file="value" -->`). This parameter defines the maximum length accepted by Nginx.

	Syntax: Numeric
	Default: `256` (characters)
	`ssi_value_length 256;`

`ssi_ignore_`
`recycled_buffers`
 	
Context: `http, server,`
`location`
	When set to on, this directive prevents Nginx from making use of recycled buffers.

	Syntax: on or off
	Default: off

`ssi_min_file_chunk`
 	
Context: `http, server,`
`location`
	If the size of a buffer is greater than `ssi_min_file_chunk`, data is stored in a file and then sent via `sendfile`. In other cases, it is transmitted directly from the memory.

	Syntax: Numeric value (size)
	Default: `1,024`

A quick note regarding possible concerns about the SSI engine resource usage—by enabling the SSI module at the `location` or `server` block level, you enable parsing of at least all `text/html` files (pretty much any page to be displayed by the client browser). While the Nginx SSI module is efficiently optimized, you might want to disable parsing for files that do not require it.

Firstly, all your pages containing SSI commands should have the `.shtml` (Server HTML) extension. Then, in your configuration, at the `location` block level, enable the SSI engine under a specific condition. The name of the served file must end with `.shtml`:

```
server {
    server_name website.com;
    location ~* \.shtml$ {
        ssi on;
    }
}
```

On one hand, all HTTP requests submitted to Nginx will go through an additional regular expression pattern matching. On the other hand, static HTML files or files to be processed by other interpreters (.php, for instance) will not be parsed unnecessarily.

Finally, the SSI module enables two variables:

- `$date_local`: Returns the current time according to the current system time zone
- `$date_gmt`: Returns the current GMT time, regardless of the server time zone

SSI Commands

Once you have the SSI engine enabled for your web pages, you are ready to start writing your first dynamic HTML page. Again, the principle is simple — design the pages of your website using regular HTML code, inside which you will insert SSI commands.

These commands respect a particular syntax — at first sight, they look like regular HTML comments: `<!-- A comment -->`, and that is the good thing about it — if you accidentally disable SSI parsing of your files, the SSI commands do not appear on the client browser; they are only visible in the source code as actual HTML comments. The full syntax is as follows:

```
<!--# command param1="value1" param2="value2" … -->
```

File includes

The main command of the Server Side Include module is obviously the `include` command. It comes in two different fashions.

First, you are allowed to make a simple file include:

```
<!--# include file="header.html" -->
```

This command generates an HTTP sub-request to be processed by Nginx. The body of the response that was generated is inserted instead of the command itself.

The second possibility is to use the `include virtual` command:

```
<!--# include virtual="/sources/header.php?id=123" -->
```

This also performs a sub-request to the server; the difference lies within the way that Nginx fetches the specified file (when using `include file`, the `wait` parameter is automatically enabled). Indeed, two parameters can be inserted within the `include` command tag. By default, all SSI requests are issued simultaneously, in parallel. This can cause slowdowns and timeouts in the case of heavy loads. Alternatively, you can use the `wait="yes"` parameter to specify that Nginx should wait for the completion of the request before moving on to other includes:

```
<!--# include virtual="header.php" wait="yes" -->
```

If the result of your `include` command is empty or triggered an error (`404`, `500`, and so on), Nginx inserts the corresponding error page with its HTML: `<html> [...] 404 Not Found</body></html>`. The message is displayed at the exact same place where you inserted the `include` command. If you wish to revise this behavior, you have the possibility to create a named block. By linking the block to the `include` command, the contents of the block will show at the location of the `include` command tag, in case an error occurs:

```
<html>
<head><title>SSI Example</title></head>
<body>
<center>
  <!--# block name="error_footer" -->Sorry, the footer file was not
found.<!--# endblock -->
  <h1>Welcome to nginx</h1>
  <!--# include virtual="footer.html" stub="error_footer" -->
</center>
</body>
</html>
```

The result as output in the client browser is shown as follows:

As you can see, the contents of the `error_footer` block were inserted at the location of `include` command, after the `<h1>` tag.

Working with variables

The Nginx SSI module also offers the possibility to work with variables. Displaying a variable (in other words, inserting the variable value into the final HTML source code) can be done with the `echo` command:

```
<!--# echo var="variable_name" -->
```

The command accepts the following three parameters:

- `var`: The name of the variable you want to display, for example, REMOTE_ADDR to display the IP address of the client.

- `default`: A string to be displayed in case the variable is empty. If you don't specify this parameter, the output is `(none)`.

- `encoding`: Encoding method for the string. The accepted values are `none` (no particular encoding), `url` (encode text like a URL—a blank space becomes `%20`, and so on) and `entity` (uses HTML entities: & becomes `&amp;`).

You may also affect your own variables with the `set` command:

```
<!--# set var="my_variable" value="your value here" -->
```

The `value` parameter is itself parsed by the engine; as a result, you are allowed to make use of existing variables:

```
<!--# echo var="MY_VARIABLE" -->
<!--# set var="MY_VARIABLE" value="hello" -->
<!--# echo var="MY_VARIABLE" -->
<!--# set var="MY_VARIABLE" value="$MY_VARIABLE there" -->
<!--# echo var="MY_VARIABLE" -->
```

Here is the code that Nginx outputs for each of the three `echo` commands from the example above:

```
(none)
hello
hello there
```

Conditional structure

The following set of commands will allow you to include text or other directives depending on a condition. The conditional structure can be established with the following syntax:

```
<!--# if expr="expression1" -->
[...]
<!--# elif expr="expression2" -->
```

```
[...]
<!--# else -->
[...]
<!--# endif -->
```

The expression can be formulated in three different ways:

- Inspecting a variable: `<!--# if expr="$variable" -->`. Similar to the `if` block in the Rewrite module, the condition is true if the variable is not empty.

- Comparing two strings: `<!--# if expr="$variable = hello" -->`. The condition is true if the first string is equal to the second string. Use `!=` instead of `=` to revert the condition (the condition is true if the first string is not equal to the second string).

- Matching a regular expression pattern: `<!--# if expr="$variable = / pattern/" -->`. Note that the pattern must be enclosed with / characters, otherwise it is considered to be a simple string (for example, `<!-- # if expr="$MY_VARIABLE = /^/documents//" -->`). Similar to the comparison, use `!=` to negate the condition. Captures in regular expressions are supported.

The content that you insert within a condition block can contain regular HTML code or additional SSI directives, with one exception—you cannot nest `if` blocks.

Configuration

Last and probably least (for once) of the SSI commands offered by Nginx is the `config` command. It allows you to configure two simple parameters.

First, the message that appears when the SSI engine faces an error is malformed tags or invalid expressions. By default, Nginx displays `[an error occurred while processing the directive]`. If you want it to display something else, enter the following:

```
<!--# config errmsg="Something terrible happened" -->
```

Additionally, you can configure the format of the dates that are returned by the `$date_local` and `$date_gmt` variables using the `timefmt` parameter:

```
<!--# config timefmt="%A, %d-%b-%Y %H:%M:%S %Z" -->
```

The string you specify here is passed as the format string of the `strftime` C function. For more information about the arguments that can be used in the format string, please refer to the documentation of the `strftime` C language function at `http:// www.opengroup.org/onlinepubs/009695399/functions/strftime.html`.

Additional modules

The first half of this chapter covered two of the most important Nginx modules, namely, the Rewrite module and the SSI module. There are a lot more modules that will greatly enrich the functionality of the web server; they are regrouped here, by thematic.

Among the modules described in this section, some are included in the default Nginx build, but some are not. This implies that unless you specifically configured your Nginx build to include these modules (as described in *Chapter 1, Downloading and Installing Nginx*), they will not be available to you.

Website access and logging

The following set of modules allows you to configure how visitors access your website and the way your server logs requests.

Index

The Index module provides a simple directive named `index`, which lets you define the page that Nginx will serve by default if no filename is specified in the client request (in other words, it defines the website index page). You may specify multiple filenames; the first file to be found will be served. If none of the specified files are found, Nginx will either attempt to generate an automatic index of the files, if the `autoindex` directive is enabled (check the HTTP Autoindex module), or return a `403 Forbidden` error page.

Optionally, you may insert an absolute filename (such as `/page.html`) but only as the last argument of the directive.

Syntax: `index file1 [file2...] [absolute_file];`

Default value: `index.html`

```
index index.php index.html index.htm;
index index.php index2.php /catchall.php;
```

This directive is valid in the following contexts: `http`, `server`, `location`.

Autoindex

If Nginx cannot provide an index page for the requested directory, the default behavior is to return a `403 Forbidden HTTP` error page. With the following set of directives, you enable an automatic listing of the files that are present in the requested directory:

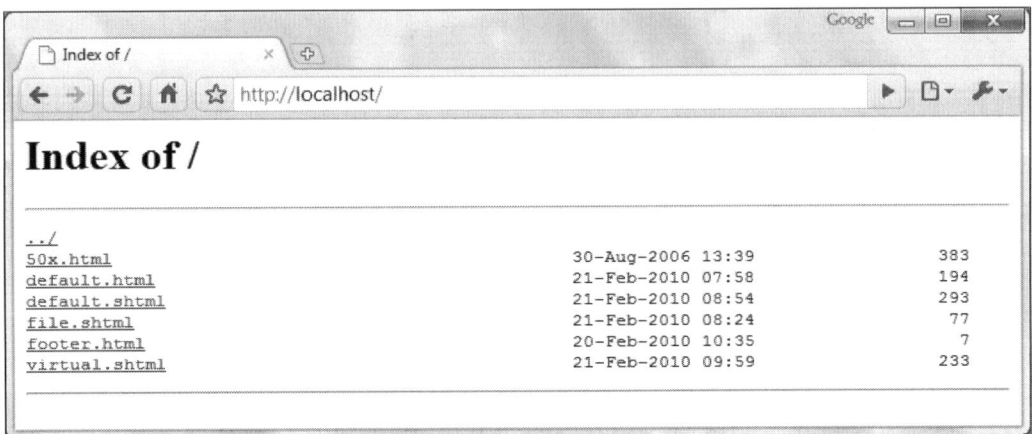

Three columns of information appear for each file—the filename, the file date and time, and the file size in bytes.

Directive	Description
`autoindex` Context: `http, server, location`	Enables or disables automatic directory listing for directories missing an index page. Syntax: `on` or `off`
`autoindex_exact_size` Context: `http, server, location`	If set to `on`, this directive ensures that the listing displays file sizes in bytes. Otherwise, another unit is employed, such as KB, MB, or GB. Syntax: `on` or `off` Default value: `on`
`autoindex_localtime` Context: `http, server, location`	By default, this directive is set to `off`, so the date and time of files in the listing appears as GMT time. Set it to `on` to make use of the local server time. Syntax: `on` or `off` Default value: `off`

Random index

This module enables a simple directive, `random_index`, which can be used within a `location` block in order for Nginx to return an index page selected randomly among the files of the specified directory.

> This module is not included in the default Nginx build.

Syntax: `on` or `off`

Log

This module controls the behavior of Nginx regarding access logs. It is a key module for system administrators as it allows analyzing the runtime behavior of web applications. It is composed of three essential directives:

Directive	Description
`access_log` Context: `http, server, location`	This parameter defines the access log file path, the format of entries in the access log by selecting a template name, or disables access logging. Syntax: `access_log path [format [buffer=size]] | off;` Some remarks concerning the directive syntax: • Use `access_log off` to disable access logging at the current level • The format argument corresponds to a template declared with the `log_format` directive, described below • If the format argument is not specified, the default format is employed (combined) • You may use variables in the file path

Directive	Description
| `log_format`<br><br>Context: `http, server, location` | Defines a template to be utilized by the `access_log` directive, describing the contents that should be included in an entry of the access log.<br><br>Syntax: `log_format template_name format_string;`<br><br>The default template is called `combined` and matches the following example:<br><br>```
log_format combined '$remote_addr - $remote_user
[$time_local] '"$request" $status
$body_bytes_sent '"$http_referer"
"$http_user_agent"';
# Other example
log_format simple '$remote_addr $request';
``` |
| `open_log_file_cache`

Context: `http, server, location` | Configures the cache for log file descriptors. Please refer to the `open_file_cache` directive of the HTTP Core module for additional information.

Syntax: `open_log_file_cache max=N [inactive=time] [min_uses=N] [valid=time] | off;`

The arguments are similar to the `open_file_cache` and other related directives; the difference being that this applies to access log files only. |

The Log module also enables several new variables, though they are only accessible when writing log entries:

- `$connection`: The connection number
- `$pipe`: The variable is set to "p" if the request was pipelined
- `$time_local`: Local time (at the time of writing the log entry)
- `$msec`: Local time (at the time of writing the log entry) to the microsecond
- `$request_time`: Total length of the request processing, in milliseconds
- `$status`: Response status code
- `$bytes_sent`: Total number of bytes sent to the client
- `$body_bytes_sent`: Number of bytes sent to the client for the response body
- `$apache_bytes_sent`: Similar to `$body_bytes`, which corresponds to the `%B` parameter of Apache's `mod_log_config`
- `$request_length`: Length of the request body
```

Limits and restrictions

The following modules allow you to regulate access to the documents of your websites — require users to authenticate, match a set of rules, or simply restrict access to certain visitors.

Auth_basic module

The auth_basic module enables the basic authentication functionality. With the two directives that it reveals, you can make it so that a specific location of your website (or your server) is restricted to users that authenticate using a username and password:

```
location /admin/ {
    auth_basic "Admin control panel";
    auth_basic_user_file access/password_file;
}
```

The first directive, auth_basic, can be set to either off or a text message usually referred to as *authentication challenge* or *authentication realm*. This message is displayed by web browsers in a username/password box when a client attempts to access the protected resource.

The second one, auth_basic_user_file, defines the path of the password file relative to the directory of the configuration file. A password file is formed of lines respecting the following syntax: username:password[:comment]. The password must be encrypted with the crypt(3) function, for example, using the htpasswd command-line utility from Apache.

> If you aren't too keen on installing Apache on your system just for the sake of the htpasswd tool, you may resort to online tools as there are plenty of them available. Fire up your favorite search engine and type "*online htpasswd*".

Access

Two important directives are brought up by this module: allow and deny. They let you allow or deny access to a resource for a specific IP address or IP address range.

Both directives have the same syntax: `allow IP | CIDR | all`, where `IP` is an IP address, CIDR is an IP address range (CIDR syntax), and `all` specifies that the directive applies to all clients:

```
location {
    allow 127.0.0.1; # allow local IP address
    deny all; # deny all other IP addresses
}
```

Note that rules are processed from top-down—if your first instruction is `deny all`, all possible `allow` exceptions that you place afterwards will have no effect. The opposite is also true—if you start with `allow all`, all possible `deny` directives that you place afterwards will have no effect, as you already allowed all IP addresses.

Limit connections

The mechanism induced by this module is a little more complex than regular ones. It allows you to define the maximum amount of simultaneous connections to the server for a specific *zone*.

The first step is to define the zone using the `limit_conn_zone` directive:

- Directive syntax: `limit_conn_zone $variable zone=name:size;`
- `$variable` is the variable that will be used to differentiate one client from another, typically `$binary_remote_addr`—the IP address of the client in binary format (more efficient than ASCII)
- `name` is an arbitrary name given to the zone
- `size` is the maximum size you allocate to the table storing session states

The following example defines zones based on the client IP addresses:

```
limit_conn_zone $binary_remote_addr zone=myzone:10m;
```

Now that you have defined a zone, you may limit connections using `limit_conn`:

```
limit_conn zone_name connection_limit;
```

When applied to the previous example it becomes:

```
location /downloads/ {
    limit_conn myzone 1;
}
```

As a result, requests that share the same `$binary_remote_addr` are subject to the connection limit (one simultaneous connection). If the limit is reached, all additional concurrent requests will be answered with a `503 Service unavailable` HTTP response. If you wish to log client requests that are affected by the limits you have set, enable the `limit_conn_log_level` directive and specify the log level (`info` | `notice` | `warn` | `error`).

Limit request

In a similar fashion, the *Limit request* module allows you to limit the amount of requests for a defined zone.

Defining the zone is done via the `limit_req_zone` directive; its syntax differs from the *Limit zone* equivalent directive:

```
limit_req_zone $variable zone=name:max_memory_size rate=rate;
```

The directive parameters are identical, except for the trailing `rate:` expressed in requests per second (r/s) or requests per minute (r/m). It defines a request rate that will be applied to clients where the zone is enabled. To apply a zone to a location, use the `limit_req` directive:

```
limit_req zone=name burst=burst [nodelay];
```

The `burst` parameter defines the maximum possible bursts of requests — when the amount of requests received from a client exceeds the limit defined in the zone, the responses are delayed in a manner that respects the rate that you defined. To a certain extent, only a maximum of `burst` requests will be accepted simultaneously. Past this limit, Nginx returns a `503 Service Unavailable` HTTP error response:

```
limit_req_zone $binary_remote_addr zone=myzone:10m rate=2r/s;
[...]
location /downloads/ {
    limit_req zone=myzone burst=10;
}
```

If you wish to log client requests that are affected by the limits you have set, enable the `limit_req_log_level` directive and specify the log level (`info` | `notice` | `warn` | `error`).

Content and encoding

The following set of modules provides functionalities having an effect on the contents served to the client, either by modifying the way the response is encoded, by affecting the headers, or by generating a response from scratch.

Empty GIF

The purpose of this module is to provide a directive that serves a *1 x 1* transparent GIF image from the memory. Such files are sometimes used by web designers to tweak the appearance of their website. With this directive, you get an empty GIF straight from the memory instead of reading and processing an actual GIF file from the storage space.

To utilize this feature, simply insert the `empty_gif` directive in the location of your choice:

```
location = /empty.gif {
    empty_gif;
}
```

FLV and MP4

FLV and MP4 are separate modules enabling a simple functionality that becomes useful when serving Flash (FLV) or MP4 video files. It parses a special argument of the request, `start`, which indicates the offset of the section the client wishes to download or pseudo-stream. The video file must thus be accessed with the following URI: `video.flv?start=XXX`. This parameter is prepared automatically by mainstream video players such as JWPlayer.

 This module is not included in the default Nginx build.

To utilize this feature, simply insert the `flv` or `mp4` directive in the location of your choice:

```
location ~* \.flv {
    flv;
}
location ~* \.mp4 {
    mp4;
}
```

Be aware that in case Nginx fails to seek to the requested position within the video file, the request will result in a `500 Internal Server Error` HTTP response. JWPlayer sometimes misinterprets this error and simply displays a "Video not found" error message.

HTTP headers

Two directives are introduced by this module that will affect the header of the response sent to the client.

First, `add_header Name value` lets you add a new line in the response headers, respecting the following syntax: `Name: value`. The line is added only for responses of the following code: `200`, `201`, `204`, `301`, `302`, and `304`. You may insert variables in the `value` argument.

Additionally, the `expires` directive allows you to control the value of the *Expires and Cache-Control HTTP header* sent to the client, affecting requests of the same code, as listed above. It accepts a single value among the following:

- `off`: Does not modify either headers.
- A time value: The expiration date of the file is set to *the current time +, the time you specify*. For example, `expires 24h` will return an expiry date set to 24 hours from now.
- `epoch`: The expiration date of the file is set to January 1, 1970. The Cache-Control header is set to `no-cache`.
- `max`: The expiration date of the file is set to December 31, 2037. The Cache-Control header is set to 10 years.

Addition

The Addition module allows you (through simple directives) to add content before or after the body of the HTTP response.

 This module is not included in the default Nginx build.

The two main directives are:

```
add_before_body file_uri;
add_after_body file_uri;
```

As stated previously, Nginx triggers a sub-request for fetching the specified URI. Additionally, you can define the type of files to which the content is appended in case your `location` block pattern is not specific enough (default: `text/html`):

```
addition_types mime_type1 [mime_type2...];
addition_types *;
```

Substitution

Along the lines of the previous module, the Substitution module allows you to search and replace text directly from the response body:

```
sub_filter searched_text replacement_text;
```

 This module is not included in the default Nginx build.

Two additional directives provide more flexibility:

- `sub_filter_once` (on or off, default on): Only replaces the text once and stops after the first occurrence.
- `sub_filter_types` (default text/html): Affects additional MIME types that will be eligible for the text replacement. The * wildcard is allowed.

Gzip filter

This module allows you to compress the response body with the Gzip algorithm before sending it to the client. To enable Gzip compression, use the `gzip` directive (on or off) at the http, server, location, and even the if level (though that is not recommended). The following directives will help you further configure the filter options:

Directive	Description
`gzip_buffers` Context: http, server, location	Defines the amount and size of buffers to be used for storing the compressed response.
	Syntax: `gzip_buffers amount size;`
	Default: `gzip_buffers 4 4k` (or 8 k depending on the OS).
`gzip_comp_level` Context: http, server, location	Defines the compression level of the algorithm. The specified value ranges from 1 (low compression, faster for the CPU) to 9 (high compression, slower).
	Syntax: Numeric value.
	Default: 1
`gzip_disable` Context: http, server, location	Disables Gzip compression for requests where the User-Agent HTTP header matches the specified regular expression.
	Syntax: Regular expression
	Default: None

Directive	Description

`gzip_http_version`
 	
Context: `http,`
`server, location`
	Enables Gzip compression for the specified protocol version.
	
	Syntax: `1.0` or `1.1`
	
	Default: `1.1`

`gzip_min_length`
 	
Context: `http,`
`server, location`
	If the response body length is inferior to the specified value, it is not compressed.
	
	Syntax: Numeric value (size)
	
	Default: `0`

`gzip_proxied`
 	
Context: `http,`
`server, location`
	Enables or disables Gzip compression for the body of responses received from a proxy (see reverse-proxying mechanisms in later chapters).
	
	The directive accepts the following parameters; some can be combined:
	
	• `off`/`any`: Disables or enables compression for all requests
	
	• `expired`: Enables compression if the *Expires* header prevents caching
	
	• `no-cache`/`no-store`/`private`: Enables compression if the *Cache-Control* header is set to no-cache, no-store, or private
	
	• `no_last_modified`: Enables compression in case the *Last-Modified* header is not set
	
	• `no_etag`: Enables compression in case the *ETag* header is not set
	
	• `auth`: Enables compression in case an *Authorization* header is set

`gzip_types`
 	
Context: `http,`
`server, location`
	Enables compression for types other than the default `text/html` MIME type.
	
	Syntax:
	
	`gzip_types mime_type1 [mime_type2...];`
	`gzip_types *;`
	
	Default: `text/html` (cannot be disabled)

`gzip_vary`
 	
Context: `http,`
`server, location`
	Adds the *Vary: Accept-Encoding* HTTP header to the response.
	
	Syntax: `on` or `off`
	
	Default: `off`

Directive	Description
gzip_window Context: http, server, location	Sets the size of the window buffer (windowBits argument) for Gzipping operations. This directive value is used for calls to functions from the Zlib library.
	Syntax: Numeric value (size)
	Default: MAX_WBITS constant from the Zlib library
gzip_hash Context: http, server, location	Sets the amount of memory that should be allocated for the internal compression state (memLevel argument). This directive value is used for calls to functions from the Zlib library.
	Syntax: Numeric value (size)
	Default: MAX_MEM_LEVEL constant from the Zlib prerequisite library
postpone_ gzipping Context: http, server, location	Defines a minimum data threshold to be reached before starting the Gzip compression.
	Syntax: Size (numeric value)
	Default: 0
gzip_no_buffer Context: http, server, location	By default, Nginx waits until at least one buffer (defined by gzip_buffers) is filled with data before sending the response to the client. Enabling this directive disables buffering.
	Syntax: on or off
	Default: off

Gzip static

This module adds a simple functionality to the Gzip filter mechanism — when its gzip_static directive (on or off) is enabled, Nginx will automatically look for a .gz file corresponding to the requested document before serving it. This allows Nginx to send pre-compressed documents instead of compressing documents on-the-fly at each request.

[This module is not included in the default Nginx build.]

If a client requests /documents/page.html, Nginx checks for the existence of a /documents/page.html.gz file. If the .gz file is found, it is served to the client. Note that Nginx does not generate .gz files itself, even after serving the requested files.

Charset filter

With the *Charset filter* module, you can control the character set of the response body more accurately. Not only are you able to specify the value of the `charset` argument of the Content-Type HTTP header (such as `Content-Type: text/html; charset=utf-8`), but Nginx can also re-encode data to a specified encoding method automatically.

Directive	Description
`charset` Context: `http`, `server`, `location`, `if`	This directive adds the specified encoding to the Content-Type header of the response. If the specified encoding differs from the `source_charset` one, Nginx re-encodes the document. Syntax: `charset encoding | off;` Default: `off` Example: `charset utf-8;`
`source_charset` Context: `http`, `server`, `location`, `if`	Defines the initial encoding of the response; if the value specified in the `charset` directive differs, Nginx re-encodes the document. Syntax: `source_charset encoding;`
`override_charset` Context: `http`, `server`, `location`, `if`	When Nginx receives a response from the proxy or FastCGI gateway, this directive defines whether or not the character encoding should be checked and potentially overridden. Syntax: on or off Default: `off`

`charset_types`
 	
Context: `http`, `server`, `location`
	Defines the MIME types that are eligible for re-encoding.
	
	Syntax:
	`charset_types mime_type1 [mime_type2...];`
	`charset_types * ;`
	
	Default: `text/html`, `text/xml`, `text/plain`, `text/vnd.wap.wml`, `application/x-javascript`, `application/rss+xml`

`charset_map` Context: `http`	Lets you define character re-encoding tables. Each line of the table contains two hexadecimal codes to be exchanged. You will find re-encoding tables for the `koi8-r` character set in the default Nginx configuration folder (`koi-win` and `koi-utf`). Syntax: `charset_map src_encoding dest_encoding { ... }`

Memcached

Memcached is a daemon application that can be connected to via sockets. Its main purpose, as the name suggests, is to provide an efficient distributed key/value memory caching system. The *Nginx Memcached* module provides directives allowing you to configure access to the Memcached daemon.

Directive	Description
memcached_pass Context: location, if	Defines the hostname and port of the Memcached daemon. Syntax: memcached_pass hostname:port; Example: memcached_pass localhost:11211;
memcached_bind Context: http, server, location	Forces Nginx to use the specified local IP address for connecting to the Memcached server. This can come in handy if your server has multiple network cards connected to different networks. Syntax: memcached_bind IP_address; Example: memcached_bind 192.168.1.2;
memcached_connect_timeout Context: http, server, location	Defines the connection timeout in milliseconds (default: 60,000). Example: memcached_connect_timeout 5000;
memcached_send_timeout Context: http, server, location	Defines the data writing operations timeout in milliseconds (default: 60,000). Example: memcached_send_timeout 5,000;
memcached_read_timeout Context: http, server, location	Defines the data reading operations timeout in milliseconds (default: 60,000). Example: memcached_read_timeout 5,000;
memcached_buffer_size Context: http, server, location	Defines the size of the read and write buffer, in bytes (default: page size). Example: memcached_buffer_size 8k;
memcached_next_upstream Context: http, server, location	When the memcached_pass directive is connected to an upstream block (see Upstream module), this directive defines the conditions that should be matched in order to skip to the next upstream server. Syntax: Values selected among error timeout, invalid_response, not_found, or off Default: error timeout Example: memcached_next_upstream off;

Additionally, you will need to define the $memcached_key variable that defines the key of the element that you are placing or fetching from the cache. You may, for instance, use set $memcached_key $uri or set $memcached_key $uri?$args.

Note that the Nginx Memcached module is only able to retrieve data from the cache; it does not store the result of requests. Storing data in the cache should be done by a server-side script. You just need to make sure to employ the same key naming scheme in both your server-side scripts and the Nginx configuration. As an example, we could decide to use memcached to retrieve data from the cache before passing the request to a proxy, if the requested URI is not found (see *Chapter 7, From Apache to Nginx*, for more details about the Proxy module):

```
server {
    server_name example.com;
    [...]
    location / {
        set $memcached_key $uri;
        memcached_pass 127.0.0.1:11211;
        error_page 404 @notcached;
    }
    location @notcached {
        internal;
        # if the file is not found, forward request to proxy
        proxy_pass 127.0.0.1:8080;
    }
}
```

Image filter

This module provides image processing functionalities through the *GD Graphics Library* (also known as *gdlib*).

 This module is not included in the default Nginx build.

Make sure to employ the following directives on a `location` block that filters image files only, such as `location ~* \.(png|jpg|gif)$ { … }`.

Directive	Description
`image_filter` Context: `location`	Lets you apply a transformation on the image before sending it to the client. There are five options available: • `test`: Makes sure that the requested document is an image file, returns a `415 Unsupported media type` HTTP error if the test fails. • `size`: Composes a simple JSON response indicating information about the image such as the size and type (for example; `{ "img": { "width":50, "height":50, "type":"png"}}`). If the file is invalid, a simple `{}` is returned. • `resize width height`: Resizes the image to the specified dimensions. • `crop width height`: Selects a portion of the image of the specified dimensions. • `rotate 90	180	270`: Rotates the image by the specified angle (in degrees).  Example: `image_filter resize 200 100;`
`image_filter_buffer` Context: `http, server, location`	Defines the maximum file size for images to be processed. Default: `image_filter_buffer 1m;`
`image_filter_jpeg_quality` Context: `http, server, location`	Defines the quality of output JPEG images. Default: `image_filter_jpeg_quality 75;`
`image_filter_transparency` Context: `http, server, location`	By default, PNG and GIF images keep their existing transparency during operations you perform using the Image Filter module. If you set this directive to `off`, all existing transparency will be lost but the image quality will be improved. Syntax: on or `off` Default: on
`image_filter_sharpen` Context: `http, server, location`	Sharpens the image by specified percentage (value may exceed 100). Syntax: Numeric value Default: 0

Please note that when it comes to JPG images, Nginx automatically strips off metadata (such as EXIF) if it occupies more than 5 percent of the total space of the file.

XSLT

The Nginx XSLT module allows you to apply an XSLT transform on an XML file or response received from a backend server (proxy, FastCGI, and so on) before serving the client.

[This module is not included in the default Nginx build.]

Directive	Description

`xml_entities`
 	
Context: `http,`
`server, location`
	Specifies the DTD file containing symbolic element definitions.
	
	Syntax: File path
	
	Example: `xml_entities xml/entities.dtd;`

`xslt_stylesheet` Context: `location`	Specifies the XSLT template file path with its parameters. Variables may be inserted in the parameters. Syntax: `xslt_stylesheet template [param1] [param2...];` Example: `xslt_stylesheet xml/sch.xslt param=value;`

`xslt_types`
 	
Context: `http,`
`server, location`
	Defines additional MIME types to which the transforms may apply, other than `text/xml`.
	
	Syntax: MIME type
	
	Example:
	`    xslt_types text/xml text/plain;`
	`    xslt_types *;`

`xslt_paramxslt_`
`string_param`
 	
Context: `http,`
`server, location`
	Both directives allow defining parameters for XSLT stylesheets. The difference lies in the way the specified value is interpreted: using `xslt_param`, XPath expressions in the value are processed; while `xslt_string_param` should be used for plain character strings.
	
	Syntax: `xslt_param key value;`

About your visitors

The following set of modules provides extra functionality that will help you find out more information about the visitors, such as by parsing client request headers for browser name and version, assigning an identifier to requests presenting similarities, and so on.

Browser

The Browser module parses the User-Agent HTTP header of the client request in order to establish values for variables that can be employed later in the configuration. The three variables produced are:

- `$modern_browser`: If the client browser is identified as being a modern web browser, the variable takes the value defined by the `modern_browser_value` directive.

- `$ancient_browser`: If the client browser is identified as being an old web browser, the variable takes the value defined by `ancient_browser_value`.

- `$msie`: This variable is set to 1 if the client is using a Microsoft IE browser.

To help Nginx recognize web browsers, telling the old from the modern, you need to insert multiple occurrences of the `ancient_browser` and `modern_browser` directives:

```
modern_browser opera 10.0;
```

With this example, if the User-Agent HTTP header contains Opera 10.0, the client browser is considered modern.

Map

Just like the Browser module, the Map module allows you to create maps of values depending on a variable:

```
map $uri $variable {
  /page.html    0;
  /contact.html    1;
  /index.html    2;
  default 0;
}
rewrite ^ /index.php?page=$variable;
```

Note that the `map` directive can only be inserted within the `http` block. Following this example, `$variable` may have three different values. If `$uri` was set to `/page.html`, `$variable` is now defined as 0; if `$uri` was set to `/contact.html`, `$variable` is now 1; if `$uri` was set to `/index.html`, `$variable` now equals 2. For all other cases (default), `$variable` is set to 0. The last instruction rewrites the URL accordingly. Apart from `default`, the `map` directive accepts another special keyword: `hostnames`. It allows you to match hostnames using wildcards such as `*.domain.com`.

Two additional directives allow you to tweak the way Nginx manages the mechanism in memory:

- `map_hash_max_size`: Sets the maximum size of the hash table holding a map
- `map_hash_bucket_size`: The maximum size of an entry in the map

Regular expressions may also be used in patterns if you prefix them with ~ (case sensitive) or ~* (case insensitive):

```
map $http_referer $ref {
~google "Google";
    ~* yahoo "Yahoo";
    \~bing "Bing"; # not a regular expression due to the \ before the
tilde
default $http_referer; # variables may be used
}
```

Geo

The purpose of this module is to provide functionality that is quite similar to the map directive—affecting a variable based on client data (in this case, the IP address). The syntax is slightly different in the extent that you are allowed to specify address ranges (in CIDR format):

```
geo $variable {
   default unknown;
   127.0.0.1    local;
   123.12.3.0/24  uk;
   92.43.0.0/16  fr;
}
```

Note that the above block is being presented to you just for the sake of the example and does not actually detect U.K. and French visitors; you'll want to use the GeoIP module if you wish to achieve proper geographical location detection. In this block, you may insert a number of directives that are specific to this module:

- `delete`: Allows you to remove the specified subnetwork from the mapping.
- `default`: The default value given to `$variable` in case the user's IP address does not match any of the specified IP ranges.
- `include`: Allows you to include an external file.
- `proxy`: Defines a subnet of trusted addresses. If the user IP address is among the trusted, the value of the X-Forwarded-For header is used as IP address instead of the socket IP address.

- **proxy_recursive**: If enabled, this will look for the value of the X-Forwarded-For header even if the client IP address is not trusted.

- **ranges**: If you insert this directive as the first line of your geo block, it allows you to specify IP ranges instead of CIDR masks. The following syntax is thus permitted: 127.0.0.1-127.0.0.255   LOCAL;

GeoIP

Although the name suggests some similarities with the previous one, this optional module provides accurate geographical information about your visitors by making use of the *MaxMind* (www.maxmind.com) GeoIP binary databases. You need to download the database files from the MaxMind website and place them in your Nginx directory.

 This module is not included in the default Nginx build.

All you have to do then is specify the database path with either directive:

```
geoip_country country.dat; # country information db
geoip_city city.dat; # city information db

geoip_org geoiporg.dat; # ISP/organization db
```

The first directive enables several variables: $geoip_country_code (two-letter country code), $geoip_country_code3 (three-letter country code), and $geoip_country_name (full country name). The second directive includes the same variables but provides additional information: $geoip_region, $geoip_city, $geoip_postal_code, $geoip_city_continent_code, $geoip_latitude, $geoip_longitude, $geoip_dma_code, $geoip_area_code, $geoip_region_name. The third directive offers information about the organization or ISP that owns the specified IP address, by filling up the $geoip_org variable.

 If you need the variables to be encoded in UTF-8, simply add the utf8 keyword at the end of the geoip_ directives.

UserID filter

This module assigns an identifier to clients by issuing cookies. The identifier can be accessed from variables `$uid_got` and `$uid_set` further in the configuration.

Directive	Description
`userid` Context: `http, server, location`	Enables or disables issuing and logging of cookies. The directive accepts four possible values: • `on`: Enables v2 cookies and logs them • `v1`: Enables v1 cookies and logs them • `log`: Does not send cookie data but logs incoming cookies • `off`: Does not send cookie data Default value: `userid off;`
`userid_service` Context: `http, server, location`	Defines the IP address of the server issuing the cookie. Syntax: `userid_service ip;` Default: IP address of the server
`userid_name` Context: `http, server, location`	Defines the name assigned to the cookie. Syntax: `userid_name name;` Default value: The user identifier
`userid_domain` Context: `http, server, location`	Defines the domain assigned to the cookie. Syntax: `userid_domain domain;` Default value: None (the domain part is not sent)
`userid_path` Context: `http, server, location`	Defines the path part of the cookie. Syntax: `userid_path path;` Default value: /
`userid_expires` Context: `http, server, location`	Defines the cookie expiration date. Syntax: `userid_expires date	max;` Default value: No expiration date
`userid_p3p` Context: `http, server, location`	Assigns a value to the P3P header sent with the cookie. Syntax: `userid_p3p data;` Default value: None

Referer

A simple directive is introduced by this module: `valid_referers`. Its purpose is to check the Referer HTTP header from the client request and possibly to deny access based on the value. If the referrer is considered invalid, `$invalid_referer` is set to 1. In the list of valid referrers, you may employ three kinds of values:

- None: The absence of a referrer is considered to be a valid referrer
- Blocked: A masked referrer (such as xxxxx) is also considered valid
- A server name: The specified server name is considered to be a valid referrer

Following the definition of the `$invalid_referer` variable, you may, for example, return an error code if the referrer was found invalid:

```
valid_referers none blocked *.website.com *.google.com;
  if ($invalid_referer) {
  return 403;
}
```

Be aware that spoofing the Referer HTTP header is a very simple process, so checking the referrer of client requests should not be used as a security measure.

Real IP

This module provides one simple feature—it replaces the client IP address by the one specified in the *X-Real-IP* HTTP header for clients that visit your website behind a proxy or for retrieving IP addresses from the proper header if Nginx is used as a backend server (it essentially has the same effect as Apache's `mod_rpaf`, see *Chapter 7, From Apache to Nginx*, for more details). To enable this feature, you need to insert the `real_ip_header` directive that defines the HTTP header to be exploited—either `X-Real-IP` or `X-Forwarded-For`. The second step is to define trusted IP addresses. In other words, the clients that are allowed to make use of those headers. This can be done thanks to the `set_real_ip_from` directive, which accepts both IP addresses and CIDR address ranges:

```
real_ip_header X-Forwarded-For;
set_real_ip_from 192.168.0.0/16;
set_real_ip_from 127.0.0.1;
set_real_ip_from unix:; # trusts all UNIX-domain sockets
```

 This module is not included in the default Nginx build.

Split Clients

The Split Clients module provides a resource-efficient way to split the visitor base into subgroups based on the percentages that you specify. To distribute visitors into one group or another, Nginx hashes a value that you provide (such as the visitor's IP address, cookie data, query arguments, and so on) and decides which group the visitor should be affected to. The following example configuration divides visitors up into three groups based on their IP address. If a visitor is affected to the first 50 percent, the value of $variable will be set to group1:

```
split_clients "$remote_addr" $variable {
  50% "group1";
  30% "group2";
  20% "group3";
}
location ~ \.php$ {
  set $args "${query_string}&group=${variable}";
}
```

SSL and security

Nginx provides secure HTTP functionalities through the SSL module but also offers an extra module called *Secure Link* that helps you protect your website and visitors in a totally different way.

SSL

The SSL module enables HTTPS support, HTTP over SSL/TLS in particular. It gives you the possibility to serve secure websites by providing a certificate, a certificate key, and other parameters defined with the following directives:

 This module is not included in the default Nginx build.

Directive	Description
ssl Context: http, server	Enables HTTPS for the specified server. This directive is the equivalent of listen 443 ssl or listen port ssl more generally. Syntax: on or off Default: ssl off;

Directive	Description
ssl_certificate	Sets the path of the PEM certificate.
Context: http, server	Syntax: File path
ssl_certificate_key	Sets the path of the PEM secret key file.
Context: http, server	Syntax: File path
ssl_client_certificate	Sets the path of the client PEM certificate.
Context: http, server	Syntax: File path
ssl_crl Context: http, server	Orders Nginx to load a CRL (Certificate Revocation List) file, which allows checking the revocation status of certificates.
ssl_dhparam	Sets the path of the *Diffie-Hellman* parameters file.
Context: http, server	Syntax: File path.
ssl_protocols	Specifies the protocol that should be employed.
Context: http, server	Syntax: ssl_protocols [SSLv2] [SSLv3] [TLSv1] [TLSv1.1] [TLSv1.2];
	Default: ssl_protocols SSLv2 SSLv3 TLSv1;
ssl_ciphers Context: http, server	Specifies the ciphers that should be employed. The list of available ciphers can be obtained running the following command from the shell: openssl ciphers.
	Syntax: ssl_ciphers cipher1[:cipher2...];
	Default: ssl_ciphers ALL:!ADH:RC4+RSA:+HIGH:+MEDIUM:+LOW:+SSLv2:+EXP;
ssl_prefer_server_ciphers	Specifies whether server ciphers should be preferred over client ciphers.
Context: http, server	Syntax: on or off
	Default: off
ssl_verify_client Context: http, server	Enables verifying certificates transmitted by the client and sets the result in the $ssl_client_verify. The optional_no_ca value verifies the certificate if there is one, but does not require it to be signed by a trusted CA certificate.
	Syntax: on | off | optional | optional_no_ca
	Default: off
ssl_verify_depth Context: http, server	Specifies the verification depth of the client certificate chain.
	Syntax: Numeric value
	Default: 1

Directive	Description
`ssl_session_cache` Context: `http, server`	Configures the cache for SSL sessions. Syntax: `off`, `none`, `builtin:size` or `shared:name:size` Default: `off` (disables SSL sessions)
`ssl_session_timeout` Context: `http, server`	When SSL sessions are enabled, this directive defines the timeout for using session data. Syntax: Time value Default: 5 minutes

Additionally, the following variables are made available:

- `$ssl_cipher`: Indicates the cipher used for the current request
- `$ssl_client_serial`: Indicates the serial number of the client certificate
- `$ssl_client_s_dn` and `$ssl_client_i_dn`: Indicates the value of the Subject and Issuer DN of the client certificate
- `$ssl_protocol`: Indicates the protocol at use for the current request
- `$ssl_client_cert` and `$ssl_client_raw_cert`: Returns client certificate data, which is raw data for the second variable
- `$ssl_client_verify`: Set to SUCCESS if the client certificate was successfully verified
- `$ssl_session_id`: Allows you to retrieve the ID of an SSL session

Setting up an SSL certificate

Although the SSL module offers a lot of possibilities, in most cases only a couple of directives are actually useful for setting up a secure website. This guide will help you configure Nginx to use an SSL certificate for your website (in the example, your website is identified by `secure.website.com`). Before doing so, ensure that you already have the following elements at your disposal:

- A `.key` file generated with the following command: `openssl genrsa -out secure.website.com.key 1024` (other encryption levels work too).
- A `.csr` file generated with the following command: `openssl req -new -key secure.website.com.key -out secure.website.com.csr`.
- Your website certificate file, as issued by the Certificate Authority, for example, `secure.website.com.crt`. (Note: In order to obtain a certificate from the CA, you will need to provide your `.csr` file.)
- The CA certificate file as issued by the CA (for example, `gd_bundle.crt` if you purchased your certificate from `GoDaddy.com`).

The first step is to merge your website certificate and the CA certificate together with the following command:

```
cat secure.website.com.crt gd_bundle.crt > combined.crt
```

You are then ready to configure Nginx to serve secure content:

```
server {
    listen 443;
    server_name secure.website.com;
    ssl on;
    ssl_certificate /path/to/combined.crt;
    ssl_certificate_key /path/to/secure.website.com.key;
    [...]
}
```

Secure link

Totally independent from the SSL module, Secure link provides a basic protection by checking the presence of a specific hash in the URL before allowing the user to access a resource:

```
location /downloads/ {
secure_link_md5  "secret";
secure_link $arg_hash,$arg_expires;
    if ($secure_link = "") {
      return 403;
    }
}
```

With such a configuration, documents in the /downloads/ folder must be accessed via a URL containing a query string parameter hash=xxx (note the $arg_hash in the example), where xxx is the MD5 hash of the secret you defined through the secure_link_md5 directive. The second argument of the secure_link directive is a UNIX timestamp defining the expiration date. The $secure_link variable is empty if the URI does not contain the proper hash or if the date has expired. Otherwise, it is set to 1.

[This module is not included in the default Nginx build.]

Other miscellaneous modules

The remaining three modules are optional (which all need to be enabled at compile time) and provide additional advanced functionality.

Stub status

The Stub status module was designed to provide information about the current state of the server, such as the amount of active connections, the total handled requests, and more. To activate it, place the stub_status directive in a location block. All requests matching the location block will produce the status page:

```
location = /nginx_status {
    stub_status on;
    allow 127.0.0.1; # you may want to protect the information
    deny all;
}
```

 This module is not included in the default Nginx build.

An example result produced by Nginx:

```
Active connections: 1
server accepts handled requests
 10 10 23
Reading: 0 Writing: 1 Waiting: 0
```

It's interesting to note that there are several server monitoring solutions such as *Monitorix* that offer Nginx support through the stub status page by calling it at regular intervals and parsing the statistics.

Degradation

The HTTP Degradation module configures your server to return an error page when your server runs low on memory. It works by defining a memory amount that is to be considered low, and then specifies the locations for which you wish to enable the degradation check:

```
degradation sbrk=500m; # to be inserted at the http block level
degrade 204; # in a location block, specify the error code (204 or
444) to return in case the server condition has degraded
```

Google-perftools

This module interfaces the Google Performance Tools profiling mechanism for the Nginx worker processes. The tool generates a report based on performance analysis of the executable code. More information can be discovered from the official website of the project `http://code.google.com/p/google-perftools/`.

 This module is not included in the default Nginx build.

In order to enable this feature, you need to specify the path of the report file that will be generated using the `google_perftools_profiles` directive:

```
google_perftools_profiles logs/profiles;
```

WebDAV

WebDAV is an extension of the well-known HTTP protocol. While HTTP was designed for visitors to download resources from a website (in other words, reading data) WebDAV extends the functionality of web servers by adding write operations such as creating files and folders, moving and copying files, and more. The Nginx WebDAV module implements a small subset of the WebDAV protocol:

 This module is not included in the default Nginx build.

Directive	Description
`dav_methods` Context: `http, server, location`	Selects the DAV methods you want to enable. Syntax: `dav_methods [off | [PUT] [DELETE] [MKCOL] [COPY] [MOVE]];` Default: `off`
`dav_access` Context: `http, server, location`	Defines access permissions at the current level. Syntax: `dav_access [user:r|w|rw] [group:r|w|rw] [all:r|w|rw];` Default: `dav_access user:rw;`
`create_full_put_path` Context: `http, server, location`	This directive defines the behavior when a client requests to create a file in a directory that does not exist. If set to `on`, the directory path is created. If set to `off`, the file creation fails. Syntax: `on` or `off` Default: `off`

Directive	Description
min_delete_depth Context: http, server, location	This directive defines a minimum URI depth for deleting files or directories when processing the DELETE command. Syntax: Numeric value Default: 0

Third-party modules

The Nginx community has been growing larger over the past few years and many additional modules were written by third-party developers. These can be downloaded from the official wiki website http://wiki.nginx.org/nginx3rdPartyModules.

The currently available modules offer a wide range of new possibilities, among which are:

- An *Access Key* module to protect your documents in a similar fashion as Secure link, by *Mykola Grechukh*
- A *Fancy Indexes* module that improves the automatic directory listings generated by Nginx, by *Adrian Perez de Castro*
- The *Headers More* module that improves flexibility with HTTP headers, by *Yichun Zhang* (*agentzh*)
- Many more features for various parts of the web server

To integrate a third-party module into your Nginx build, you need to follow these three simple steps:

1. Download the .tar.gz archive associated with the module you wish to download.
2. Extract the archive with the following command: tar xzf module.tar.gz.
3. Configure your Nginx build with the following command:

   ```
   ./configure --add-module=/module/source/path […]
   ```

Once you finished building and installing the application, the module is available just like a regular Nginx module with its directives and variables.

If you are interested in writing Nginx modules yourself, *Evan Miller* published an excellent walkthrough: *Emiller's Guide to Nginx Module Development*. The complete guide may be consulted from his personal website at http://www.evanmiller.org/.

Summary

All throughout this chapter, we have been discovering modules that help you improve or fine-tune the configuration of your web server. Nginx fiercely stands up to other concurrent web servers in terms of functionality, and its approach with virtual hosts and the way they are configured will probably convince many administrators to make the switch.

Three additional modules were left out though. Firstly, the FastCGI module will be approached in the next chapter, as it will allow us to configure a gateway to applications such as PHP or Python. Secondly, the proxy module that lets us design complex setups will be described in *Chapter 7, From Apache to Nginx*. Finally, the Upstream module is tied to both, so it will be detailed in parallel.

5
PHP and Python with Nginx

The 2000s have been the decade of server-side technologies. Over the past fifteen years or so, an overwhelming majority of websites have migrated from simple static HTML content to highly and fully dynamic pages, taking the Web to an entirely new level in terms of interaction with visitors. Software solutions emerged quickly, including open source ones, and some became mature enough to process high-traffic websites. In this chapter, we will study the ability of Nginx to interact with these applications. We have selected two for different reasons. The first one is obviously PHP. According to a January 2013 Netcraft survey, nearly 40 percent of the World Wide Web is powered by PHP. The second one is Python. The reason being the way it's installed and configured to work with Nginx. The mechanism effortlessly applies to other applications such as Perl or Ruby on Rails.

This chapter covers the following topics:

- Discovering the CGI and FastCGI technologies
- The Nginx FastCGI and similar modules
- Load balancing via the Upstream module
- Setting up PHP and PHP-FPM
- Setting up Python and Django
- Configuring Nginx to work with PHP and Python

Introduction to FastCGI

Before we begin, you should know that (as the name suggests) FastCGI is actually a variation of CGI. Therefore, explaining CGI first is in order. The improvements introduced by FastCGI are detailed in the following sections.

Understanding the CGI mechanism

The original purpose of a web server was merely to answer requests from clients by serving files located on a storage device. The client sends a request to download a file and the server processes the request and sends the appropriate response: 200 OK if the file can be served normally, 404 if the file was not found, and other variants.

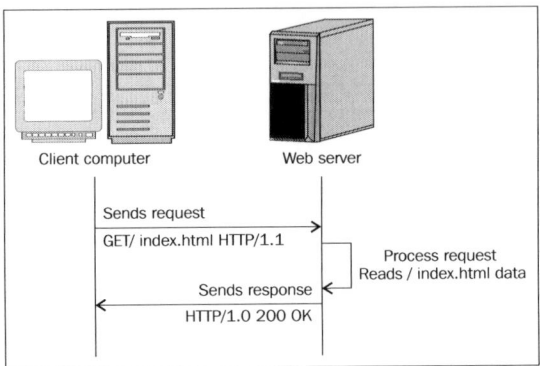

This mechanism has been in use since the beginning of the World Wide Web and it still is. However, as stated before, static websites are being progressively abandoned at the expense of dynamic ones that contain scripts that are processed by applications such as PHP and Python among others. The web serving mechanism thus evolved into the following:

When a client attempts to visit a dynamic page, the web server receives the request and forwards it to a third-party application. The application processes the script independently and returns the produced response to the web server, which then forwards the response back to the client.

In order for the web server to communicate with that application, the CGI protocol was invented in the early 1990s.

Common Gateway Interface (CGI)

As stated in RFC 3875 (CGI protocol v1.1), designed by the **Internet Society** (**ISOC**):

> *The Common Gateway Interface (CGI) allows an HTTP server and a CGI script to share responsibility for responding to client requests. [...] The server is responsible for managing connection, data transfer, transport, and network issues related to the client request, whereas the CGI script handles the application issues such as data access and document processing.*

CGI is the protocol that describes the way information is exchanged between the web server (Nginx) and the gateway application (PHP, Python, and so on). In practice, when the web server receives a request that should be forwarded to the gateway application, it simply executes the command corresponding to the desired application, for example, /usr/bin/php. Details about the client request (such as the User Agent and other request information) are passed either as command-line arguments or in environment variables, while actual data from POST or PUT requests is transmitted via the standard input. The invoked application then writes the processed document contents to the standard output, which is recaptured by the web server.

While this technology seems simple and efficient enough at first sight, it comes with a few major drawbacks, which are discussed as follows:

- A unique process is spawned for each request. Memory and other context information are lost from one request to another.

- Starting up a process can be resource-consuming for the system. Massive amounts of simultaneous requests (each spawning a process) could quickly clutter a server.

- Designing an architecture where the web server and the gateway application would be located on different computers seems difficult, if not impossible.

Fast Common Gateway Interface (FastCGI)

The issues mentioned in the *Common Gateway Interface (CGI)* section render the CGI protocol relatively inefficient for servers that are subject to heavy load. The will to find solutions led Open Market in the mid-90s to develop an evolution of CGI: FastCGI. It has become a major standard over the past fifteen years and most web servers now offer the functionality, even proprietary server software such as Microsoft IIS.

Although the purpose remains the same, FastCGI offers significant improvements over CGI with the establishment of the following principles:

- Instead of spawning a new process for each request, FastCGI employs persistent processes that come with the ability to handle multiple requests.

- The web server and the gateway application communicate with the use of sockets such as TCP or POSIX Local IPC sockets. Consequently, both processes may be on two different computers on a network.

- The web server forwards the client request to the gateway and receives the response within a single connection. Additional requests may also follow without needing to create additional connections. Note that on most web servers, including Nginx and Apache, the implementation of FastCGI does not (or at least not fully) support multiplexing.

- Since FastCGI is a socket-based protocol, it can be implemented on any platform with any programming language.

Throughout this chapter, we will be setting up PHP and Python via FastCGI. Additionally, you will find the mechanism to be relatively similar in the case of other applications, such as Perl or Ruby on Rails.

Designing a FastCGI-powered architecture is actually not as complex as one might imagine. As long as you have the web server and the processing application running, the only difficulty that remains is to establish the connection between both parties. The first step in that perspective is to configure the way Nginx will communicate with the FastCGI application. FastCGI compatibility with Nginx is introduced by the FastCGI module. This section details the directives that are made available by the module.

uWSGI and SCGI

Before reading the rest of the chapter, you should know that Nginx offers two other CGI-derived module implementations:

- The **uWSGI** module allows Nginx to communicate with applications through the **uwsgi** protocol, itself derived from **Web Server Gateway Interface (WSGI)**. The most commonly used (if not the unique) server implementing the uwsgi protocol is the unoriginally named uWSGI server. Its latest documentation can be found at `http://uwsgi-docs.readthedocs.org`. This module will prove useful to Python adepts seeing as the uWSGI project was designed mainly for Python applications.

- **SCGI**, which stands for Simple Common Gateway Interface, is a variant of the CGI protocol, much like FastCGI. Younger than FastCGI since its specification was first published in 2006, SCGI was designed to be easier to implement and as its name suggests: simple. It is not related to a particular programming language. SCGI interfaces and modules can be found in a variety of software projects such as Apache, IIS, Java, Cherokee, and a lot more.

There are no major differences in the way Nginx handles the FastCGI, uwsgi and SCGI protocols: each of these have their respective module, containing similarly named directives. The following table lists a couple of directives from the FastCGI module, which are detailed in following sections, and their uWSGI and SCGI equivalents:

FastCGI module	uWSGI equivalent	SCGI equivalent
`fastcgi_pass`	`uwsgi_pass`	`scgi_pass`
`fastcgi_cache`	`uwsgi_cache`	`scgi_cache`
`fastcgi_temp_path`	`uwsgi_temp_path`	`scgi_temp_path`

Directive names and syntaxes are identical. In addition, the Nginx development team has been maintaining all three modules in parallel. New directives or directive updates are always applied to all of them. As such, the following sections will be documenting Nginx's implementation of the FastCGI protocol, but they also apply to uWSGI and SCGI.

Main directives

The FastCGI, uWSGI, and SCGI modules are included in the default Nginx build. You do not need to enable them manually at compile time. The directives listed in the following table allow you to configure the way Nginx *passes* requests to the FastCGI/uWSGI/SCGI application. Note that you will find `fastcgi_params`, `uwsgi_params`, and `scgi_params` files in the Nginx configuration folder that define directive values that are valid for most situations.

Directive	Description

`fastcgi_pass`
 	
Context: `location, if`
	This directive specifies that the request should be passed to the FastCGI server, by indicating its location:
	
	• For TCP sockets, the syntax is:
	`fastcgi_pass hostname:port;`
	
	• For Unix Domain sockets, the syntax is:
	`fastcgi_pass unix:/path/to/fastcgi.socket;`
	
	• You may also refer to upstream blocks (read the following sections for more information):
	`fastcgi_pass myblock;`
	
	Examples:
	
	`fastcgi_pass localhost:9000;`
	`fastcgi_pass 127.0.0.1:9000;`
	`fastcgi_pass unix:/tmp/fastcgi.socket;`
	`# Using an upstream block`
	`upstream fastcgi {`
	` server 127.0.0.1:9000;`
	` server 127.0.0.1:9001;`
	`}`
	`location ~* \.php$ {`
	`    fastcgi_pass fastcgi;`
	`}`

Directive	Description

`fastcgi_param`
 	
Context: `http, server, location`
	This directive allows you to configure the request passed to FastCGI. Two parameters are strictly required for all FastCGI requests: `SCRIPT_FILENAME` and `QUERY_STRING`.
	
	Example:
	
	`fastcgi_param SCRIPT_FILENAME /home/website.com/www$fastcgi_script_ name;`
	`fastcgi_param QUERY_STRING $query_ string;`
	
	As for POST requests, additional parameters are required: `REQUEST_METHOD`, `CONTENT_TYPE`, and `CONTENT_LENGTH`:
	
	`fastcgi_param REQUEST_METHOD $request_ method;`
	`fastcgi_param CONTENT_TYPE $content_ type;`
	`fastcgi_param CONTENT_LENGTH $con tent_length;`
	
	The `fastcgi_params` file that you will find in the Nginx configuration folder already includes all of the necessary parameter definitions, except for the `SCRIPT_FILENAME`, which you need to specify for each of your FastCGI configurations.
	
	If the parameter name begins with `HTTP_`, it will override potentially existing HTTP headers of the client request.
	
	You may optionally specify the `if_not_empty` keyword, forcing Nginx to transmit the parameter only if the specified value is not empty.
	
	Syntax: `fastcgi_param PARAM value [if_not_ empty];`

`fastcgi_bind` Context: `http, server, location`	This directive binds the socket to a local IP address, allowing you to specify the network interface you want to use for FastCGI communications. Syntax: `fastcgi_bind IP_address;`

Directive	Description
`fastcgi_pass_header` Context: `http`, `server`, `location`	This directive specifies the additional headers that should be passed to the FastCGI server. Syntax: `fastcgi_pass_header headername;` Example: `fastcgi_pass_header Authorization;`
`fastcgi_hide_header` Context: `http`, `server`, `location`	This directive specifies the headers that should be hidden from the FastCGI server (headers that Nginx does not forward). Syntax: `fastcgi_hide_header headername;` Example: `fastcgi_hide_header X-Forwarded-For;`
`fastcgi_index` Context: `http`, `server`, `location`	The FastCGI server does not support automatic directory indexes. If the requested URI ends with a /, Nginx appends the value `fastcgi_index`. Syntax: `fastcgi_index filename;` Example: `fastcgi_index index.php;`
`fastcgi_ignore_client_abort` Context: `http`, `server`, `location`	This directive lets you define what happens if the client aborts their request to the web server. If the directive is turned on, Nginx ignores the abort request and finishes processing the request. If it's turned off, Nginx does not ignore the abort request. It interrupts the request treatment and aborts related communication with the FastCGI server. Syntax: on or `off` Default: `off`
`fastcgi_intercept_errors` Context: `http`, `server`, `location`	This directive defines whether or not Nginx should process the errors returned by the gateway or directly return error pages to the client. (Note: Error processing is done via the `error_page` directive of Nginx.) Syntax: on or `off` Default: `off`

Directive	Description
`fastcgi_read_timeout` Context: `http, server, location`	This directive defines the timeout for the response from the FastCGI application. If Nginx does not receive the response after this period, the `504 Gateway Timeout` HTTP error is returned. Syntax: Numeric value (in seconds) Default: 60 seconds
`fastcgi_connect_timeout` Context: `http, server, location`	This directive defines the backend server connection timeout. This is different than the read/send timeout. If Nginx is already connected to the backend server, the `fastcgi_connect_timeout` is not applicable. Syntax: Time value (in seconds) Default: 60 seconds
`fastcgi_send_timeout` Context: `http, server, location`	This is the timeout for sending data to the backend server. The timeout isn't applied to the entire response delay but rather between two write operations. Syntax: Time value (in seconds) Default value: `60`

`fastcgi_split_path_info`
 	
Context: `location`
	A directive particularly useful for URLs of the following form: `http://website.com/page.php/param1/param2/`.
	
	The directive splits the path information according to the specified regular expression:
	
	`fastcgi_split_path_info ^(.+\.php)(.*)$;`
	
	This affects two variables:
	
	• `$fastcgi_script_name`: The filename of the actual script to be executed (in the example: `page.php`)
	• `$fastcgi_path_info`: The part of the URL that is after the script name (in the example: `/param1/param2/`)
	
	These can be employed in further parameter definitions:
	
	`fastcgi_param SCRIPT_FILENAME /home/website.com/www$fastcgi_script_name;`
	`fastcgi_param PATH_INFO $fastcgi_path_info;`
	
	Syntax: Regular expression

Directive	Description
`fastcgi_store` Context: `http, server, location`	This directive enables a simple *cache store* where responses from the FastCGI application are stored as files on the storage device. When the same URI is requested again, the document is directly served from the cache store instead of forwarding the request to the FastCGI application. This directive enables or disables the cache store. Syntax: `on` or `off`
`fastcgi_store_access` Context: `http, server, location`	This directive defines the access permissions applied to the files created in the context of the cache store. Syntax: `fastcgi_store_access [user:r|w|rw] [group:r|w|rw] [all:r|w|rw];` Default: `fastcgi_store_access user:rw;`
`fastcgi_temp_path` Context: `http, server, location`	This directive sets the path of temporary and cache store files. Syntax: File path Example: `fastcgi_temp_path /tmp/nginx_fastcgi;`
`fastcgi_max_temp_file_ size` Context: `http, server, location`	Set this directive to 0 to disable the use of temporary files for FastCGI requests or to specify a maximum file size. Default value: 1 GB Syntax: Size value Example: `fastcgi_max_temp_file_size 5m;`
`fastcgi_temp_file_write_ size` Context: `http, server, location`	This directive sets the write buffer size when saving temporary files to the storage device. Syntax: Size value Default value: `2 * proxy_buffer_size`
`fastcgi_buffers` Context: `http, server, location`	This directive sets the amount and size of buffers that will be used for reading the response data from the FastCGI application. Syntax: `fastcgi_buffers amount size;` Default: 8 buffers, 4 k or 8 k each, depending on platform Example: `fastcgi_buffers 8 4k;`

Directive	Description
`fastcgi_buffer_size` Context: `http`, `server`, `location`	This directive sets the size of the buffer for reading the beginning of the response from the FastCGI application, which usually contains simple header data. The default value corresponds to the size of 1 buffer, as defined by the previous directive (`fastcgi_buffers`). Syntax: Size value Example: **`fastcgi_buffer_size 4k;`**
`fastcgi_send_lowat` Context: `http`, `server`, `location`	This option allows you to make use of the `SO_SNDLOWAT` flag for TCP sockets under FreeBSD only. This value defines the minimum number of bytes in the buffer for output operations. Syntax: Numeric value (size) Default value: `0`

`fastcgi_pass_request_body`
 	
`fastcgi_pass_request_headers`
 	
Context: `http`, `server`, `location`
	This directive defines whether or not, respectively, the request body and extra request headers should be passed on to the backend server.
	
	Syntax: `on` or `off`;
	
	Default: `on`

`fastcgi_ignore_headers` Context: `http`, `server`, `location`	This directive prevents Nginx from processing one or more of the following headers from the backend server response: • `X-Accel-Redirect` • `X-Accel-Expires` • `Expires` • `Cache-Control` • `X-Accel-Limit-Rate` • `X-Accel-Buffering` • `X-Accel-Charset` Syntax: `fastcgi_ignore_headers header1 [header2...];`

Directive	Description

`fastcgi_next_upstream`
 	
Context: `http, server, location`
	When `fastcgi_pass` is connected to an upstream block, this directive defines the cases where requests should be abandoned and re-sent to the next upstream server of the block. The directive accepts a combination of values among the following:
	
	• `error`: An error occurred while communicating or attempting to communicate with the server
	
	• `timeout`: A timeout occurs during transfers or connection attempts
	
	• `invalid_header`: The backend server returned an empty or invalid response
	
	• `http_500, http_502, http_503, http_504, http_404`: In case such HTTP errors occur, Nginx switches to the next upstream
	
	• `off`: Forbids from using the next upstream server
	
	Examples:
	
	`fastcgi_next_upstream error timeout http_504;`
	`fastcgi_next_upstream timeout invalid_header;`

`fastcgi_catch_stderr` Context: `http, server, location`	This directive allows you to intercept some of the error messages sent to `stderr` (Standard Error stream) and store them in the Nginx error log. Syntax: `fastcgi_catch_stderr filter;` Example: `fastcgi_catch_stderr "PHP Fatal error:";`
`fastcgi_keep_conn` Context: `http, server, location`	When set to `on`, Nginx will conserve the connection to the FastCGI server, thus reducing overhead. Syntax: `on` or `off` (default: `off`). Note that there is no equivalent directive in the uWSGI and SCGI modules.

FastCGI caching

Once you have correctly configured Nginx to work with your FastCGI application, you may optionally make use of the following directives,which will help you improve the overall server performance by setting up a cache system.

Directive	Description
`fastcgi_cache` Context: `http`, `server`, `location`	This directive defines a cache zone. The identifier given to the zone is to be reused in further directives. Syntax: `fastcgi_cache zonename;` Example: `fastcgi_cache cache1;`
`fastcgi_cache_key` Context: `http`, `server`, `location`	This directive defines the cache key. In other words, what differentiates a cache entry from another. If the cache key is set to `$uri`, as a result, all requests with a similar `$uri` will correspond to the same cache entry. It's not enough for most dynamic websites, you also need to include the query string arguments in the cache key so that `/index.php` and `/index.php?page=contact` do not point to the same cache entry. Syntax: `fastcgi_cache_key key;` Example: `fastcgi_cache "$scheme$host$request_uri $cookie_user";`
`fastcgi_cache_methods` Context: `http`, `server`, `location`	This directive defines the HTTP methods eligible for caching. `GET` and `HEAD` are included by default and cannot be disabled. You may, for example, enable caching of `POST` requests. Syntax: `fastcgi_cache_methods METHOD;` Example: `fastcgi_cache_methods POST;`
`fastcgi_cache_min_uses` Context: `http`, `server`, `location`	This directive defines the minimum amount of hits before a request is eligible for caching. By default, the response of a request is cached after one hit (next requests with the same cache key will receive the cached response). Syntax: Numeric value Example: `fastcgi_cache_min_uses 1;`

Directive	Description
`fastcgi_cache_path` Context: `http, server, location`	This directive indicates the directory for storing cached files, as well as other parameters. Syntax: `fastcgi_cache_path path [levels=numbers] keys_zone=name:size [inactive=time] [max_size=size] [loader_files=number] [loader_sleep=time] [loader_threshold=time];` The additional parameters are: • `levels`: Indicates the depth of subdirectories (1:2 indicates that subfolders will be created down to two levels) • `keys_zone`: Selects the zone you previously declared with the `fastcgi_cache` directive, and indicates the size to occupy in memory • `inactive`: If a cached response is not used within the specified time frame, it's removed from the cache (default: 10 minutes) • `max_size`: Defines the maximum size of the entire cache • `loader_files, loaded_sleep, loader_threshold`: Configures the cache loader: the amount of files it processes in one read cycle (`loader_files`, default: 100 files), the pause time between read cycles (`loader_sleep`, default: 50ms), and the maximum duration of a read cycle (`loader_threshold`, default: 200ms). Example: `fastcgi_cache_path /tmp/nginx_cache levels=1:2 zone=zone1:10m inactive=10m max_size=200M;`
`fastcgi_cache_use_stale` Context: `http, server, location`	This directive defines whether or not Nginx should serve stale cached data in certain circumstances (in regards to the gateway). If you use `fastcgi_cache_use_stale timeout`, and if the gateway times out, then Nginx will serve cached data. Syntax: `fastcgi_cache_use_stale [updating] [error] [timeout] [invalid_header] [http_500];` Example: `fastcgi_cache_use_stale error timeout;`

Directive	Description

fastcgi_cache_valid
 	
Context: http, server,
location
	This directive allows you to customize the caching time for different kinds of response codes. You may cache responses associated to 404 error codes for 1 minute, and on the opposite cache, 200 OK responses for 10 minutes or more. This directive can be inserted more than once, demonstrated as follows:
	
	`fastcgi_cache_valid 404 1m;`
	`fastcgi_cache_valid 500 502 504 5m;`
	`fastcgi_cache_valid 200 10;`
	
	Syntax: fastcgi_cache_valid code1 [code2...] time;

fastcgi_no_cache Context: http, server, location	You may want to disable caching for requests that meet certain conditions. The directive accepts a series of variables. If at least one of these variables has a value (not an empty string, and not 0), this request will not be stored in cache. Syntax: fastcgi_no_cache $variable1 [$variable2] [...]; Example: fastcgi_no_cache $args_nocaching;
fastcgi_cache_bypass Context: http, server, location	This directive functions in a similar manner to fastcgi_no_cache, except that it tells Nginx whether or not the request should be *loaded* from cache, if it can be (as opposed to deciding whether to *store* the request result in cache). Syntax: fastcgi_cache_bypass $variable1 [$variable2] [...]; Example: fastcgi_cache_bypass $cookie_bypass_cache;

fastcgi_cache_lock,
fastcgi_cache_lock_timeout
 	
Context: http, server,
location
	If set to on, fastcgi_cache_lock prevents repopulating existing cache elements for the duration specified by fastcgi_cache_lock_timeout.
	
	Example:
	
	`fastcgi_cache_lock on;`
	`fastcgi_cache_lock_timeout 10s;`

Here is a full Nginx FastCGI cache configuration example, making use of most of the cache-related directives described in the preceding table:

```
fastcgi_cache phpcache;
fastcgi_cache_key "$scheme$host$request_uri"; # $request_uri includes
the request arguments (such as /page.php?arg=value)
```

```
fastcgi_cache_min_uses 2; # after 2 hits, a request receives a cached
response
fastcgi_cache_path /tmp/cache levels=1:2 keys_zone=phpcache:10m inac
tive=30m max_size=500M;
fastcgi_cache_use_stale updating timeout;
fastcgi_cache_valid 404 1m;
fastcgi_cache_valid 500 502 504 5m;
```

Since these directives are valid for pretty much any virtual host configuration, you may want to save these in a separate file (`fastcgi_cache`) that you include at the appropriate place:

```
server {
    server_name website.com;
    location ~* \.php$ {
        fastcgi_pass 127.0.0.1:9000;
        fastcgi_param SCRIPT_FILENAME
/home/website.com/www$fastcgi_script_name;
        fastcgi_param PATH_INFO $fastcgi_script_name;
        include fastcgi_params;
        include fastcgi_cache;
    }
}
```

Upstream blocks

With the FastCGI module, and as you will discover in the next chapter with the Proxy module too, Nginx forwards requests to backend servers. It communicates with processes using either FastCGI or simply by behaving like a regular HTTP client. Either way, the backend server (a FastCGI application, another web server, and so on) may be hosted on a different server in the case of load-balanced architectures:

The general issue with applications (such as PHP) is that they are quite resource-consuming, especially in terms of CPU. Therefore, you may find yourself forced to balance the load across multiple servers, resulting in the following architecture:

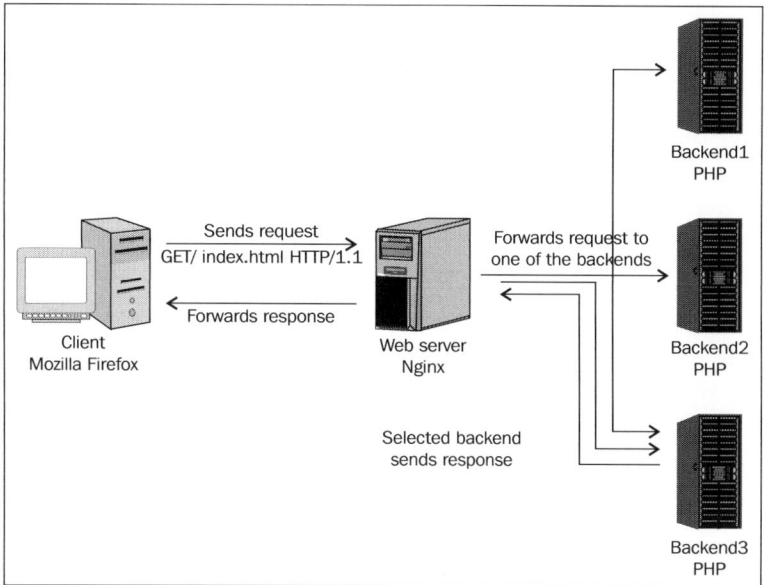

In this case, Nginx is connected to multiple backend servers. To establish such a configuration, a new module comes into play: the **upstream module**.

Module syntax

The upstream module allows you to declare named `upstream` blocks that define lists of servers:

```
upstream phpfpm {
    server 192.168.0.50:9000;
    server 192.168.0.51:9000;
    server 192.168.0.52:9000;
}
```

When defining the FastCGI configuration, connect to the `upstream` block:

```
server {
    server_name website.com;
    location ~* \.php$ {
        fastcgi_pass phpfpm;
        [...]
    }
}
```

In this case, requests eligible to FastCGI will be forwarded to one of the backend servers defined in the upstream block.

A question you might ask is, how does Nginx decide which backend server is to be employed for each request? And the answer is simple: the default method of the Upstream module is round robin. However, this method is not necessarily the best. Two requests from the same visitor might be processed by two different servers, and that could be a problem for many reasons (for example, when PHP sessions are stored on the backend server and are not replicated across the other servers).

To ensure that requests from a same visitor always get processed by the same backend server, you may enable the `ip_hash` option when declaring the `upstream` block:

```
upstream phpfpm {
   ip_hash;
   server 192.168.0.50:9000;
   server 192.168.0.51:9000;
   server 192.168.0.52:9000;
}
```

This will distribute requests based on the visitors IP address employing a regular round robin algorithm. However, be aware that client IP addresses are sometimes subject to change for various reasons such as dynamic IP refresh, proxy switching, Tor. Consequently, the `ip_hash` mechanism cannot fully guarantee that clients will always be involved to the same upstream server. Alternatively, you may force Nginx to select the backend server that currently has the last amount of active connections, through the use of the `least_conn` directive.

Server directive

The server directive that you place within upstream blocks accepts several parameters that influence the backend selection by Nginx:

- `weight=n`: This lets you indicate a numeric value that will affect the weight of the backend server. If you create an `upstream` block with two backend servers, and set the weight of the first one to 2, it will be selected twice more often:

```
upstream php {
   server 192.168.0.1:9000 weight=2;
   server 192.168.0.2:9000;
}
```

- `max_fails=n`: This defines the number of communication failures that should occur (in the time frame specified with the `fail_timeout` parameter below) before Nginx considers the server inoperative.

- `fail_timeout=n`: This defines the time frame within which the maximum failure count applies. If Nginx fails to communicate with the backend server `max_fails` times over `fail_timeout` seconds, the server is considered inoperative.

- `down`: If you mark a backend server as `down`, the server is no longer used. This only applies when the `ip_hash` directive is enabled.

- `backup`: If you mark a backend server as `backup`, Nginx will not make use of the server until all other servers (servers not marked as `backup`) are down or inoperative.

These parameters are all optional and can be used altogether:

```
upstream phpbackend {
  server localhost:9000 weight=5;
  server 192.168.0.1 max_fails=5 fail_timeout=60s;
  server unix:/tmp/backend backup;
}
```

> Inserting the `keepalive` directive in your upstream block enables a connection cache to your backend servers. Requests can then be processed faster since the socket connection and disconnection times are eliminated. For example, `keepalive 32` will maintain up to 32 connections (per worker process) to your backend servers.

PHP with Nginx

We are now going to configure PHP to work together with Nginx via FastCGI. Why FastCGI in particular, as opposed to the other two alternatives SCGI and uWSGI? The answer came with the release of PHP version 5.3.3. As of this version, all releases come with an integrated FastCGI process manager allowing you to easily connect applications implementing the FastCGI protocol. The only requirement is for your PHP build to have been configured with the `--enable-fpm` argument. If you are unsure whether your current setup includes the necessary components, worry not, a section of this chapter is dedicated to building PHP with everything we need.

Architecture

Before starting the setup process, it's important to understand the way PHP will interact with Nginx. We have established that FastCGI is a communication protocol running through sockets, which implies that there is a client and a server. The client is obviously Nginx. As for the server, well, the answer is actually more complicated than just "PHP."

By default, PHP supports the FastCGI protocol. The PHP binary processes scripts and is able to interact with Nginx via sockets. However, we are going to use an additional component to improve the overall process management: the FastCGI Process Manager, also known as **PHP-FPM**:

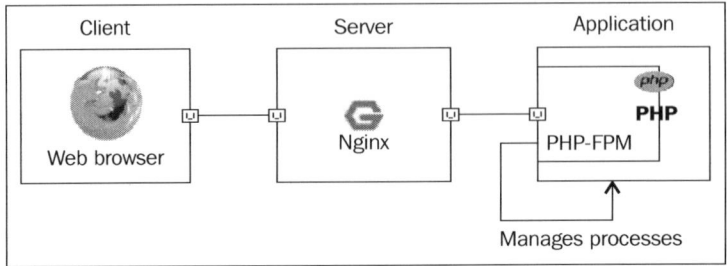

PHP-FPM takes FastCGI support to an entirely new level. Its numerous features are detailed in the next section.

PHP-FPM

The process manager, as its name suggests, is a script that manages PHP processes. It awaits and receives instructions from Nginx and runs the requested PHP scripts under the environment that you configure. In practice, PHP-FPM introduces a number of possibilities such as:

- Automatically *daemonizing* PHP (turning it into a background process)
- Executing scripts in a *chrooted* environment
- Improved logging, IP address restrictions, pool separation, and many more

Setting up PHP and PHP-FPM

In this section, we will detail the process of downloading and compiling a recent version of PHP. You will need to go through this particular step if you are currently running an earlier version of PHP (<5.3.3).

Downloading and extracting

At the time of writing these lines, the latest stable version of PHP is 5.4.14. Download the tar ball via the following command:

```
[user@local ~]$ wget http://php.net/get/php-5.4.14.tar.gz/from/www.php.
net/mirror
```

Once downloaded, extract the PHP archive with the `tar` command:

```
[user@local ~]$ tar xzf php-5.4.14.tar.gz
```

Requirements

There are two main requirements for building PHP with PHP-FPM: the `libevent` and `libxml` development libraries. If these are not already installed on your system, you will need to install them with your system's package manager.

For Red Hat-based systems and other systems using Yum as the package manager:

```
[root@local ~]# yum install libevent-devel libxml2-devel
```

For Ubuntu, Debian, and other systems that use `apt-get` or `aptitude`:

```
[root@local ~]# aptitude install libxml2-dev libevent-dev
```

Building PHP

Once you have installed all of the dependencies, you may start building PHP. Similar to other applications and libraries that were previously installed, you will basically need three commands: `configure`, `make`, and `make install`. Be aware that this will install a new instance of the application. If you already have PHP set up on your system, the new instance will not override it, but instead be installed in a different location that is revealed to you during the `make install` command execution.

The first step (`configure`) is critical here as you will need to enable the PHP-FPM options in order for PHP to include the required functionality. There is a great variety of configuration arguments that you can pass to the `configure` command, some are necessary to enable important features such as database interaction, regular expressions, file compression support, web server integration, and so on. All of the possible configure options are listed when you run this command:

```
[user@local php-5.4.14]$ ./configure --help
```

A minimal command may be also used, but be aware that a great deal of features will be missing. If you wish to include other components, additional dependencies may be needed, which are not documented here. In all cases, the `--enable-fpm` switch should be included:

```
[user@local php-5.4.14]$ ./configure --enable-fpm [...]
```

The next step is to build the application and install it at the same time:

```
[user@local php-5.4.14]$ make && make install
```

This process may take a while depending on your system specifications. Take good note of (some of) the information given to you during the build process. If you did not specify the location of the compiled binaries and configuration files, they will be revealed to you at the end of this step.

Post-install configuration

Begin by configuring your newly installed PHP, for example, copying the php.ini of your previous setup over the new one.

> Due to the way Nginx forwards script file and request information to PHP, a security breach might be caused by the use of the cgi.fix_pathinfo=1 configuration option. It is highly recommended that you set this option to 0 in your php.ini file. For more information about this particular security issue, please consult the following article:
>
> http://cnedelcu.blogspot.com/2010/05/nginx-php-via-fastcgi-important.html

The next step is to configure PHP-FPM. Open up the php-fpm.conf file which located in /usr/local/php/etc/ by default. We cannot detail all aspects of the PHP-FPM configuration here (they are largely documented in the configuration file itself anyway), but there are important configuration directives that you shouldn't miss:

- Edit the user(s) and group(s) used by the worker processes and optionally the UNIX sockets

- Address(es) and port(s) on which PHP-FPM will be listening

- Amount of simultaneous requests that will be served

- IP address(es) allowed to connect to PHP-FPM

Running and controlling

Once you have made the appropriate changes to the PHP-FPM configuration file, you may start it with the following command (the file paths may vary depending on your build configuration):

```
[user@local ~]# /usr/local/php/sbin/php-fpm -c /usr/local/php/etc/php.ini
--pid /var/run/php-fpm.pid --fpm-config=/usr/local/php/etc/php-fpm.conf
-D
```

The preceding command includes several important arguments:

- `-c /usr/local/php/etc/php.ini` sets the path of the PHP configuration file
- `--pid /var/run/php-fpm.pid` sets the path of the PID file, which can be useful for controlling the process via an init script
- `--fpm-config=/usr/local/php/etc/php-fpm.conf` forces PHP-FPM to use the specified configuration file
- `-D` *daemonizes* PHP-FPM (ensures it runs in the background)

Other command-line arguments can be obtained by running `php-fpm -h`.

 Stopping PHP-FPM can be done via the `kill` or `killall` commands. Alternatively, you may use an init script to start and stop the process, provided the version of PHP you installed came with one.

Nginx configuration

If you have managed to configure and start PHP-FPM correctly, you are ready to tweak your Nginx configuration file to establish the connection between both parties. The following server block is a simple, valid template on which you can base your own website configuration:

```
server {
    server_name .website.com; # server name, accepting www
    listen 80; # listen on port 80
    root /home/website/www; # our root document path
    index index.php; # default request filename: index.php

    location ~* \.php$ { # for requests ending with .php
        # specify the listening address and port that you configured
previously
        fastcgi_pass 127.0.0.1:9000;
        # the document path to be passed to PHP-FPM
        fastcgi_param SCRIPT_FILENAME $document_root$fastcgi_script_
name;
        # the script filename to be passed to PHP-FPM
        fastcgi_param PATH_INFO $fastcgi_script_name;
        # include other FastCGI related configuration settings
        include fastcgi_params;
    }
}
```

After saving the configuration file, reload Nginx using one of the following commands:

```
/usr/local/nginx/sbin/nginx -s reload
service nginx reload
```

Create a simple script at the root of your website to make sure PHP is being correctly interpreted:

```
[user@local ~]# echo "<?php phpinfo(); ?>" >/home/website/www/index.php
```

Fire up your favorite web browser and load `http://localhost/` (or your website URL). You should be seeing something similar to the following screenshot, which is the PHP server information page:

Note that you may run into the occasional `403 Forbidden` HTTP error if the file and directory access permissions are not properly configured. If that is the case, make sure that you specified the correct user and group in the `php-fpm.conf` file and that the directory and files are readable by PHP.

Python and Nginx

Python is a popular object-oriented programming language available on many platforms, from Unix-based systems to Windows. It is also available for Java and the Microsoft .NET platform. If you are interested in configuring Python to work with Nginx, it's likely that you already have a clear idea of what Python does. We are going to use Python as server-side web programming language, with the help of the Django framework.

Django

Django is an open source web development framework for Python that aims at making web development simple and easy, as its slogan states:

The Web framework for perfectionists with deadlines.

More information is available on the project website at www.djangoproject.com.

Among other interesting features, such as a dynamic administrative interface, a caching framework, and unit tests, Django comes with a FastCGI manager. It's going to make things much simpler for us from the perspective of running Python scripts through Nginx.

Setting up Python and Django

We will now install Python and Django on your Linux operating system, along with its prerequisites. The process is relatively smooth and mostly consists of running a couple of commands that rarely cause trouble.

Python

Python should be available on your package manager repositories. To install it, run the following commands. For Red Hat-based systems and other systems using Yum as the package manager, use:

```
yum install python python-devel
```

For Ubuntu, Debian, and other systems that use Apt or Aptitude, use:

```
aptitude install python python-dev
```

The package manager will resolve dependencies by itself.

Django

In order to install Django, we will use a different approach. We will be downloading the source directly from the Django SVN in order to make sure we get the latest version.

> **SVN** is an acronym for **Subversion**, a file management and revision system. Its main purpose is to maintain a collaborative working environment for development projects, and to conserve historical versions of source code and other files. By connecting to an SVN repository, you are able to download specific versions of a project's source code.

Therefore, the first step is to install Subversion, the tool that will allow us to synchronize with the Django repository. For Red Hat-based systems and other systems using Yum as the package manager, use:

```
yum install subversion
```

For Ubuntu, Debian, and other systems that use Apt or Aptitude, use:

```
aptitude install subversion
```

The package manager will resolve dependencies by itself.

Once Subversion is installed, we can download the source files into a dedicated folder, and install Django:

```
[root@website.com ~]# mkdir django && cd django
[root@website.com django]# svn co http://code.djangoproject.com/svn/
django/trunk/
[...]
[root@website.com django]# cd trunk
[root@website.com trunk]# python setup.py install
```

Finally, there is one last component required for running the Python FastCGI manager: the `flup` library. This provides the actual FastCGI protocol implementation. For Red Hat-based systems and other systems using Yum as the package manager (EPEL repositories must be enabled, otherwise you will need to build from source), use:

```
yum install python-flup
```

For Ubuntu, Debian, and other systems that use Apt or Aptitude, use:

```
aptitude install python-flup
```

Starting the FastCGI process manager

The process of beginning to build a website with the Django framework will not be detailed here. Once that part is done, you will find a `manage.py` Python script that comes with the default project template. Move to the directory of this file, and run the following command:

```
[root@website.com www]# python manage.py runfcgi method=prefork
host=127.0.0.1 port=9000 pidfile=/var/run/ django.pid
```

If everything was correctly configured, and the dependencies are properly installed, running this command should produce no output, which is often a good sign. The FastCGI process manager is now running in the background waiting for connections. You can verify that the application is running with the `ps` command (for example, by executing `ps aux | grep python`). All we need to do now is to set up the virtual host in the Nginx configuration file.

Nginx configuration

The Nginx configuration is similar to the PHP one:

```
server {
    server_name .website.com;
    listen 80;
    root /home/website/www;
    index index.html;

    location / {
        fastcgi_pass 127.0.0.1:9000;
        fastcgi_param SCRIPT_FILENAME  $document_root$fastcgi_script_
name;
        fastcgi_param PATH_INFO $fastcgi_script_name;
        include fastcgi_params;
    }
}
```

Summary

Whether you use PHP, Python, or any other CGI application, you should now have a clear idea of how to get your scripts processed behind Nginx. There are all sorts of implementations on the Web for mainstream programming languages and the FastCGI protocol. Due to its well-acknowledged efficiency, it is starting to take over server-integrated solutions such as Apache's `mod_php`, `mod_wsgi`, and many others.

If you are unsure about connecting Nginx directly to those server applications, because you already have a well-functioning system architecture in place (for example, Apache with `mod_php`), you may want to consider the option offered in the next chapter, *Installing Nginx on top of Your Existing Apache Setup*.

6
Apache and Nginx Together

If you are reading this book, chances are you already have some good knowledge of the Apache web server with its 51 percent market share (as of April 2013 according to a Netcraft Survey). In fact, a lot of the administrators interested in Nginx are people who have encountered issues with the former regarding slowdowns, being complex to configure, unresponsive at times, and has a variety of other problems. Consequently, the first idea that comes to mind is to replace **Apache** with an alternative web server such as **Nginx**. However, there is a possibility that is not often considered as it sounds a little far-fetched at first — running both Nginx and Apache at the same time. When you look into it, this solution offers a great deal of advantages, especially for administrators looking for a quick and efficient solution to the aforementioned issues.

This chapter covers:

- An introduction to the reverse proxy mechanism
- The advantages and disadvantages of the architecture
- Discovering the proxy module of Nginx
- Configuring Nginx to work with Apache
- Reconfiguring Apache to work as a backend server
- Additional tweaks and notes

Nginx as reverse proxy

First, let's make it clear, the reverse proxy mechanism that we are going to describe in this chapter cannot be considered to be perfect server architecture. At best, it is a temporary solution and should be employed in problematic cases such as the following:

- When you already have Apache installed with complex configuration files that can hardly be ported to Nginx, or if you do not have the time or the will to completely switch to Nginx

- When your system operates a frontend system management panel such as Parallels Plesk, cPanel, or other solutions that generate automatically Apache configuration files

- When a functionality that your project or architecture requires is available with Apache but not with Nginx

In most of the other cases, a complete switch to Nginx is in order. *Chapter 7, From Apache to Nginx* provides a good description of the process.

Understanding the issue

The reverse proxy mechanism mainly addresses one issue — the overall serving speed of Apache. Due to the massive amount of modules and other components that Apache loads in memory (for each HTTP request that it receives), your server may rapidly clutter when massive influxes of requests come in at the same time. One could say that Apache focuses on functionality at the expense of optimization and processing speeds. In practice, this results in excessive memory and CPU overhead. Oppositely, Nginx has proven to be both lightweight and stable while serving a larger amount of requests (using lesser RAM and CPU time in comparison to Apache).

What do we make of that? Before answering this question, it would be interesting to analyze the type of content that will be delivered by your server. Let us visit a regular web page that millions of people load every day: www.yahoo.com. While it's not fully representative of the World Wide Web, our analysis will be valid for a large number of websites and the Yahoo! homepage is the perfect illustration to the problem that we face.

When a regular user visits www.yahoo.com, the web browser actually needs to download a great amount of data. Here are the different files that the browser downloads:

Media type	File/Request count	Total size	Total Gzipped Size
HTML source code	1	157.6 KB	52.5 KB
JavaScript (.js) code files and libraries	6	382.1 KB	112.3 KB
Cascading Style Sheet (.css) files	3	256.8 KB	42.8 KB
Flash animations (.swf)	2	61.4 KB	61.4 KB
Images linked from CSS files (.png, .gif)	18	43.0 KB	43.0 KB
Regular images (.gif, .jpg)	11	73.3 KB	73.3 KB
TOTAL	41	974.2 KB	385.3 KB

 These figures reflect a snapshot taken at the time of writing these lines, as visited by a US-based visitor. Results may differ slightly according to your geographical location, date of visit, and other criteria.

The amount of data to download may not be too surprising. After all, the 385.3 KB (make that 400-450 KB including cookie data and other overhead) can be transferred in less than a second with the fast Internet connections that are now being offered in many countries.

A much bigger problem, in our case, is the amount of requests that the server will have to handle. For all of the first-time visitors, and for any web browser that does not use cached data to load this page, a minimum of 41 HTTP requests will be processed by the web server. Thankfully, a great portion of people will have most of the files cached, but that is never good if you have something to update. Besides, cached data is bound to expire one day or another.

Can your web server process 41 HTTP requests in less than a second? Can it process 41,000 (1,000 page views/second)? Can it process 410,000? If so, you probably have the infrastructure to support such a load. Either way, you are better off with Nginx as you have noticed, 40 out of the 41 requests are for static content — image files, CSS, JavaScript code files, and so on. Provided the speed at which Nginx serves those files, we could design an architecture that lets Nginx serve static files and Apache to handle dynamic content.

The reverse proxy mechanism

Somewhat like the **FastCGI architecture**, described in the previous chapter, we are going to be running Nginx as a frontend server. In other words, it will be in direct communication with the outside world whereas Apache will be running as a backend server and will only exchange data with Nginx:

There are now two web servers running and processing requests:

- Nginx positioned as a frontend server (in other words, as reverse proxy), receives all the requests coming from the outside world. It filters them, either serving static files directly to the client or forwarding dynamic content requests to Apache.

- Apache runs as a backend server and it only communicates with Nginx. It may be hosted on the same computer as the frontend, in which case, the listening port must be edited to leave port 80 available to Nginx. Alternatively, you can employ multiple backend servers (using the upstream block, as seen in *Chapter 6, Apache and Nginx Together*) on different machines and share the load.

To communicate and interact with each other, neither processes will be using FastCGI. Instead, as the name suggests, Nginx acts as a simple proxy server — it receives HTTP requests from client (acting as HTTP server) and forwards them to the backend server (acting as HTTP client). There is, thus, no new protocol or software involved. The mechanism is handled by the proxy module of Nginx (detailed later in the chapter).

Advantages and disadvantages of the mechanism

The main purpose of setting up Nginx as a frontend server and giving Apache a simple backend role is to improve the serving speed. As we established, a great amount of requests coming from clients are for static files, and static files are served much faster by Nginx. The overall performance sharply improves both on the client side and server side.

On a lesser scale, Apache has experienced quite a number of security issues in the past, pushing forward new releases. You are forced to keep your system up-to-date in order to make sure you have a completely secure web server. It is reasonable to say that the more popular a web server is, the more likely bugs and security issues are to be discovered. Oppositely, the latest stable versions of Nginx have so far been apparently secure and the author had no other choice than to focus his rare updates on new functionality over security fixes.

Eventually, if you adopt this solution, you will find it particularly easy to set up as you nearly have no modification to make when it comes to Apache configuration. All it requires is a simple port change, but that isn't even necessary if you set up Nginx and Apache on different servers. Your setup works as it is, which is particularly useful if you already spent hours configuring Apache to work with server-side preprocessors, such as PHP, Python, or others.

On the other hand, you are still deporting requests for dynamic content to Apache, which is, slower than a combination of Nginx and FastCGI most of the time. The optimal solution would be to completely switch to Nginx and leave out Apache.

Besides, since Nginx that is installed as the frontend, it implies that it receives raw requests from users. This implies that the **URI (Uniform Resource Identifier)** comes in its original form, which can lead to confusion for Nginx as it will not be able to make the difference between static and dynamic content. You have two choices to solve this issue. You can either port your rewrite rules to Nginx or redirect any request that results in a 404 error to the Apache backend. To explain the latter, a request such as `/articles/43515-us-economy-strengthens.html` most likely does not correspond to any file on your system — it's meant to be rewritten. You may then check for the existence of such a file from within the Nginx configuration and if it doesn't exist, redirect the request to Apache.

Last but not the least, and this will be further discussed in the last section of this chapter, there may be some issues with control panel software such as Parallels Plesk, cPanel, and others. These panels are very useful for administrators, as they automate some of the most bothersome tasks like adding virtual hosts to the Apache configuration, creating e-mail accounts, configuring the DNS daemon, and many more. The two main issues being:

- These control panels allow you to apply changes on the web server configuration, and based on your changes, they automatically generate valid configuration files for the server. Unfortunately, so far these control panels only offer Apache compatibility, they do not generate Nginx configuration files. So any change that you make will have no effect.

- Whether you completely replace Apache by Nginx or go for the reverse proxy mechanism, Nginx usually ends up running on port 80. The control panel software generating configuration files is unaware of this fact and might be stubborn. When generating configuration files, it will systematically reset the Apache port to 80, creating conflicts with Nginx.

Both issues will be discussed again later in the chapter.

Nginx proxy module

Similar to the previous chapter, the first step towards establishing the new architecture will be to discover the appropriate module. The default Nginx build comes with the proxy module, which allows forwarding of HTTP requests from the client to a backend server. We will be configuring multiple aspects of the module:

- Basic address and port information on the backend server
- Caching, buffering, and temporary file options
- Limits, timeout, and error behavior
- Other miscellaneous options

All these options are available via directives which we will learn to configure throughout this section.

Main directives

The first set of directives will allow you to establish basic configuration such as the location of the backend server, information to be passed, and how it should be passed.

Directive	Description

`proxy_pass`
 	
Context: `location, if`
	Specifies that the request should be forwarded to the backend server by indicating its location:
	
	For TCP sockets, the syntax is `proxy_pass http://hostname:port;`
	
	For Unix domain sockets, the syntax is: `proxy_pass http://unix:/path/to/file.socket;`
	
	You may also refer to upstream blocks: `proxy_pass http://myblock;`
	
	Instead of `http://`, you can use `https://` for secure traffic. Additional URI parts as well as the use of variables are allowed.
	
	Examples:
	
	`proxy_pass http://localhost:8080;`
	
	`proxy_pass http://127.0.0.1:8080;`
	
	`proxy_pass http://unix:/tmp/nginx.sock;`
	
	`proxy_pass https://192.168.0.1;`
	
	`proxy_pass http://localhost:8080/uri/;`
	
	`proxy_pass http://unix:/tmp/nginx.sock:/uri/;`
	
	`proxy_pass http://$server_name:8080;`
	
	`# Using an upstream block`
	
	<pre> upstream backend {
	        server 127.0.0.1:8080;
	        server 127.0.0.1:8081;
	    }
	
	    location ~* \.php$
	    {
	        proxy_pass http://backend;
	    }</pre>

`proxy_method` Context: `http, server, location`	Allows overriding the HTTP method of the request to be forwarded to the backend server. If you specify POST, for example, all requests forwarded to the backend server will be POST requests. Syntax: `proxy_method method;` Example: `proxy_method POST;`

Directive	Description
`proxy_hide_header` Context: `http, server, location`	By default, as Nginx prepares the response received from the backend server to be forwarded back to the client, it ignores some of the headers, such as `Date`, `Server`, `X-Pad`, and `X-Accel-*`. With this directive, you can specify an additional header line to be hidden from the client. You may insert this directive multiple times with one header name for each. Syntax: `proxy_hide_header header_name;` Example: `proxy_hide_header Cache-Control;`
`proxy_pass_header` Context: `http, server, location`	Related to the above directive, this directive forces some of the ignored headers to be passed on to the client. Syntax: `proxy_pass_header headername;` Example: `proxy_pass_header Date;`

`proxy_pass_ request_body`
 	
`proxy_pass_ request_headers`
 	
Context: `http, server, location`
	Defines whether or not, respectively, the request body and extra request headers should be passed on to the backend server.
	
	Syntax: on or `off;`
	
	Default: on

`proxy_redirect`
 	
Context: `http, server, location`
	Allows you to rewrite the URL appearing in the Location HTTP header on redirections triggered by the backend server.
	
	Syntax: `off`, `default`, or the URL of your choice
	
	`off`: Redirections are forwarded *as it is*.
	
	`default`: The value of the `proxy_pass` directive is used as the hostname and the current path of the document is appended. Note that the `proxy_redirect` directive must be inserted after the `proxy_pass` directive as the configuration is parsed sequentially.
	
	URL: Replace a part of the URL by another.
	
	Additionally, you may use variables in the rewritten URL.
	
	Examples:
	
	`proxy_redirect off;`
	
	`proxy_redirect default;`
	
	`proxy_redirect http://localhost:8080/ http:// example.com/;`
	
	`proxy_redirect http://localhost:8080/wiki/ /w/;`
	
	`proxy_redirect http://localhost:8080/ http://$host/;`

Directive	Description

`proxy_next_upstream`
 	
Context: `http, server, location`
	When `proxy_pass` is connected to an upstream block, this directive defines the cases where requests should be abandoned and resent to the next upstream server of the block. The directive accepts a combination of values among the following:
	
	`error`: An error occurred while communicating or attempting to communicate with the server
	
	`timeout`: A timeout occurs during transfers or connection attempts
	
	`invalid_header`: The backend server returned an empty or invalid response
	
	`http_500, http_502, http_503, http_504, http_404`: In case such HTTP errors occur, Nginx switches to the next upstream
	
	`off`: Forbids from using the next upstream server
	
	Examples:
	
	`proxy_next_upstream error timeout http_504;`
	
	`proxy_next_upstream timeout invalid_header;`

Caching, buffering, and temporary files

Ideally, as much as possible, you should reduce the amount of requests being forwarded to the backend server. The following directive will help you build a caching system, as well as control buffering options and the way Nginx handles temporary files:

Directive	Description
`proxy_buffer_size` Context: `http, server, location`	Sets the size of the buffer for reading the beginning of the response from the backend server, which usually contains simple header data. The default value corresponds to the size of 1 buffer, as defined by the directive above (`proxy_buffers`). Syntax: `Numeric value` (size) Example: `proxy_buffer_size 4k;`

Directive	Description
`proxy_buffering` Context: `http, server, location`	Defines whether or not the response from the backend server should be buffered. If set to `on`, Nginx will store the response data in memory using the memory space offered by the buffers. If the buffers are full, the response data will be stored as a temporary file. If the directive is set to `off`, the response is directly forwarded to the client. Syntax: `on` or `off` Default: `on`
`proxy_buffers` Context: `http, server, location`	Sets the amount and size of buffers that will be used for reading the response data from the backend server. Syntax: `proxy_buffers amount size;` Default: 8 buffers, 4 k or 8 k each depending on platform Example: `fastcgi_buffers 8 4k;`
`proxy_busy_buffers_size` Context: `http, server, location`	When the backend-received data accumulated in buffers exceeds the specified value, buffers are flushed and data is sent to the client. Syntax: `Numeric value` (size) Default: `2 * proxy_buffer_size`
`proxy_cache` Context: `http, server, location`	Defines a cache zone. The identifier given to the zone is to be reused in further directives. Syntax: `proxy_cache zonename;` Example: `proxy_cache cache1;`
`proxy_cache_key` Context: `http, server, location`	This directive defines the cache key, in other words, it differentiates one cache entry from another. If the cache key is set to `$uri`, as a result, all requests with this `$uri` will work as a single cache entry. But that's not enough for most dynamic websites. You also need to include the query string arguments in the cache key, so that `/index.php` and `/index.php?page=contact` do not point to the same cache entry. Syntax: `proxy_cache_key key;` Example: `proxy_cache_key "$scheme$host$request_uri $cookie_user";`

Directive	Description
proxy_cache_path Context: http	Indicates the directory for storing cached files, as well as other parameters. Syntax: `proxy_cache_path path [levels=numbers keys_zone=name:size inactive=time max_size=size];` The additional parameters are: `levels`: Indicates the depth level of subdirectories (usually 1:2 is enough) `keys_zone`: Lets you make use of the zone you previously declared with the `proxy_cache` directive and indicates the size to occupy in memory `inactive`: If a cached response is not used within the specified time frame, it is removed from the cache `max_size`: Defines the maximum size of the entire cache Example: `proxy_cache_path /tmp/nginx_cache levels=1:2 zone=zone1:10m inactive=10m max_size=200M;`
proxy_cache_methods Context: http, server, location	Defines the HTTP methods eligible for caching. GET and HEAD are included by default and cannot be disabled. Syntax: `proxy_cache_methods METHOD;` Example: `proxy_cache_methods OPTIONS;`
proxy_cache_min_uses Context: http, server, location	Defines the minimum amount of hits before a request is eligible for caching. By default, the response of a request is cached after one hit (next requests with the same cache key will receive the cached response). Syntax: `Numeric value` Example: `proxy_cache_min_uses 1;`

proxy_cache_valid
 	
Context: http, server, location
	This directive allows you to customize the caching time for different kinds of response codes. You may cache responses associated with 404 error codes for 1 minute, and on the opposite cache, 200 OK responses for 10 minutes or more. This directive can be inserted more than once:
	
	`proxy_cache_valid 404 1m;`
	
	`proxy_cache_valid 500 502 504 5m;`
	
	`proxy_cache_valid 200 10;`
	
	Syntax: `proxy_cache_valid code1 [code2...] time;`

Directive	Description
`proxy_cache_use_stale` Context: `http, server, location`	Defines whether or not Nginx should serve stale cached data in certain circumstances (in regard to the gateway). If you use `proxy_cache_use_stale timeout`, and if the gateway times out, then Nginx will serve cached data.
	Syntax: `proxy_cache_use_stale [updating] [error] [timeout] [invalid_header] [http_500];`
	Example: `proxy_cache_use_stale error timeout;`
`proxy_max_temp_file_size` Context: `http, server, location`	Set this directive to `0` to disable the use of temporary files for requests eligible to proxy forwarding or specify a maximum file size.
	Syntax: `Size value`
	Default value: `1 GB`
	Example: `proxy_max_temp_file_size 5m;`
`proxy_temp_file_write_size` Context: `http, server, location`	Sets the write buffer size when saving temporary files to the storage device.
	Syntax: `Size value`
	Default value: `2 * proxy_buffer_size`
`proxy_temp_path` Context: `http, server, location`	Sets the path of temporary and cache store files.
	Syntax: `proxy_temp_path path [level1 [level2...]]`
	Examples:
	`proxy_temp_path /tmp/nginx_proxy;`
	`proxy_temp_path /tmp/cache 1 2;`

Limits, timeouts, and errors

The following directives will help you define timeout behavior, as well as various limitations regarding communications with the backend server:

Directive	Description
`proxy_connect_timeout` Context: `http, server, location`	Defines the backend server connection timeout. This is different from the read/send timeout. If Nginx is already connected to the backend server, the `proxy_connect_timeout` is not applicable.
	Syntax: `Time value` (in seconds)
	Example: `proxy_connect_timeout 15;`

Directive	Description
proxy_read_timeout Context: http, server, location	The timeout for reading data from the backend server. This timeout isn't applied to the entire response delay but between two read operations instead. Syntax: Time value (in seconds) Default value: 60 Example: proxy_read_timeout 60;
proxy_send_timeout Context: http, server, location	This timeout is for sending data to the backend server. The timeout isn't applied to the entire response delay but between two write operations instead. Syntax: Time value (in seconds) Default value: 60 Example: proxy_send_timeout 60;
proxy_ignore_client_abort Context: http, server, location	If set to on, Nginx will continue processing the proxy request, even if the client aborts its request. In the other case (off), when the client aborts its request, Nginx also aborts its request to the backend server. Default value: off
proxy_intercept_errors Context: http, server, location	By default, Nginx returns all error pages (HTTP status code 400 and higher) sent by the backend server directly to the client. If you set this directive to on, the error code is parsed and can be matched against the values specified in the error_page directive. Default value: off
proxy_send_lowat Context: http, server, location	An option allowing you to make use of the SO_SNDLOWAT flag for TCP sockets under BSD-based operating systems only. This value defines the minimum number of bytes in the buffer for output operations. Syntax: Numeric value (size) Default value: 0

Other directives

Finally, the last set of directives available in the proxy module is uncategorized and is as follows:

Directive	Description
`proxy_headers_hash_max_size` Context: `http`, `server`, `location`	Sets the maximum size for the proxy headers hash tables. Syntax: `Numeric value` Default value: `512`
`proxy_headers_hash_bucket_size` Context: `http`, `server`, `location`	Sets the bucket size for the proxy headers hash tables. Syntax: `Numeric value` Default value: `64`
`proxy_ignore_headers` Context: `http`, `server`, `location`	Prevents Nginx from processing one of the following four headers from the backend server response: `X-Accel-Redirect`, `X-Accel-Expires`, `Expires`, and `Cache-Control`. Syntax: `proxy_ignore_headers header1 [header2...];`
`proxy_set_body` Context: `http`, `server`, `location`	Allows you to set a static request body for debugging purposes. Variables may be used in the directive value. Syntax: `String value` (any value) Example: `proxy_set_body test;`
`proxy_set_header` Context: `http`, `server`, `location`	This directive allows you to redefine header values to be transferred to the backend server. It can be declared multiple times. Syntax: `proxy_set_header Header Value;` Example: `proxy_set_header Host $host;`

`proxy_store`
 	
Context: `http`, `server`, `location`
	Specifies whether or not the backend server response should be stored as a file. Stored response files can be reused for serving other requests.
	
	Possible values: `on`, `off`, or a path relative to the document root (or alias). You may also set this to `on` and define the `proxy_temp_path` directive.
	
	Examples:
	
	`proxy_store on;`
	
	`proxy_temp_path /temp/store;`

Directive	Description
`proxy_store_access` Context: `http, server, location`	This directive defines file access permissions for the stored response files.
	Syntax: `proxy_store_access [user:[r|w|rw]] [group:[r|w|rw]] [all:[r|w|rw]];`
	Example: `proxy_store_access user:rw group:rw all:r;`
`proxy_http_version` Context: `http, server, location`	Sets the HTTP version to be used for communicating with the proxy backend. HTTP 1.0 is the default value, but if you are going to enable keepalive connections, you might want to set this directive to `1.1`.
	Syntax: `proxy_http_version 1.0 | 1.1;`

`proxy_cookie_domain`
 	
`proxy_cookie_path`
 	
Context: `http, server, location`
	Applies an on-the-fly modification to the domain or path attributes of a cookie (case insensitive).

	Syntaxes: `proxy_cookie_domain off | domain replacement;` `proxy_cookie_path off | domain replacement ;`

Variables

The proxy module offers several variables that can be inserted in various locations, for example, in the `proxy_set_header` directive or in the logging-related directives such as `log_format`. The available variables are:

- `$proxy_host`: Contains the hostname of the backend server used for the current request.

- `$proxy_port`: Contains the port of the backend server used for the current request.

- `$proxy_add_x_forwarded_for`: This variable contains the value of the `X-Forwarded-For` request header, followed by the remote address of the client. Both values are separated by a comma. If the `X-Forwarded-For` request header is unavailable, the variable only contains the client remote address.

- `$proxy_internal_body_length`: Length of the request body (set with the `proxy_set_body` directive or 0).

Configuring Apache and Nginx

After having reviewed the proxy module, which allows us to establish our reverse proxy configuration architecture, it's now time to put all these principles into practice. There are basically two main parts involved in the configuration, one relating to Apache and one relating to Nginx. The order in which you decide to apply those modifications does not make any difference whatsoever.

Note that while we have chosen to describe the process specifically for Apache, this method can be applied to any other HTTP server. The only point that differs is the exact configuration sections and directives that you will need to edit. Otherwise, the principle of reverse proxy can be applied, regardless of the server software you are using.

Reconfiguring Apache

There are two main aspects of your Apache configuration that will need to be edited in order to allow both Apache and Nginx to work together at the same time. But let us first clarify where we are coming from and where we are going.

Configuration overview

At this point, you probably have the following architecture set up on your server:

- A web server application running on port 80, such as Apache
- A dynamic server-side script processing application such as PHP, communicating with your web server via CGI, FastCGI, or as a server module

The new configuration we are going towards will resemble the following:

- Nginx running on port 80
- Apache (or another web server) running on a different port, accepting requests coming from local sockets only
- The script processing application configuration will remain unchanged

As you can tell, only two main configuration changes will be applied to Apache, as well as the other web server that you are running. Firstly, change the port number in order to avoid conflicts with Nginx, which will then be running as the frontend server. Secondly, (although this is optional) you may want to disallow requests coming from the outside and only allow requests forwarded by Nginx. Both configuration steps are detailed in the next sections.

Resetting the port number

Depending on how your web server was set up (manual build or automatic configuration from server panel managers such as cPanel, Plesk), you may find yourself with a lot of configuration files to edit. The main configuration file is often found in /etc/httpd/conf/ or /etc/apache2/, and there might be more, depending on how your configuration is structured. Some server panel managers create extra configuration files for each virtual host.

There are three main elements you need to replace in your Apache configuration:

- The Listen directive is set to listen on port 80 by default. You will have to replace that port by another such as 8080. This directive is usually found in the main configuration file.

- You must make sure that the following configuration directive is present in the main configuration file: NameVirtualHost A.B.C.D:8080, where A.B.C.D is the IP address of the main network interface on which server communications go through.

- The port you just selected needs to be reported in all your virtual host configuration sections.

The virtual host sections must be transformed from the following template:

```
<VirtualHost A.B.C.D:80>
   ServerName    example.com
   ServerAlias   www.example.com
   [...]
</VirtualHost>
```

to the following:

```
<VirtualHost A.B.C.D:8080>
   ServerName    example.com:8080
   ServerAlias   www.example.com
[...]
</VirtualHost>
```

In this example, A.B.C.D is the IP address of the virtual host and example.com is the virtual host's name. The port must be edited on the first two lines.

Accepting local requests only

There are many ways by which you can restrict Apache to only accept local requests and deny access to the outside world. But first, why would you want to do that? As an extra layer positioned between the client and Apache, Nginx provides a certain comfort in terms of security. Visitors no longer have direct access to Apache, which decreases the potential risk regarding all security issues the web server may have. Globally, it's not necessarily a bad idea to only allow access to your frontend server.

The first method consists of changing the listening network interface in the main configuration file. The `Listen` directive of Apache lets you specify a port, but also an IP address. However, by default, no IP address is selected which results in communications coming from all interfaces. All you have to do is replace the `Listen 8080` directive by `Listen 127.0.0.1:8080`, Apache should then only listen on the local IP address. If you do not host Apache on the same server, you will need to specify the IP address of the network interface that can communicate with the server hosting Nginx.

The second alternative is to establish per-virtual-host restrictions:

```
<VirtualHost A.B.C.D:8080>
   ServerName    example.com:8080
   ServerAlias   www.example.com
   [...]
   Order deny,allow
   allow from 127.0.0.1
   allow from 192.168.0.1
   deny all
</VirtualHost>
```

Using the `allow` and `deny` Apache directives, you are able to restrict the allowed IP addresses accessing your virtual hosts. This allows for a finer configuration, which can be useful in case some of your websites cannot be fully served by Nginx.

Once all your changes are done, don't forget to reload the server to make sure the new configuration is applied, such as `service httpd reload` or `/etc/init.d/httpd reload`.

Configuring Nginx

There are only a couple of simple steps to establish a working configuration of Nginx, although it can be tweaked more accurately as seen in the next section.

Enabling proxy options

The first step is to enable proxying of requests from your location blocks. Since the proxy_pass directive cannot be placed at the http or server level, you need to include it in every single place that you want to be forwarded. Usually, a location / { fallback block suffices since it encompasses all requests, except those that match location blocks containing a break statement.

The following is a simple example using a single static backend hosted on the same server:

```
server {
    server_name .example.com;
    root /home/example.com/www;
    [...]
    location / {
        proxy_pass http://127.0.0.1:8080;
    }
}
```

In the following example, we make use of an upstream block allowing us to specify multiple servers, as described in *Chapter 6, Apache and Nginx Together*:

```
upstream apache {
    server 192.168.0.1:80;
    server 192.168.0.2:80;
    server 192.168.0.3:80 weight=2;
    server 192.168.0.4:80 backup;
}
    server {
    server_name .example.com;
    root /home/example.com/www;
    [...]
    location / {
        proxy_pass http://apache;
    }
}
```

So far, with such a configuration, all requests are proxied to the backend server. We are now going to separate the content into two categories:

- **Dynamic files**: Files that require processing before being sent to the client, such as PHP, Perl, and Ruby scripts, will be served by Apache
- **Static files**: All other content that does not require additional processing, such as images, CSS files, static HTML files, and media, will be served directly by Nginx

Therefore, we somehow need to separate the dynamic from the static content to be provided by either server.

Separating content

In order to establish this separation, we can simply use two different location blocks, one that will match the dynamic file extensions and another one encompassing all the other files. This example passes requests for .php files to the proxy:

```
server {
    server_name .example.com;
    root /home/example.com/www;
    [...]
    location ~* \.php.$ {
      # Proxy all requests with an URI ending with .php*
      # (includes PHP, PHP3, PHP4, PHP5…)
        proxy_pass http://127.0.0.1:8080;
    }
    location / {
        # Your other options here for static content
        # for example cache control, alias…
        expires 30d;
    }
}
```

This method, although simple, will cause trouble with websites using URL rewriting. Most Web 2.0 websites now use links that hide file extensions such as http://example.com/articles/us-economy-strengthens/; some even replace file extensions with links such as http://example.com/us-economy-strengthens.html.

When building a reverse proxy configuration, you have two options:

- Port your Apache rewrite rules to Nginx (usually found in the .htaccess file at the root of the website), in order for Nginx to know the actual file extension of the request and proxy it to Apache correctly.

- If you do not wish to port your Apache rewrite rules, the default behavior shown by Nginx is to return 404 errors for such requests. However, you can alter this behavior in multiple ways, for example, by handling 404 requests with the error_page directive, or by testing the existence of files before serving them. Both solutions are detailed in the following.

Here is an implementation of this mechanism, using the error_page directive:

```
server {
    server_name .example.com;
    root /home/example.com/www;
    [...]
    location / {
        # Your static files are served here
        expires 30d;
        [...]
        # For 404 errors, submit the query to the @proxy
        # named location block
        error_page 404 @proxy;
    }

    location @proxy {
        proxy_pass http://127.0.0.1:8080;
    }
}
```

Alternatively, making use of the if directive from the rewrite module:

```
server {
    server_name .example.com;
    root /home/example.com/www;
    [...]
    location / {
      # If the requested file extension ends with .php,
      # forward the query to Apache
      if ($request_filename ~* \.php.$) {
        break; # prevents further rewrites
        proxy_pass http://127.0.0.1:8080;
      }
      # If the requested file does not exist,
      # forward the query to Apache
      if (!-f $request_filename) {
        break; # prevents further rewrites
        proxy_pass http://127.0.0.1:8080;
      }
      # Your static files are served here
      expires 30d;
    }
}
```

There is no real performance difference between either solution, as they will transfer the same amount of requests to the backend server. You should work on porting your Apache rewrite rules to Nginx if you are looking to get optimal performance.

Advanced configuration

For now, we have only made use of one directive offered by the proxy module. There are many more features that we can employ to optimize our design. The table below lists a handful of settings that are valid for most of your reverse proxy configurations, although they need to be verified individually. Since they can be employed multiple times, you can also place them in a separate configuration file that you will include in your location blocks.

Start by creating a `proxy.conf` text file that you place in the Nginx configuration directory. Insert the directives described in the following in that file. Then, for each location of your `if` blocks that forward requests to a backend server or upstream block, insert the following line after the `proxy_pass` directive:

```
include proxy.conf;
```

Suggested values for some of the settings:

Setting	Description
`proxy_redirect off;`	Lets Nginx forward redirections to the client as it is without processing the response itself.
`proxy_set_header Host $host;`	The Host HTTP header in the request forwarded to the backend server defaults to the proxy hostname, as specified in the configuration file. This setting lets Nginx use the original Host from the client request instead.
`proxy_set_header X-Real-IP $remote_addr;`	Since the backend server receives a request from Nginx, the IP address it communicates with is not that of the client. Use this setting to forward the actual client IP address into a new header, X-Real-IP.
`proxy_set_header X-Forwarded-For $proxy_add_x_forwarded_for;`	Similar to the header above, except that if the client already uses a proxy on his/her own end, the actual IP address of the client should be contained in the X-Forwarded-For request header. Using $proxy_add_x_forwarded_for ensures that both the IP address of the communicating socket and possibly the original IP address of the client (behind a proxy) gets forwarded to the backend server.

Setting	Description
`client_max_body_size 10m;`	Limits the maximum size of the request body to `10` megabytes. Actually, this setting is referenced here to make sure that you adjust the value to the same level as your backend server. Otherwise, a request that is correctly received and processed by Nginx may not be successfully forwarded to the backend.
`client_body_buffer_size 128k;`	Defines the minimum size of the memory buffer that will hold a request body. Past this size, the content is saved in a temporary file. Adjust it according to the expected size of requests your visitors will be sending, similar to `client_max_body_size`.
`proxy_connect_timeout 15;`	If you are working with a backend server on a local network, make sure to keep this value reasonably low (`15` seconds here, but it depends on the average load). The maximum value for this directive is `75` seconds anyway.
`proxy_send_timeout 15;`	Make sure you define a timeout for write operations (timeout between two write operations during a communication to the backend server).
`proxy_read_timeout 15;`	Similar to the previous directive, except for read operations.

Many other directives may be configured here. However, default values are appropriate for most setups.

Improving the reverse proxy architecture

There are a few more additional steps that you may be interested in if you want to perfect your reverse proxy architecture. Three main issues are discussed here: the issue of IP addresses and how to ensure that the backend server retrieves the correct one, how to handle HTTPS requests with such a setup, and finally a few words about server control panels (cPanel, Plesk, and others).

Forwarding the correct IP address

Nowadays, a good portion of websites make use of the visitor's IP address for all kinds of reasons:

- Storing the IP address of a visitor posting a comment on a blog or a discussion forum
- Geo-targeted advertising or other services
- Limiting services to specific IP address ranges

Therefore, it is important for those websites to ensure that the web server correctly receives the IP address of the visitor.

As explained before, since Apache, or more generally the backend server uses the IP address of the socket it communicates with, the IP that will appear in our design will always be the IP of the server hosting Nginx. We discussed a solution already — inserting the `proxy_set_header X-Real-IP $remote_addr;` directive in the configuration in order to forward the client IP address in the `X-Real-IP` header.

Unfortunately, that is not enough as some web applications are not configured to make use of the `X-Real-IP` header. The client remote address needs to be replaced somehow by that value. When it comes to Apache, a module was written to do just that: `mod_rpaf`. Details on how to install and configure it are not discussed here; you may find more documentation over at the official website: `http://stderr.net/apache/rpaf/`.

SSL issues and solutions

If your website is going to serve secure web pages, you need to somehow allow visitors to connect to your infrastructure via **SSL (Secure Sockets Layer)** on port 443. Two solutions are possible at this point: either you do not make use of Nginx at all and keep your Apache SSL configuration unmodified, or you configure Nginx to accept communications on port 443.

The first solution is clearly the simplest — do not change the port of your virtual hosts as configured in Apache. Your website should still be fully accessible from the outside, unless your backend server is hosted on another computer on the local network.

The alternative is to configure Nginx to accept secure connections via the SSL module, as described in *Chapter 5, PHP and Phython with Nginx*. Once your `server` block is correctly configured, you can establish a proxied configuration to forward secure requests to your Apache server. Note that if your backend server is hosted on the same machine, you will need to edit the configuration in order to avoid port conflicts between the frontend and backend.

Server control panel issues

A lot of server administrators rely on control panel software to simplify many aspects of their work: managing hosted domains, e-mail accounts, network settings, and much more. Advanced software solutions such as Parallels Plesk or cPanel are able to generate configuration files for many server applications (web, e-mail, database, and so on) on-the-fly. Unfortunately, most of them only support Apache as a unique web server application; Nginx is often left behind.

If you followed the steps of the reverse proxy configuration process, you noticed that at some point, the Apache configuration files had to be manually edited. We replaced the listening port and edited or inserted some configuration directives. Obviously, when the control panel software generates configuration files, it is unaware of the manual changes we made. Therefore, it erases our modifications. When you restart Apache, you are greeted with error messages and conflicts.

At this point, there is no other solution than to apply the changes again after each configuration rebuild. With the growing popularity of Nginx, developers will hopefully implement full Nginx support in their software, or at least allow those configuration settings to be edited that are required to use Nginx as a reverse proxy.

 Facing the growing popularity of Nginx, web control panel developers are indeed starting to take steps towards full or partial support of Nginx. As of version 11, Parallels Plesk now offers support for Nginx as a frontend server.

Summary

Configuring Nginx as a reverse proxy for our architecture introduces a lot of advantages in terms of loading speeds and server load. However, a few obstacles might stand in your way, especially if you are running control panel software solutions to manage your services. Moreover, you do not get to make the most of Nginx as you are not using it for all your requests.

If you are seeking to find an even more efficient solution, you may want to look into completely replacing Apache by Nginx. The next chapter will detail this process, step-by-step, from virtual hosts to rewrite rules to FastCGI.

7
From Apache to Nginx

Every experienced system administrator will tell you the same story. When your web infrastructure works fine and client requests are served at a good speed, the last thing you want to do is modify the architecture that you have spent days, weeks, or even months putting together. In reality, as your website grows more popular, problems pertaining to scalability tend to occur inevitably (and the said problems are not as documented as mainstream ones), regardless of the effort you originally involved in your initial server configuration. Eventually you have to start looking for solutions. In that extent, there are multiple reasons why you would want to completely adopt Nginx at the expense of your previous web server application. Whether you have decided that Nginx could be more efficient as a unique server rather than working as a reverse proxy, or simply because you want to get rid of Apache once and for all, this chapter will guide you through the complete process of replacing the latter by the former.

This chapter covers:

- An in-depth comparison between **Apache** and **Nginx**
- A full guide to porting your Apache configuration
- How to port your Apache rewrite rules to Nginx
- Rewrite rule walkthroughs for a few popular web applications

Nginx versus Apache

This section will provide answers to the main questions that one would ask about Nginx — how does it stand apart from the other servers? How does it compare to Apache? Whether you were using Apache before or considered it as a replacement for your current web server, why would you decide to adopt Nginx at the expense of the web server that empowers nearly half of the Internet websites worldwide?

Features

With the reverse proxy configuration that was elaborated in the previous chapter, the presence or absence of specific features wasn't much of a problem. This is because Nginx would simply have to differentiate between static and dynamic content, and in consequence, serve static file requests and forward dynamic file requests to a backend server.

However, when you start to consider Nginx as a possible full replacement for your current web server, you better make sure of what's in the box. If your projected architecture requires specific components, the first thing you would usually do is check the application features. The table below lists a few of the major features and describes how Nginx performs in comparison to Apache.

Core and functioning

Features	Nginx	Apache
Request management: This specifies how the web server processes the requests.	**Event-driven architecture:** In this architecture, requests are accepted using asynchronous sockets and aren't processed in separate threads, in order to reduce memory and CPU overhead.	**Synchronous sockets, threads, and processes**: In this, each request is in a separate thread or process and uses synchronous sockets.
Programming language: This specifies the language the web server is written in.	**C:** The C language is notably low-level and offers more accurate memory management.	**C and C++:** Although Apache was written in C, many modules were designed with C++.
Portability: This specifies the operating systems that are supported.	**Multiplatform:** Nginx runs under Windows, GNU/Linux, Unix, BSD, Mac OS X, and Solaris.	**Multiplatform:** Apache runs under Windows, GNU/Linux, Unix, BSD, Mac OS X, Solaris, Novell NetWare, OS/2, TPF, OpenVMS, eCS, AIX, z/OS, HP-UX, and more.
Year of birth: This specifies the time when the development started.	**2002:** While Nginx is younger than Apache, it was intended for a more modern era.	**1994:** Apache is one of the numerous open source projects initiated in the 90s that contributed to making the World Wide Web what it is today.

General functionality

This section mainly focuses on differences between Apache and Nginx rather than listing all sorts of features that have already been covered in previous chapters:

Feature	Nginx	Apache
HTTPS support: This specifies whether the web server can deliver secure web pages.	**Supported as module**: If you want HTTPS support, you need to make sure to compile Nginx with the proper module.	**Supported as module**: Apache comes with HTTPS support via a module included by default.
Virtual Hosting: This specifies whether the web server can host multiple websites on the same computer.	**Supported natively**: Nginx natively supports virtual hosting, but is not configured by default to accept per-virtual-host configuration files (more details are provided further in this chapter).	**Supported natively**: Apache natively supports virtual hosting and offers the possibility to include one configuration file per folder (.htaccess).
CGI Support: This specifies whether the web server support CGI based protocols.	**FastCGI, uWSGI, SCGI**: Nginx supports FastCGI, uWSGI and SCGI via modules that are included by default at compile time.	**CGI, FastCGI**: Most CGI protocols are exploitable via modules that can be loaded into Apache.
Module system: This specifies how the web server handles the modules.	**Static module system**: Modules must be included at compile time.	**Dynamic module system**: Modules can be loaded and unloaded dynamically from configuration files.

Generally speaking, Apache has a lot more to offer, notably a much larger number of modules available. Most of its functionality, even core functions for the application core, is modularized. At this time, the official Apache module website references over 500 modules for various version branches, versus a little more than 90 for Nginx. This state of facts is mainly caused by the following reasons:

Flexibility and community

This is another criterion for establishing an honest comparison between two applications of Nginx and Apache family. In today's information technology industry, one cannot simply regard the raw functionality of a server application without considering questions such as:

- Where am I going to get help if I get stuck?
- Am I going to find documentation about the features offered by the server?

- Are more modules going to be implemented in the future?

- Is the project still active and being updated by its developers?

- Has the server security been tested by a large enough number of administrators?

These questions generally answer themselves when the server gets popular enough. In the case of Apache, saying that it is a mainstream application would be an understatement. Documentation is easily found, developers have released hundreds of modules over the years, and it has received regular updates for the past fifteen years.

What about Nginx, how does it stand on those matters? That is definitely a sensitive issue. To begin with, there are some solid websites, centralizing information such as the official wiki. If you have a problem with Apache, a simple search engine query suffices to find multiple articles, answering the exact question you have been asking yourself. If you have an overly specific problem with Nginx though, you will likely have to resort to newsgroups, mailing lists, or web forums.

On the updates and security side though, Nginx is frequently updated by its author Igor Sysoev and his team. Those updates rarely include security fixes as the server has been built on solid and reliable foundations from the start. Although it doesn't serve as many websites as Apache does, Nginx still empowers some of the most popular online platforms such as Facebook, SourceForge, WordPress, ImageShack, and many more. This contributes to conferring it undeniable legitimacy in the domain of high-performance web servers.

Performance

While features and community-related matters are important in general, the aspect that can make all the difference is performance. Administrators naturally tend to favor the server that will provide optimal comfort for the end user, characterized by minimal page load times and maximum download speeds.

Chapter 2, Basic Nginx Configuration provided a first approach to HTTP server performance testing. The same tests can be applied to Apache in order to establish direct performance comparisons. In fact, many admin bloggers and technicians have already done so, and the general trend is unquestionably in favor of Nginx on all aspects, such as the following:

- The RPS rate is generally much higher with Nginx, sometimes twice higher than Apache's. In other words, Nginx is able to serve twice as many pages as Apache in the same lapse of time.

- Response times are lower on Nginx. As the request count grows, Apache becomes slower and slower to serve pages.

- Apache tends to use slightly more bandwidth than Nginx for serving the same requests. This can be interpreted in two ways — either Apache generates more traffic overhead, or it is able to transfer data at a faster rate by better occupying the available bandwidth (it's still unsure as to which of these assumptions is the most valid).

In conclusion on the field of performance, Nginx wins hands down. It's clearly the main reason why so many have switched to the lightweight Russian web server.

Usage

The reason why Nginx is so far ahead of Apache performance-wise is because it's precisely the reason it was written for. Originally, Igor Sysoev created Nginx to empower an extremely high-traffic Russian website (`www.rambler.ru`), which received hundreds of millions of requests every day. This was probably not part of the original plans of the Apache designers when they initiated the project back in the early 90s.

More generally, it is said that Nginx was designed to address the **C10k problem**. This expression designates a common observation according to which the current state of computer technology and network scalability only allows a computer (from the mainstream industry) to maintain up to 10,000 simultaneous network connections, due to operating system and software limitations. While that number isn't representative anymore due to the progress of the technology, at the time, the issue was considered very seriously and it triggered the development of major web servers such as Lighttpd, Cherokee, and obviously Nginx.

Conclusion

There is one famous quote going around the Nginx community that summarizes the situation pretty accurately:

"Apache is like Microsoft Word, it has a million options but you only need six. Nginx does those six things, and it does five of them 50 times faster than Apache." – Chris Lea, `ChrisLea.com`

Other notable testimonies help build the reputation of Nginx:

"I currently have Nginx doing reverse proxy of over tens of millions of HTTP requests per day (that's a few hundred per second) on a *single server*. At peak load, it uses about 15 MB RAM and 10 percent of my CPU on my particular configuration (FreeBSD 6). Under the same kind of load, Apache falls over (after using 1,000 or so processes and god knows how much RAM), Pound falls over (too many threads, and using 400 MB+ of RAM for all the thread stacks), and Lighty leaks more than 20 MB per hour (and uses more CPU, but not significantly more)." – Bob Ippolito, `MochiMedia.com`

If you are in the market for high-scale projects with limited resources at your disposal, Nginx comes in as a great solution. Apache is a good option to get your projects started when your knowledge of web servers and hosting is limited, but as soon as you meet success, you, your server, and your visitors may eventually find it inconsistent.

Porting your Apache configuration

That's it. You've had enough of Apache. You finally decided to make a complete switch to Nginx. There are quite a few steps ahead of you now, the first of which is to adapt your previous configuration in a way to ensure that your existing websites work 1:1 after the switch.

Directives

This first section will summarize some of the common Apache configuration directives and attempt to provide equivalent or replacement solutions from Nginx. The list follows the order of the default Apache configuration file:

Apache directive	Nginx equivalent
`ServerTokens`: Apache allows you to configure the information transmitted in request headers regarding the server OS and software name and versions.	`server_tokens`: In Nginx, you may enable or disable transmission of server information by using the `server_tokens` directive from the main HTTP module.
`ServerRoot`: Lets you define the `root` folder of the server, which will contain the configuration and logs folder.	`--prefix` build-time option: With Nginx, this option is defined at compile time with the `--prefix` switch of the configure script or at execution time with the -p command line option.
PID file: Defines the path of the application PID file.	`PID`: The exact equivalent directive is PID.
`TimeOut`: This directive defines three elements: • The maximum execution time of a GET request • The maximum allowed delay between two TCP packets in POST and PUT requests • The maximum allowed delay between two TCP ACK packets	**Multiple directives:** There are multiple directives allowing a similar behavior: • `send_timeout`: Defines the maximum allowed delay between two read operations by the client • `client_body_timeout`: Defines the timeout for reading client request body • `client_header_timeout`: Defines the timeout for reading client request headers

Apache directive	Nginx equivalent
`KeepAlive`, `MaxKeepAliveRequests`, `KeepAliveTimeout`: These three directives control the keep-alive behavior of Apache.	`keepalive_timeout`, `keepalive_requests`: These two directives are the direct equivalents to the Apache ones, except that if you want to completely disable keepalives, set `keepalive_timeout` or `keepalive_requests` to 0.
`Listen`: Defines the interface and port on which Apache will listen for connections.	`Listen`: In Nginx, this directive is only defined at the virtual host level (`server` block).
`LoadModule`: With this directive, Apache offers the possibility to load modules dynamically.	`--with_****_module`: Nginx cannot load modules dynamically; these need to be included at compile time. Once incorporated in Nginx, they cannot be disabled.
`Include`: File inclusion directive supports wildcards.	`Include`: The `include` directive of Nginx is identical.
`User`, `Group`: Allows you to define the user and group under which the daemon will be running.	`User`: The `user` directive of Nginx lets you specify both the user and the group.
`ServerAdmin`, `ServerSignature`: Let's you specify the e-mail address of the server administrator and a signature message to be displayed on error and diagnostic pages.	No equivalent As of Version 1.2.9, there is no equivalent for Nginx. Error pages do not show the e-mail address of the server administrator or other information. Look into the `error_page` directive to customize your site's error pages.
`UseCanonicalName`: Defines how Apache constructs self-referential URLs.	No direct equivalent Although there is no direct equivalent for this Apache directive, the construction of self-referential URLs can be defined via module-specific settings (proxy, FastCGI, and so on).
`DocumentRoot`: Defines the `root` folder from which Apache will serve files. The directive can be used at the server and virtual host levels.	`Root`: The `root` directive can be inserted to define the document root at all levels: `http`, `server`, `location`, and `if` blocks.
`DirectoryIndex`, `IndexOptions`, `IndexIgnore`: Define directory index and file listing options.	`index`, `autoindex`, `random_index`, `fancyindex` (third party): Nginx also offers a good variety of options for managing indexes.
`AccessFileName`: Defines the filename of `.htaccess` files that are included dynamically on page execution.	No equivalent Nginx, as of Version 1.2.9, has no such feature as `.htaccess` files. Read the further sections for more information.

Apache directive	Nginx equivalent
`TypesConfig`, `DefaultType`: Defines MIME type options.	`types`, `default_type`: Equivalent directives exist in Nginx, although with a different syntax.
`HostNameLookups`: Allows looking up of hostnames for client IP addresses for logging or access control purposes.	No equivalent As of Nginx 1.2.9, there is no equivalent functionality.
`ErrorLog`, `LogLevel`, `LogFormat`, `CustomLog`: Logging activation and format settings.	`access_log`, `log_format`: Nginx also allows a large variety of options, but they are combined in fewer directives.
`Alias`, `AliasMatch`, `ScriptAlias`: Directory aliasing options.	`Alias`: The `alias` equivalent directive is offered by Nginx, but nothing for the other two.

Modules

As we have learned earlier in *Chapter 1, Downloading and Installing Nginx*, modules in Nginx cannot be loaded dynamically and must be included at compile time. Additionally, they cannot be disabled at runtime since they are completely compiled and integrated in the main binary. Consequently, you should carefully consider your choice of modules when you build Nginx.

> If you are worried about the impact on performance of the modules you selected, you should be aware that the only noticeable differences will come from filter modules. This name is given to modules that apply a filter to the content of requests and/or responses, and therefore they are always activated. Examples of filter modules: Addition, Charset, Gzip, SSI, and more. In the case of non-filter modules (such as Autoindex, FastCGI, Stub Status, and others), if none of their directives are used, the module handler is never executed.

The following table lists some modules that Apache and Nginx have in common. Note that there might be equivalent modules, but they do not necessarily provide the exact same functionality and directives are likely to be different in all cases. You should check the documentation of these modules in their respective chapter:

Apache Module	Nginx Module	Status	Configure switch
`mod_auth_basic`	`auth_basic`	Included by default	`--without-http_auth_basic_module`
`mod_autoindex`	`autoindex`	Included by default	`--without-http_autoindex_module`

Apache Module	Nginx Module	Status	Configure switch
`mod_charset_lite`	`charset`	Included by default	`--without-http_charset_module`
`mod_dav`	`dav`	Optional	`--with-http_dav_module`
`mod_deflate`	`gzip`	Included by default	`--without-http_gzip_module`
`mod_expires`	`headers`	Included by default	Cannot be disabled
`mod_fcgid`	`fastcgi`	Included by default	`--without-http_fastcgi_module`
`mod_headers`	`Headers`	Included by default	Cannot be disabled
`mod_include`	`ssi`	Included by default	`--without-http_ssi_module`
`mod_log_config`	`log`	Included by default	Cannot be disabled
`mod_proxy`	`proxy`	Included by default	`--without-http_proxy_module`
`mod_rewrite`	`rewrite`	Included by default	`--without-http_rewrite_module`
`mod_ssl`	`ssl`	Optional	`--with-http_ssl_module`
`mod_status`	`stub_status`	Optional	`--with-http_stub_status_module`
`mod_substitute`	`sub`	Optional	`--with-http_sub_module`
`mod_uid`	`userid`	Included by default	`--without-http_userid_module`

Virtual hosts and configuration sections

Just like Nginx allows you to define configuration settings at various levels (`http`, `server`, `location`, `if`), Apache also has its own sections. The section list is described as follows and along with a configuration example.

Configuration sections

The following table provides a translation of Apache sections into Nginx configuration blocks. Some Apache sections have no direct Nginx equivalent, but for most cases, identical behavior can be reproduced in a slightly different syntax.

Apache section	Nginx section	Description
Default	http	The settings placed at the root of the Apache configuration files correspond to the settings placed at the root of the Nginx configuration file and also those placed in the http block (as opposed to other blocks such as mail or imap used for mail server proxying functionality).
<VirtualHost>	server	Apache settings placed in the <VirtualHost> sections should be placed in the server blocks of the Nginx configuration file.
<Location> <LocationMatch>	location	The behavior of the <Location> and <LocationMatch> (regular expression) can be reproduced with the Nginx location block.
None	if	Nginx offers dynamic conditional structure with the if block. There is no exact equivalent in Apache. The closest equivalence is the RewriteCond directive from the Rewrite module.
<Directory> <DirectoryMatch> <Files> <FilesMatch>	None	Apache allows you to apply settings to specific locations of the local file system while Nginx only offers per-URI settings.
<IfDefine>	None	Applies a set of directives if the specified condition is true on startup. This feature is not available on Nginx.
<IfModule>	None	Applies a set of directives on startup if the specified module is loaded. Since Nginx does not support dynamic module loading, this feature is not available.
<Proxy> <ProxyMatch>	None	Applies a set of directives to proxied resources by specifying a wildcard URI or a regular expression. This section has no equivalent on Nginx.

Creating a virtual host

In Apache, virtual hosts are optional. You are allowed to define server settings at the root of the configuration file:

```
Listen 80
ServerName example.com
ServerAlias www.example.com
DocumentRoot "/home/example.com/www"
[...]
```

However, this behavior is useful only if you are going to host one website on the server, or if you want to define the default settings for incoming requests that do not match other virtual host access rules.

In Nginx, however, all the websites you will be hosting must be placed in a `server` block which allows the creation of a virtual host, equivalent to the `<VirtualHost>` section in Apache. The following table describes the translation of an Apache `<VirtualHost>` section to an Nginx `server` block:

Apache virtual host	Nginx virtual host equivalent
`<VirtualHost 12.34.56.78:80>`	`server {`
`ServerName    example.com:80`	`listen 12.34.56.78:80;`
`ServerAlias   www.example.com`	`server_name example.com www.example.com;`
`UseCanonicalName Off`	# No equivalent
`SuexecUserGroup user group`	# No equivalent
`ServerAdmin  "admin@example.com"`	# No equivalent
`DocumentRoot /home/example.com/www`	`root  /home/example.com/www;`
`CustomLog  /home/example.com/logs/access_log cust`	`access_log/home/example.com/logs/access_log cust;`
	# Note that the `cust` format must be declared beforehand with `log_format`.
`ErrorLog  /home/example.com/logs/error_log`	`error_log /home/example.com/logs/error_log;`

`<Location /documents/>`
`  Options +Indexes`
`</Location>`
	`location /documents/ {`
	`    autoindex on;`
	`}`

`<IfModule mod_ssl.c>`
`SSLEngine off`
`</IfModule>`
	# there is no equivalent for `IfModule`.
	`ssl off;`

Apache virtual host	Nginx virtual host equivalent

``
<Directory /home/example.com/
www>
  <IfModule mod_fcgid.c>
  <Files ~ (\.php)>
    SetHandler fcgid-script
    FCGIWrapper /usr/bin/php-
cgi .php
    Options +ExecCGI
    allow from all
  </Files>
  </IfModule>
  Options -Includes -ExecCGI
</Directory>
``
	# There is no equivalent to the Directory section. The location block only applies per-URI settings. The location block applies settings for all requests relative to the virtual host root folder. We use it to apply settings to the .php files.
	
	``
	location ~ \.php {
	``
	# Insert your FCGI settings
	``
	    fastcgi_pass 127.0.0.1:9000;
	    fastcgi_param SCRIPT_FILENAME
	/home/example.com/ www$fastcgi_
	script_name;
	    fastcgi_param PATH_INFO
	$fastcgi_script_name;
	    include fastcgi_params; # Your
	additional FastCGI settings
	}
	``
	# Other directives have no direct equivalent or are not necessary with Nginx.

```</VirtualHost>```	```}```

This translation guide is valid for regular virtual hosts, serving non-secure web pages. There are a few differences when creating a secure virtual host using **SSL**. The following table focuses on the SSL-related directives, although directives from the previous table can still be used:

Apache virtual host	Nginx virtual host
```<VirtualHost 12.34.56.78:443>```	```server {```
```ServerName example.com:443``` ```ServerAlias www.example.com```	```listen 12.34.56.78:443;``` ```server_name example.com www.example.com;```

```SSLEngine on```
```SSLVerifyClient none```
```SSLCertificateFile /home/```
```example.com/cert/certchL9435```
	```ssl on;```
	```ssl_verify_client off;```
	```ssl_certificate /home/example.com/cert/cert.pem;```
	```ssl_certificate_key /home/example.com/cert/cert.key;```

Apache virtual host	Nginx virtual host

`<Directory /home/example.com/`
`www>`
`SSLRequireSSL`
`</Directory>`
	# There is no equivalent required with Nginx.

`</VirtualHost>`	}

.htaccess files

This section approaches the tricky problem of `.htaccess` files and the underlying thematic of shared hosting. There is indeed no such mechanism in Nginx, which among other reasons, renders shared hosting difficult to achieve.

Reminder on Apache .htaccess files

`.htaccess` files are small independent configuration files that webmasters are allowed to place in every single folder of their website. Upon receiving a request for accessing a particular folder, Apache checks for the presence of such a file and applies it to the request context. This allows webmasters to apply separate settings at multiple levels. Have a look at the following screenshot:

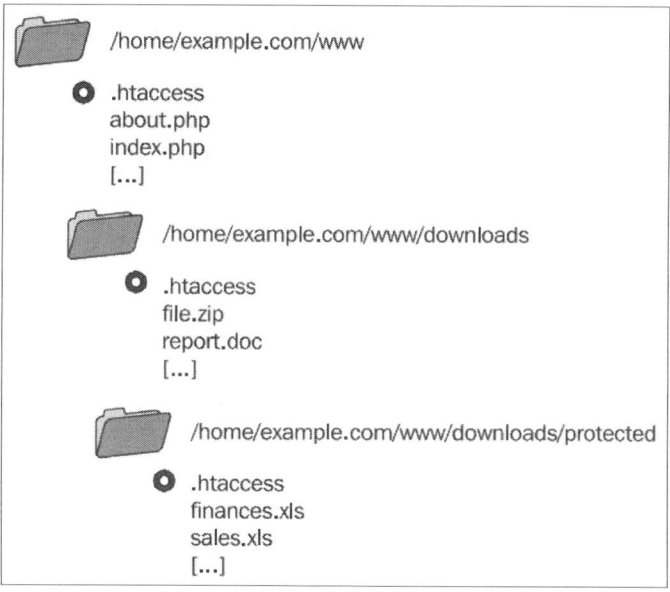

In the context of a client request for `/downloads/protected/finances.xls`, all three `.htaccess` files would be applied in the following order:

1. `/home/example.com/www/.htaccess`
2. `/home/example.com/www/downloads/.htaccess`
3. `/home/example.com/www/downloads/protected/.htaccess`

The settings precedence is given to the last `.htaccess` file read — if the same setting is defined in `/www/.htaccess` and `/www/downloads/.htaccess`, the latter file has priority over the former.

Nginx equivalence

Unfortunately, there is no such mechanism in Nginx. We can, however, find replacement solutions by making the most of directives that we have at our disposal.

There are three major uses for `.htaccess` files in Apache:

- Creating access and authentication rules for specific directories
- Defining rewrite rules at the top level (usually not folder-specific)
- Setting flags for modules such as `mod_php`, `mod_perl`, or `mod_python`

 When it comes to the latter, the use of flags is only achievable when the pre-processors are set up as Apache modules. If your server runs PHP through CGI or FastCGI, flags will not be recognized and generate a `500 Internal Server Error`. In our case, connecting Nginx to such applications can only be done via FastCGI or HTTP; consequently flags are not allowed.

Depending on how you declare your virtual hosts, there are two solutions for implementing an `.htaccess`-like behavior or at least something remotely similar.

The first solution, if you are going to list all virtual hosts from a unique configuration file, is to insert an `include` directive in the `server` block that refers to an extra configuration file located in the `/www/` folder. We should not forget that this configuration file should be hidden and not downloadable by clients:

```
server {
    listen 80;
    server_name .example.com;
    root /home/example.com/www;
    [...]
    # Include extra configuration files
```

```
    location / {
        include /home/example.com/www/.ngconf*;
    }
    # Deny access if someone tries to download the file
    location ~ \.ngconf {
        return 404;
    }
}
```

This will include any file with a name starting with `.ngconf` from the `/www/` folder of the virtual host. Note the `*` in the `include` directive. If you specify a filename without a wildcard, Nginx will consider the configuration to be invalid if the file is missing. If you use the wildcard, the absence of such a file does not generate any error.

The `.ngconf` file would then include directives related to the virtual host itself:

```
autoindex off; # Disable directory listing
location /downloads/ {
    autoindex on; # Allow directory listing in /downloads/
}
[...]
```

This solution seems relatively secure for web hosting providers, as this only allows webmasters to define location-related settings (preventing important changes such as using a different port, different host name, and more). However, be aware that if a webmaster creates invalid `.ngconf` files, Nginx will refuse to reload until the issue is fixed.

Alternatively, you could decide to place virtual host declarations within separate files located in the `root` folder of each virtual host. In this case, you would only need the following directive in the main Nginx configuration file:

```
include /home/*/www/.ngconf;
```

The `.ngconf` file then needs to contain the complete virtual host declaration, including the port and server name. This solution should only be considered for servers that you entirely manage by yourself; you should never allow external webmasters to have so much control over your server.

That being said, there is still one major difference between Apache and Nginx:

- Apache applies settings from `.htaccess` files every time a client request is processed
- Nginx applies settings from `.ngconf` files only when you reload the configuration (such as `service nginx reload`)

At this moment, there is no work around for this last issue; Nginx does not allow on-the-fly configuration changes.

 Administrators of web servers, primarily running PHP scripts might be interested in the `htscanner` of **PECL package**. This extension offers the possibility to process `.htaccess`-like files containing PHP settings. For more details, please refer to the official page of the package: `http://pecl.php.net/package/htscanner`

Rewrite rules

The most common source of worries during an HTTP server switch is the rewrite rules. Unfortunately, Nginx is not directly compatible with the Apache rewrite rules in two regards:

- Usually, rewrite rules are placed within `.htaccess` files, as discussed in the previous section. Nginx offers no such mechanism, so rewrite rules will have to be placed in a different location.

- The syntax of the rewrite instructions and conditions is quite different and will need to be adapted.

This section will approach some of the issues encountered when porting rules to Nginx, and then will provide some prewritten rules for a couple of major web applications.

General remarks

Before studying practical examples, let us begin with a couple of important remarks regarding rewrite rules in Nginx.

On the location

With all that has been said and written about Nginx, we can safely say that it's not the most appropriate web server for web hosting companies that do shared hosting. The lack of `.htaccess` files renders it practically impossible to host websites that have their own server settings, among which are rewrite rules. While a replacement solution has been offered in the previous section, it's not optimal as it requires a configuration reload after each change, and to crown it all, reloading is only possible if the entire configuration contains no error.

The consequence of this first issue is that you will have to relocate the rewrite rules. They will have to be placed directly in the server or location blocks of your virtual host, regardless of which file contains the virtual host configuration. With Apache, rewrite rules would be located somewhere such as /home/example.com/www/. htaccess; while with Nginx, you will need to incorporate them in the virtual host configuration file (for example, /usr/local/nginx/conf/nginx.conf).

On the syntax

There are two major Apache directives that are important when it comes to porting rewrite rules to Nginx. Other directives either have no equivalent, are not supported on purpose, or their behavior is already incorporated in the offered Nginx equivalences:

- RewriteCond: This allows you to define conditions that should be matched for the URL to be rewritten
- RewriteRule: This performs the actual URL rewrite by specifying a regular expression pattern, the rewritten URL, and a set of flags

The first of those directives, RewriteCond is equivalent to Nginx's if. It is used for verifying conditions before applying a rewrite rule. The following example ensures that the requested file does not exist (!-f flag) before rewriting the URL:

```
RewriteCond %{REQUEST_FILENAME} !-f
RewriteRule . /index.php [L]
```

The Nginx equivalent, using if and rewrite, would be as follows:

```
if (!-f $request_filename) {
    rewrite . /index.php last;
}
```

It gets a little more complicated when you want to rewrite under multiple conditions. The Nginx if statement only supports one condition in the expression and does not allow imbrications of if blocks. One has to reproduce a behavior like the following one:

```
RewriteCond %{REQUEST_FILENAME} !-f # File must not exist
RewriteCond %{REQUEST_FILENAME} !-d # Directory must not exist
RewriteRule . /index.php [L] # Rewrites URL
```

There is a simple logical workaround for this particular issue — we will be using multiple `if` blocks, in which we affect a variable. After the two initial `if` blocks, a third comes in to check if the variable was affected by the first two:

```
set $check "";
# If the specified file does not exist, set $check to "A"
if (!-f $request_filename) {
    set $check "A";
}
# If the specified directory does not exist, set $check to $check + B
if (!-d $request_filename) {
    set $check "${check}B";
}
# If $check was affected in both if blocks, perform the rewrite
if ($check = "AB") {
    rewrite . /index.php last
}
```

Note that for those two particular rewrite conditions (`-f` to test file existence, `-d` to test folder existence), Nginx already offers a solution that combines both tests: `-e`. So a quicker solution would have been:

```
if (!-e $request_filename) {
    rewrite . /index.php last;
}
```

In addition to testing for file and folder existence, `-e` also checks if the specified filename corresponds to an existing symbolic link.

For more information on the `rewrite` module in general, please refer to *Chapter 5, PHP and Phython with Nginx*.

RewriteRule

The `RewriteRule` Apache directive is the direct equivalent to `rewrite` in Nginx. However, there is a subtle difference: URIs in Nginx begin with the / character. Nevertheless, the translation remains simple:

```
RewriteRule ^downloads/(.*)$ download.php?url=$1 [QSA]
```

The preceding Apache rule is transformed into the following:

```
rewrite ^/downloads/(.*)$ /download.php?url=$1;
```

Note that the `[QSA]` flag tells Apache to append the query arguments to the rewritten URL. However, Nginx does that by default. To prevent Nginx from appending query arguments, insert a trailing `?` to the substitution URL:

```
rewrite ^/downloads/(.*)$ /download.php?url=$1?;
```

The `RewriteRule` Apache directive allows additional flags; these can be matched against the ones offered by Nginx, described in *Chapter 5, PHP and Phython with Nginx*.

WordPress

WordPress is probably a familiar name to you. As of May 2013, the immensely popular open source blogging application was being used by over 65 million websites worldwide. Powered by PHP and MySQL, it's compatible with Nginx *out of the box*. Well, this statement would be entirely true if it weren't for rewrite rules.

The web application comes with a `.htaccess` file to be placed at the root of the website:

```
# BEGIN WordPress
<IfModule mod_rewrite.c>
RewriteEngine On
RewriteBase /
RewriteCond %{REQUEST_FILENAME} !-f
RewriteCond %{REQUEST_FILENAME} !-d
RewriteRule . /index.php [L]
</IfModule>
# END WordPress
```

This first example is relatively easy to understand and to translate to Nginx. In fact, most of the rewriting process consists of three steps:

1. Checking if the requested URI corresponds to an existing file, in which case, it is served normally.

2. Checking if the requested URI corresponds to a folder, in which case, it is served normally.

3. Rewrite to `index.php`, WordPress will then analyze the URI by itself from within the PHP script (by checking the `$_SERVER["REQUEST_URI"]` variable).

Since there are not a lot of complex rules to take care of and the URLs being decomposed by the PHP script itself, the translation to Nginx is rather easy. Here is a full example of a Nginx virtual host, stripped out of all unrelated directives:

```
server {
    listen 80;
    server_name blog.example.com;
```

```
    root /home/example.com/blog/www;
    index index.php;
    location / {
# If requested URI does not match any existing file,
# directory or symbolic link, rewrite the URL to index.php

        try_files $uri $uri/ index.php;
    }
    # For all PHP requests, pass them on to PHP-FPM via FastCGI
    # For more information, consult chapter 6
    location ~ \.php$ {
        fastcgi_pass 127.0.0.1:9000;
        fastcgi_param SCRIPT_FILENAME
/home/example.com/blog/www$fastcgi_script_name;
        fastcgi_param PATH_INFO $fastcgi_script_name;
        include fastcgi_params; # include extra FCGI params
    }
}
```

MediaWiki

As its name suggests, MediaWiki is the web engine that empowers the famous Wikipedia online open encyclopedia. It is currently an open source software and anyone can download and install it on their local server. The application can also be used as a **CMS (Content Management Software)**, and large companies such as Novell have found it to be a reliable solution.

Contrary to WordPress, MediaWiki does not come with a prewritten .htaccess file for prettying up URLs. Instead, the official MediaWiki website offers a wide variety of methods, which are all documented in the form of wiki articles. Webmasters can implement solutions that go as far as modifying the main Apache configuration file. However, there are simpler solutions that require no such thing. No particular Apache solution has been retained here, as three simple Nginx rewrite rules suffice to do the trick:

- The first one redirects default requests (for example, / as request URI) to /wiki/Main_Page.

- The second one rewrites all the URIs of the /wiki/abcd form into the actual URL /w/index.php?title=abcd, without forgetting to append the rest of the parameters to the request URL.

- The third one ensures that requests to /wiki get redirected to the home page /w/index.php.

The following is a full virtual host configuration example, including the rewrite rules:

```
server {
    listen 80;
    server_name wiki.example.com;
    root /home/example.com/wiki/www;
    location / {
        index index.php;
        rewrite ^/$ /wiki/Main_Page permanent;
    }
    # 2 rewrite rules
    rewrite ^/wiki/([^?]*)(?:\?(.*))? /w/index.php?title=$1&$2;
    rewrite ^/wiki /w/index.php;
    # Your FCGI configuration here
    location ~ \.php$ {
        fastcgi_pass    127.0.0.1:9000;
        fastcgi_index   index.php;
        fastcgi_param   SCRIPT_FILENAME
/home/example.com/wiki/www$fastcgi_script_name;
        include fastcgi_params;
    }
}
```

vBulletin

Discussion forums started blooming in the 2000s and a lot of popular web applications have appeared, such as vBulletin, phpBB, or Invision Board. Most of these forum software platforms have jumped in the bandwagon and now boast full SEO-friendly URL support. Unfortunately, rewrite rules often come in the form of `.htaccess` files. Indeed, the vBulletin developers have chosen to provide rewrite rules for Apache 2 and IIS, unsurprisingly forgetting Nginx. Let's teach them a lesson. The following table describes a solution for converting their Apache rewrite rules to Nginx:

Apache rule	Nginx rule
`RewriteEngine on`	# Not necessary.

`RewriteCond %{REQUEST_FILENAME}`
`-s [OR]`
`RewriteCond %{REQUEST_FILENAME}`
`-l [OR]`
`RewriteCond %{REQUEST_FILENAME}`
`-d`
`RewriteRule ^.*$ - [NC,L]`
	# Do not rewrite if the requested URI corresponds to an existing file, folder, or link on the system.
	
	`if (-e $request_filename) {`
	`    break;`
	`}`

Apache rule	Nginx rule
`RewriteRule ^threads/.*` `showthread.php [QSA]`	`rewrite ^/threads/.*$ /` `showthread.php last;`
`RewriteRule ^forums/.*` `forumdisplay.php [QSA]`	`rewrite ^/forums/.*$ /` `forumdisplay.php last;`
`RewriteRule ^members/.* member.` `php [QSA]`	`rewrite ^/members/.*$ /members.` `php last;`
`RewriteRule ^blogs/.* blog.php` `[QSA]`	`rewrite ^/blogs/.*$ /blog.php` `last;`
`ReWriteRule ^entries/.* entry.php` `[QSA]`	`rewrite ^/entries/.*$ /entry.` `php last;`

`RewriteCond %{REQUEST_FILENAME}`
`-s [OR]`
`RewriteCond %{REQUEST_FILENAME}`
`-l [OR]`
`RewriteCond %{REQUEST_FILENAME}`
`-d`
`RewriteRule ^.*$ - [NC,L]`
	# For some reason, the same set of rules appears twice in the `.htaccess` file provided by vBulletin. You do not need to insert the Nginx equivalent a second time.

`RewriteRule ^(?:(.*?)(?:/|$))`
`(.*|$)$`
`$1.php?r=$2 [QSA]`
	`rewrite ^/(?:(.*?)(?:/|$))`
	`(.*|$)$`
	`/$1.php?r=$2 last;`

Summary

Switching from Apache to Nginx may seem complex at first. There are many steps involved in the process, and you may face unsolvable problems if you are not confident and well-prepared. You need to be aware of the current limitations of Nginx: no on-the-fly configuration changes, and thus no `.htaccess` or a similar feature. Nginx does not have nearly as many modules as Apache does, at least not yet. Last but not least, you have to convert all your rewrite rules for your websites to be functional under Nginx. So yes, it does take quite a bit of work. But this is a small price to pay to get a server that will ensure long-term stability and scalability. You and your visitors will not regret it, as it generally comes with improved loading and response speeds.

The final three Appendices of this book contain full directive and module references, as well as an entire section dedicated to troubleshooting — which may come in handy if you run into unexpected issues during both configuration and production stages.

A
Directive Index

The following table lists directives from all of the available first-party Nginx modules, as of Version 1.2.9. Each directive comes with a brief description, the module providing the directive (marked with a * if the module is not included by default), and the chapter and section where you will find more information. Directives are sorted alphabetically.

Directive	Module
`accept_mutex`: Enables or disables the use of an accept mutex *Chapter 2, Events module section*	Events
`accept_mutex_delay`: Sets the delay of the accept mutex *Chapter 2, Events module section*	Events
`access_log`: Defines access log settings *Chapter 4, Website access and logging section*	Log
`add_after_body`: Adds content after response body *Chapter 4, Content and encoding section*	Addition*
`add_before_body`: Adds content before response body *Chapter 4, Content and encoding section*	Addition*
`add_header`: Adds arbitrary headers to responses *Chapter 4, Content and encoding section*	Headers
`alias`: Sets a folder alias *Chapter 3, Paths and documents section*	HTTP Core
`allow`: Allows an IP address or address range to access a resource *Chapter 4, Limits and restrictions section*	Access

Directive	Module
`ancient_browser`: Affects `$ancient_browser` if the request user agent matches a specified string	Browser
Chapter 4, About your visitors section	
`ancient_browser_value`: Sets the value to be affected to `$ancient_browser`	Browser
Chapter 4, About your visitors section	
`auth_basic`: Sets a text message to be displayed in basic authentication dialogs	Auth Basic
Chapter 4, Limits and restrictions section	
`auth_basic_user_file`: Defines the file containing usernames and passwords for basic authentication	Auth Basic
Chapter 4, Limits and restrictions section	
`autoindex`: Enables automatic folder indexes	Autoindex
Chapter 4, Website access and logging section	
`autoindex_exact_size`: Shows file sizes in bytes for automatic folder indexes	Autoindex
Chapter 4, Website access and logging section	
`autoindex_localtime`: Enables or disables adjusting file dates to match server local time	Autoindex
Chapter 4, Website access and logging section	
`break`: Prevents further URL rewrites	Rewrite
Chapter 4, Rewrite module section	
`charset`: Sets `charset` value in Content-Type HTTP header	Charset
Chapter 4, Content and encoding section	
`charset_map`: Defines character re-encoding tables	Charset
Chapter 4, Content and encoding section	
`charset_types`: Defines MIME types eligible for charset re-encoding	Charset
Chapter 4, Content and encoding section	
`chunked_transfer_encoding`: Allows disabling of chunked transfers	HTTP Core
Chapter 3, Client requests section	
`client_body_buffer_size`: Specifies the buffer size for client request body	HTTP Core
Chapter 3, Client requests section	

Directive	Module
`client_body_in_file_only`: Forces Nginx to store the client request body as a file in all cases	HTTP Core
Chapter 3, Client requests section	
`client_body_in_single_buffer`: Defines whether or not the body of client requests should be stored in a single buffer	HTTP Core
Chapter 3, Client requests section	
`client_body_temp_path`: Sets the path for storing temporary client request body files	HTTP Core
Chapter 3, Client requests section	
`client_body_timeout`: Sets inactivity timeout for reading client request body	HTTP Core
Chapter 3, Client requests section	
`client_header_buffer_size`: Sets the size of buffers allocated to request headers	HTTP Core
Chapter 3, Client requests section	
`client_header_timeout`: Sets inactivity timeout for reading client request headers	HTTP Core
Chapter 3, Client requests section	
`client_max_body_size`: Sets the maximum size for client request body	HTTP Core
Chapter 3, Client requests section	
`connection_pool_size`: Defines the size of the pool memory space to be allocated to connections	HTTP Core
Chapter 3, Socket and host configuration section	
`connections`: Deprecated (see `worker_connections`)	Events
Chapter 2, Events module section	
`create_full_put_path`: Enables or disables recursive folder creation (creates full path) for PUT requests	DAV*
Chapter 4, Other miscellaneous modules section	
`daemon`: Enables or disables daemon mode	Core
Chapter 2, Core module directives section	
`dav_access`: Defines access permissions at the current level	DAV*
Chapter 4, Other miscellaneous modules section	
`dav_methods`: Selects DAV methods to be enabled	DAV*
Chapter 4, Other miscellaneous modules section	

Directive	Module
`debug_connection`: Enables detailed logs for the specified IP address or address range	Events
Chapter 2, Events module section	
`debug_points`: Enables or disables debug points	Core
Chapter 2, Core module directives section	
`degradation`: Sets memory condition to enable degradation error page	Degradation
Chapter 4, Other miscellaneous modules section	
`degrade`: Sets error code to be returned by Nginx when low memory conditions are met	Degradation
Chapter 4, Other miscellaneous modules section	
`default_type`: Sets the default MIME type for served files	HTTP Core
Chapter 3, MIME types section	
`deny`: Denies an IP address or address range access to a resource	Access
Chapter 4, Limits and restrictions section	
`directio`: Enables or disables the use of direct I/O	HTTP Core
Chapter 3, File processing and caching section	
`directio_alignment`: Sets direct I/O byte alignment	HTTP Core
Chapter 3, File processing and caching section	
`disable_symlinks`: Defines the way Nginx should handle symbolic links	HTTP Core
Chapter 3, File processing and caching section	
`empty_gif`: Serves an empty gif from memory	Empty GIF
Chapter 4, Content and encoding section	
`env`: Defines or redefines environment variables	Core
Chapter 2, Core module directives section	
`error_log`: Specifies error logging settings	Core
Chapter 2, Core module directives section	
`error_page`: Defines behavior for specific error codes	HTTP Core
Chapter 3, Paths and documents section	
`expires`: Controls cache headers sent in responses	Headers
Chapter 4, Content and encoding section	
`fastcgi_buffer_size`: Sets the size of the FastCGI response buffer	FastCGI
Chapter 5, Main directives section	

Directive	Module
`fastcgi_buffers`: Sets buffer amount and buffer size for communications with the FastCGI backend	FastCGI
Chapter 5, Main directives section	
`fastcgi_cache`: Defines a FastCGI cache zone	FastCGI
Chapter 5, FastCGI caching section	
`fastcgi_cache_bypass`: Defines conditions for bypassing cache	FastCGI
Chapter 5, FastCGI caching section	
`fastcgi_cache_key`: Sets the key for caching FastCGI-processed requests	FastCGI
Chapter 5, FastCGI caching section	
`fastcgi_cache_lock`: Locks cache entries for a specified time	FastCGI
Chapter 5, FastCGI caching section	
`fastcgi_cache_lock_timeout`: Sets amount of time cache entries should be locked	FastCGI
Chapter 5, FastCGI caching section	
`fastcgi_cache_methods`: Sets eligible HTTP methods for FastCGI caching	FastCGI
Chapter 5, FastCGI caching section	
`fastcgi_cache_path`: Configures FastCGI caching options for a specified zone	FastCGI
Chapter 5, FastCGI caching section	
`fastcgi_cache_use_stale`: Defines whether or not stale cache data should be used in certain circumstances	FastCGI
Chapter 5, FastCGI caching section	
`fastcgi_cache_valid`: Sets caching validity period for specific response codes	FastCGI
Chapter 5, FastCGI caching section	
`fastcgi_catch_stderr`: Allows you to intercept some of the error messages sent to `stderr` and store them in the Nginx error log	FastCGI
Chapter 5, Main directives section	
`fastcgi_connect_timeout`: Defines the backend server connection timeout	FastCGI
Chapter 5, Main directives section	
`fastcgi_bind`: Binds socket to specified network interface	FastCGI
Chapter 5, Main directives section	

Directive	Module
`fastcgi_pass_request_headers`: Defines whether or not extra request headers should be passed on to the backend server	FastCGI
Chapter 5, Main directives section	
`fastcgi_read_timeout`: Sets the timeout for reading response from `FastCGI` backend	FastCGI
Chapter 5, Main directives section	
`fastcgi_send_lowat`: Allows you to make use of the `SO_SNDLOWAT` flag for TCP sockets for FastCGI communications (under BSD-based systems only)	FastCGI
Chapter 5, Main directives section	
`fastcgi_send_timeout`: Timeout for sending data to the backend server	FastCGI
Chapter 5, Main directives section	
`fastcgi_split_path_info`: Splits a URI path according to a regular expression	FastCGI
Chapter 5, Main directives section	
`fastcgi_store`: Defines FastCGI cache store settings	FastCGI
Chapter 5, Main directives section	
`fastcgi_store_access`: Sets FastCGI cache store access permissions	FastCGI
Chapter 5, Main directives section	
`fastcgi_temp_file_write_size`: Sets the write buffer size when saving temporary files to the storage device	FastCGI
Chapter 5, Main directives section	
`fastcgi_temp_path`: Sets folder path for FastCGI temporary files	FastCGI
Chapter 5, Main directives section	
`flv`: Enables seeking in FLV files	FLV*
Chapter 4, Content and encoding section	
`geo`: Defines a map of values based on the client's IP address	Geo
Chapter 4, About your visitors section	
`geoip_city`: Sets the path to your `IP-to-city` database	GeoIP*
Chapter 4, About your visitors section	
`geoip_country`: Sets the path to your `IP-to-country` database	GeoIP*
Chapter 4, About your visitors section	

Directive	Module
`gzip_types`: Sets MIME types eligible for Gzip compression	Gzip
Chapter 4, Content and encoding section	
`gzip_vary`: Enables or disables including the `Vary` HTTP header in the response	Gzip
Chapter 4, Content and encoding section	
`gzip_window`: Sets the size of the window buffer (`windowBits` argument) for Gzipping operations	Gzip
Chapter 4, Content and encoding section	
`if_modified_since`: Defines how Nginx handles the `If-Modified-Since` HTTP header	HTTP Core
Chapter 3, Paths and documents section	
`ignore_invalid_headers`: When disabled, Nginx returns a `400 Bad Request` HTTP error, in case request headers are misformed	HTTP Core
Chapter 3, Client requests section	
`image_filter`: Applies transformations on images	Image Filter*
Chapter 4, Content and encoding section	
`image_filter_buffer`: Sets the maximum file size for images	Image Filter*
Chapter 4, Content and encoding section	
`image_filter_jpeg_quality`: Sets JPEG quality for image filter output	Image Filter*
Chapter 4, Content and encoding section	
`image_filter_sharpen`: Applies a sharpening filter on images	Image Filter*
Chapter 4, Content and encoding section	
`image_filter_transparency`: Sets transparency settings for image filtering	Image Filter*
Chapter 4, Content and encoding section	
`include`: Includes an external configuration file	Core
Chapter 2, Core module directives section	
`index`: Sets the default filename(s) for folder indexes	Index
Chapter 4, Website access and logging section	
`internal`: Restricts a location block to internal sub-requests and redirects	HTTP Core
Chapter 3, Limits and restrictions section	

Directive	Module
`keepalive_disable`: Allows disabling keepalive functionality for the browser families of your choice	HTTP Core
Chapter 3, Client requests section	
`keepalive_requests`: Maximum amount of requests served over a single keepalive connection	HTTP Core
Chapter 3, Client requests section	
`keepalive_timeout`: Amount of seconds Nginx waits before closing a keepalive connection	HTTP Core
Chapter 3, Client requests section	
`large_client_header_buffers`: Sets the size of buffers for client request with larger headers	HTTP Core
Chapter 3, Client requests section	
`limit_conn`: Limits the amount of connections per zone	Limit Zone
Chapter 4, Limits and restrictions section	
`limit_except`: Sets the allowed HTTP methods	HTTP Core
Chapter 3, Limits and restrictions section	
`limit_rate`: Limits transfer rate per connection	HTTP Core
Chapter 3, Limits and restrictions section	
`limit_rate_after`: Limits transfer rate after a specified limit	HTTP Core
Chapter 3, Limits and restrictions section	
`limit_req`: Limits the amount of requests per zone	Limit Req
Chapter 4, Limits and restrictions section	
`limit_req_log_level`: Sets level required to log denied requests	Limit Req
Chapter 4, Limits and restrictions section	
`limit_req_zone`: Defines a zone to be used with `limit_req`	Limit Req
Chapter 4, Limits and restrictions section	
`limit_conn`: Sets connection limit for a zone defined with `limit_conn_zone`	Limit Conn
Chapter 4, Limits and restrictions section	
`limit_conn_log_level`: Sets level required to log denied requests	Limit Conn
Chapter 4, Limits and restrictions section	
`limit_conn_zone`: Defines a zone to be used with `limit_conn`	Limit Conn
Chapter 4, Limits and restrictions section	

Directive	Module
`lingering_close`: Controls the way Nginx closes client connections	HTTP Core
Chapter 3, *Client requests* section	
`lingering_time`: Defines behavior when a client submits a request that exceeds the maximum allowed size	HTTP Core
Chapter 3, *Client requests* section	
`lingering_timeout`: Amount of time that Nginx should wait between two read operations before closing the client connection	HTTP Core
Chapter 3, Client requests section	
`listen`: Specifies settings for listening sockets	HTTP Core
Chapter 3, Socket and Host configuration section	
`lock_file`: Sets the path of the `lock` file	Core
Chapter 2, Core module directives section	
`log_format`: Defines format of access log entries	Log
Chapter 4, Website access and logging section	
`log_not_found`: Enables or disables logging of `404 errors`	HTTP Core
Chapter 3, Other directives section	
`log_subrequest`: Enables or disables whether details about sub-requests in the logfiles will be included	HTTP Core
Chapter 3, Other directives section	
`map`: Defines a map of values to be matched against a variable; the result is stored in another variable	Map
Chapter 4, About your visitors section	
`map_hash_bucket_size`: Sets the maximum size of a map entry	Map
Chapter 4, About your visitors section	
`map_hash_max_size`: Sets the maximum amount of entries in a map	Map
Chapter 4, About your visitors section	
`master_process`: Enables or disables master process	Core
Chapter 2, Core module directives section	
`max_ranges`: Allows limiting byte ranges for clients requesting partial content	HTTP Core
Chapter 3, Client requests section	
`memcached_bind`: Binds socket to specified network interface	Memcached
Chapter 4, Content and encoding section	

Directive	Module
`memcached_buffer_size`: Sets memcached data buffer size	Memcached
Chapter 4, Content and encoding section	
`memcached_connect_timeout`: Sets memcached connect timeout	Memcached
Chapter 4, Content and encoding section	
`memcached_next_upstream`: Sets conditions for switching to the next upstream server for memcached configurations	Memcached
Chapter 4, Content and encoding section	
`memcached_pass`: Configures memcached access	Memcached
Chapter 4, Content and encoding section	
`memcached_read_timeout`: Sets memcached data read operations timeout	Memcached
Chapter 4, Content and encoding section	
`memcached_send_timeout`: Sets memcached data send operations timeout	Memcached
Chapter 4, Content and encoding section	
`merge_slashes`: Enables or disables merging of double slashes in URLs	HTTP Core
Chapter 3, Other directives section	
`min_delete_depth`: Defines a minimum URI depth for deleting files or directories when processing the `DELETE` command	DAV*
Chapter 4, Other miscellaneous modules section	
`modern_browser`: Affects the `$modern_browser` if the request user agent matches specified string	Browser
Chapter 4, About your visitors section	
`modern_browser_value`: Sets the value to be affected to `$modern_browser`	Browser
Chapter 4, About your visitors section	
`mp4`: Enables seeking in MP4 files	MP4*
Chapter 4, Content and encoding section	
`msie_padding`: Enables response padding for MSIE browsers	HTTP Core
Chapter 3, Other directives section	
`msie_refresh`: Enables MSIE-specific redirects for the MSIE browser family	HTTP Core
Chapter 3, Other directives section	

Directive	Module
`multi_accept`: Enables or disables accepting multiple connections from the queue at once	Events
Chapter 2, Events module section	
`open_file_cache`: Defines open file cache store settings	HTTP Core
Chapter 3, File processing and caching section	
`open_file_cache_errors`: Defines whether or not file errors should be cached in the open file cache store	HTTP Core
Chapter 3, File processing and caching section	
`open_file_cache_min_uses`: Defines the minimum amount of uses for a file to remain in the cache	HTTP Core
Chapter 3, File processing and caching section	
`open_file_cache_valid`: Sets the cache verification interval	HTTP Core
Chapter 3, File processing and caching section	
`open_log_file_cache`: Configures the cache of log file descriptors	Log
Chapter 4, Website access and logging section	
`override_charset`: Overrides charset for documents received via proxy or FastCGI	Charset
Chapter 4, Content and encoding section	
`pcre_jit`: Toggles Just-In-Time compilation for regular expressions	Core
Chapter 2, Core module directives section	
`pid`: Sets the path of the PID file	Core
Chapter 2, Core module directives section	
`port_in_redirect`: Enables or disables including port number for internal redirects	HTTP Core
Chapter 3, Socket and host configuration section	
`post_action`: Defines a post-completion action, a URI that will be called by Nginx after the request has been completed	HTTP Core
Chapter 3, Other directives section	
`postpone_gzipping`: Defines a minimum data threshold to be reached before starting the Gzip compression	HTTP Core
Chapter 4, Content and encoding section	
`postpone_output`: Postpones the sending of the response; this directive defines the size of data to be sent in each packet	HTTP Core
Chapter 3, Socket and host configuration section	

Directive	Module
`proxy_bind`: Binds socket to specified network interface	Proxy
Chapter 6, Main directives section	
`proxy_buffer_size`: Sets the size of backend response buffer	Proxy
Chapter 6, Caching, buffering, and temporary files section	
`proxy_buffering`: Enables or disables backend response buffering	Proxy
Chapter 6, Caching, buffering, and temporary files section	
`proxy_buffers`: Sets the amount and size of buffers for backend communications	Proxy
Chapter 6, Caching, buffering, and temporary files section	
`proxy_busy_buffers_size`: Sets the size of buffers for busy backend servers	Proxy
Chapter 6, Caching, buffering, and temporary files section	
`proxy_cache`: Defines a proxy cache zone	Proxy
Chapter 6, Caching, buffering, and temporary files section	
`proxy_cache_bypass`: Defines conditions for bypassing cache	Proxy
Chapter 6, Caching, buffering, and temporary files section	
`proxy_cache_key`: Sets the key for caching proxied requests	Proxy
Chapter 6, Caching, buffering, and temporary files section	
`proxy_cache_methods`: Sets eligible HTTP methods for proxy caching	Proxy
Chapter 6, Caching, buffering, and temporary files section	
`proxy_cache_min_uses`: Sets the amount of times a cache entry should be used before being protected from cache sweeping	Proxy
Chapter 6, Caching, buffering, and temporary files section	
`proxy_cache_path`: Configures proxy caching options for a specified zone	Proxy
Chapter 6, Caching, buffering, and temporary files section	
`proxy_cache_use_stale`: Defines whether or not stale cache data should be used in certain circumstances	Proxy
Chapter 6, Caching, buffering, and temporary files section	
`proxy_cache_valid`: Sets caching validity period for specific response codes	Proxy
Chapter 6, Caching, buffering, and temporary files section	
`proxy_connect_timeout`: Sets timeout for connecting to the backend	Proxy
Chapter 6, Limits, timeouts, and errors section	

Directive	Module
`proxy_cookie_domain`: Applies on-the-fly modification to the domain attribute of a cookie forwarded to the backend *Chapter 6, Other directives section*	Proxy
`proxy_cookie_path`: Applies on-the-fly modification to the path attribute of a cookie forwarded to the backend *Chapter 6, Other directives section*	Proxy
`proxy_headers_hash_bucket_size`: Sets the maximum size of entries in the headers hash table *Chapter 6, Other directives section*	Proxy
`proxy_headers_hash_max_size`: Sets the maximum amount of entries in the headers hash table *Chapter 6, Other directives section*	Proxy
`proxy_hide_header`: Skips specified header for reverse proxying *Chapter 6, Main directives section*	Proxy
`proxy_http_version`: Sets the HTTP version to be used for communicating with the proxy backend *Chapter 6, Other directives section*	Proxy
`proxy_ignore_client_abort`: Sets proxy module behavior when clients abort requests *Chapter 6, Limits, timeouts, and errors section*	Proxy
`proxy_ignore_headers`: Prevents Nginx from processing specified headers *Chapter 6, Other directives section*	Proxy
`proxy_intercept_errors`: Defines whether or not backend generated errors should be returned as it is *Chapter 6, Limits, timeouts, and errors section*	Proxy
`proxy_max_temp_file_size`: Sets the maximum size for temporary files *Chapter 6, Caching, buffering, and temporary files section*	Proxy
`proxy_method`: Allows additional HTTP methods for reverse proxying *Chapter 6, Main directives section*	Proxy
`proxy_next_upstream`: Defines upstream server skipping conditions *Chapter 6, Main directives section*	Proxy
`proxy_no_cache`: Sets conditions for disabling caching *Chapter 6, Caching, buffering, and temporary files section*	Proxy

Directive	Module
`proxy_temp_path`: Sets folder path for proxy temporary files	Proxy
Chapter 6, Caching, buffering, and temporary files section	
`random_index`: Enables or disables selecting a random file to be served as folder index	Random Index*
Chapter 4, Website access and logging section	
`read_ahead`: Enables file pre-reading	HTTP Core
Chapter 3, File processing and caching section	
`real_ip_header`: Sets the HTTP header to be used for the replacement IP address	Real IP*
Chapter 4, About your visitors section	
`real_ip_recursive`: Enables recursive search for client IP addresses	Real IP*
Chapter 4, About your visitors section	
`recursive_error_pages`: Enables or disables the use of recursive error pages with the `error_page` directive	HTTP Core
Chapter 3, Paths and documents section	
`referer_hash_bucket_size`: Sets the bucket size of the referers hash tables	HTTP Core
Chapter 3, Other directives section	
`referer_hash_max_size`: Sets the maximum size of the referers hash tables	HTTP Core
Chapter 3, Other directives section	
`request_pool_size`: Defines the size of the pool memory space to be allocated to requests	HTTP Core
Chapter 3, Socket and host configuration section	
`reset_timedout_connection`: Enables or disables erasing connection information after timeouts	HTTP Core
Chapter 3, Socket and host configuration section	
`resolver`: Sets the IP address of the DNS server	HTTP Core
Chapter 3, Other directives section	
`resolver_timeout`: Sets the timeout for resolving hostnames	HTTP Core
Chapter 3, Other directives section	
`return`: Interrupts request and returns specified code	Rewrite
Chapter 4, Rewrite module section	

Directive	Module
`rewrite`: Rewrites a URL	Rewrite
Chapter 4, Rewrite module section	
`rewrite_log`: Enables or disables issuing log messages from the rewrite engine at the `notice` log level	Rewrite
Chapter 4, Rewrite module section	
`root`: Sets the document root of a virtual host or virtual path	HTTP Core
Chapter 3, Paths and documents section	
`satisfy`: Defines resource access conditions	HTTP Core
Chapter 3, Limits and restrictions section	
`secure_link`: Specifies a string from which checksum and expiration date of a link should be extracted	Secure Link*
Chapter 4, SSL and security section	
`secure_link_md5`: Sets an expression to be MD5-hashed and compared to the value extracted from `secure_link`	Secure Link*
Chapter 4, SSL and security section	
`secure_link_secret`: Sets the secret word for the secure URL (note: as of Nginx 0.8.50 this directive has been deprecated so use `secure_link` and `secure_link_md5` instead)	Secure Link*
Chapter 4, SSL and security section	
`send_lowat`: Enables or disables the use of the `SO_SNDLOWAT TCP` socket flag under BSD systems for communications with the client	HTTP Core
Chapter 3, Socket and host configuration section	
`send_timeout`: The number of seconds after the last packet received before Nginx closes a client connection	HTTP Core
Chapter 3, Client requests section	
`sendfile`: Enables or disables the use of the sendfile kernel call to handle file transmissions	HTTP Core
Chapter 3, Socket and Host Configuration section	
`sendfile_max_chunk`: Maximum size of data to be used for each call to sendfile	HTTP Core
Chapter 3, Socket and Host Configuration section	
`server`: Declares a server entry in an upstream block	Upstream
Chapter 5, Upstream blocks section	
`server_name`: Sets the virtual host server names	HTTP Core
Chapter 3, Socket and Host Configuration section	

Directive	Module
`server_name_in_redirect`: Enables or disables server name for internal redirects	HTTP Core
Chapter 3, Socket and Host Configuration section	
`server_names_hash_bucket_size`: Sets the maximum size of a server name in the hash table	HTTP Core
Chapter 3, Socket and Host Configuration section	
`server_names_hash_max_size`: Sets the maximum amount of server names in the hash table	HTTP Core
Chapter 3, Socket and Host Configuration section	
`server_tokens`: Enables or disable server information display	HTTP Core
Chapter 3, Other directives section	
`set`: Sets the value of a variable	Rewrite
Chapter 4, Rewrite module section	
`set_real_ip_from`: Declares a trusted IP address, range, or socket	Real IP*
Chapter 4, About your visitors section	
`source_charset`: Sets the source charset for documents	Charset
Chapter 4, Content and encoding section	
`split_clients`: Splits visitors into groups based on the variable(s) of your choice	Split Clients
Chapter 4, About your visitors section	
`ssi`: Activates server-side includes	SSI
Chapter 4, SSI module directives and variables section	
`ssi_ignore_recycled_buffers`: Prevents Nginx from making use of recycled buffers	SSI
Chapter 4, SSI module directives and variables section	
`ssi_min_file_chunk`: Defines buffering and storage settings for SSI requests	SSI
Chapter 4, SSI module directives and variables section	
`ssi_silent_errors`: Defines whether or not SSI errors should be silent	SSI
Chapter 4, SSI module directives and variables section	
`ssi_types`: Defines MIME types eligible for SSI parsing	SSI
Chapter 4, SSI module directives and variables section	
`ssi_value_length`: Defines the maximum size for SSI tag values	SSI
Chapter 4, SSI module directives and variables section	

Directive	Module
ssl: Enables HTTPS for a virtual host	SSL*
Chapter 4, SSL and security section	
ssl_certificate: Sets the path of the PEM certificate file	SSL*
Chapter 4, SSL and security section	
ssl_certificate_key: Sets the path of the PEM secret key file	SSL*
Chapter 4, SSL and security section	
ssl_ciphers: Sets ciphers to be used by the SSL engine	SSL*
Chapter 4, SSL and security section	
ssl_client_certificate: Sets the path of the client PEM certificate file	SSL*
Chapter 4, SSL and security section	
ssl_crl: Sets the path of the **CRL** file (**Certificate Revocation List**)	SSL*
Chapter 4, SSL and security section	
ssl_dhparam: Sets the path of the DH file	SSL*
Chapter 4, SSL and security section	
ssl_engine: Specifies the name of the desired SSL engine	Core
Chapter 2, Core module directives section	
ssl_prefer_server_ciphers: Defines whether or not the server ciphers should be preferred over the client servers	SSL*
Chapter 4, SSL and security section	
ssl_protocols: Sets protocols to be used by the SSL engine	SSL*
Chapter 4, SSL and security section	
ssl_session_cache: Configures SSL session cache settings	SSL*
Chapter 4, SSL and security section	
ssl_session_timeout: Sets the timeout for SSL sessions	SSL*
Chapter 4, SSL and security section	
ssl_verify_client: Enables or disables verifying client certificates	SSL*
Chapter 4, SSL and security section	
ssl_verify_depth: Sets certificate verification depth	SSL*
Chapter 4, SSL and security section	
stub_status: Enables or disables stub status information	Stub Status*
Chapter 4, Other miscellaneous modules section	

Directive	Module
`sub_filter`: Searches and replaces text in the response	Substitution*
Chapter 4, Content and encoding section	
`sub_filter_once`: Defines whether or not `sub_filter` should search and replace only one occurrence	Substitution*
Chapter 4, Content and encoding section	
`sub_filter_types`: Defines MIME types to be affected by the search and replace filter	Substitution*
Chapter 4, Content and encoding section	
`tcp_nodelay`: Enables or disables `TCP_NODELAY` socket option for keep-alive connections	HTTP Core
Chapter 3, Socket and Host configuration section	
`tcp_nopush`: Enables or disables `TCP_NOPUSH (BSD)` or `TCP_CORK (Linux)` socket option for keep-alive connections	HTTP Core
Chapter 3, Socket and Host configuration section	
`thread_stack_size`: Sets the size of the thread stack	Core
Chapter 2, Core module directives section	
`timer_resolution`: Interval for synchronizing the internal clock	Core
Chapter 2, Core module directives section	
`try_files`: Attempts to serve files, and if none are found, jump to a named block	HTTP Core
Chapter 3, Paths and documents section	
`types`: Matches MIME types with file extensions	HTTP Core
Chapter 3, MIME types section	
`types_hash_bucket_size`: Sets the bucket size for the MIME types hash table	HTTP Core
Chapter 3, MIME types section	
`types_hash_max_size`: Defines the maximum size of the MIME types hash table	HTTP Core
Chapter 3, MIME types section	
`underscores_in_headers`: Allows or disallows underscores in HTTP header names	HTTP Core
Chapter 3, Other directives section	
`uninitialized_variable_warn`: Enables or disables logging of directives that use variables which are not initialized	Rewrite
Chapter 4, Rewrite module section	

Directive	Module
upstream: Defines an upstream block for load-balanced architectures	Upstream
Chapter 5, Upstream blocks section	
use: Sets the preferred event model	Events
Chapter 2, Events module section	
user: Sets the user and group for running worker processes	Core
Chapter 2, Core module directives section	
userid Enables or disables the user-ID module	User ID
Chapter 4, About your visitors section	
userid_domain: Sets the domain assigned to the cookie	User ID
Chapter 4, About your visitors section	
userid_expires: Sets the cookie expiration date	User ID
Chapter 4, About your visitors section	
userid_name: Sets the name assigned to the cookie	User ID
Chapter 4, About your visitors section	
userid_p3p: Sets the value of the p3p header	User ID
Chapter 4, About your visitors section	
userid_path: Sets the path part of the cookie	User ID
Chapter 4, About your visitors section	
userid_service: Sets the IP address of the service issuing the cookie	User ID
Chapter 4, About your visitors section	
valid_referers: Defines a list of accepted referrers for a location	Referrer
Chapter 4, About your visitors section	
variables_hash_bucket_size: Defines the maximum length of a variable in the variables hash table	HTTP Core
Chapter 3, Other directives section	
variables_hash_max_size: Defines the maximum size of the variables hash table	HTTP Core
Chapter 3, Other directives section	
worker_aio_requests: Sets the maximum number of outstanding asynchronous I/O operations for a single worker process	Core
Chapter 2, Core module directives section	
worker_connections: Defines the amount of simultaneous connections per worker process	Events
Chapter 2, Events Module section	

Directive	Module
`worker_cpu_affinity`: Defines affinity of worker processes with CPU cores	Core
Chapter 2, Core module directives section	
`worker_priority`: Sets the priority of worker processes	Core
Chapter 2, Core module directives section	
`worker_processes`: Sets the amount of worker processes	Core
Chapter 2, Core module directives section	
`worker_rlimit_core`: Sets the size of core files for worker processes	Core
Chapter 2, Core module directives section	
`worker_rlimit_nofile`: Sets the amount of file a worker process can use simultaneously	Core
Chapter 2, Core module directives section	
`worker_rlimit_sigpending`: Defines the amount of signals a worker process can queue	Core
Chapter 2, Core module directives section	
`worker_threads`: Enables threading (not recommended)	Core
Chapter 2, Core module directives section	
`working_directory`: Sets the working folder for worker processes	Core
Chapter 2, Core module directives section	
`xml_entities`: Specifies a DTD file containing symbolic element definitions	XSLT*
Chapter 4, Content and encoding section	
`xslt_param`: Defines an XSLT parameter	XSLT*
Chapter 4, Content and encoding section	
`xslt_string_param`: Defines an XSLT string parameter	XSLT*
Chapter 4, Content and encoding section	
`xslt_stylesheet`: Specifies the XSLT template file path with its parameters	XSLT*
Chapter 4, Content and encoding section	
`xslt_types`: Sets MIME types, on which transformations should be applied	XSLT*
Chapter 4, Content and encoding section	

B
Module Reference

This appendix summarizes the available Nginx modules, as of stable Version 1.2.9. For each module, a brief description is provided as well as some particular characteristics and a reference to the chapter where you will be able to find more information. The modules are listed in alphabetical order.

Modules marked with a * are optional modules, which are not included when you build Nginx without extra configure switches. The appropriate configure switch to enable or disable modules is detailed with each module.

Access

Allows you to grant or deny access to a resource, based on an IP address or address range.

Key directives: `allow, deny`

Configure switch: `--without-http_access_module` disables the module

Chapter 4, Limits and restrictions section

Addition*

Lets you specify content that should be added before or after the response body.

Key directives: `add_before_body, add_after_body`

Configure switch: `--with-http_addition_module` enables the module

Chapter 4, Content and encoding section

Auth_basic module

Lets you set up basic authentication settings on a specified location.

Key directives: `auth_basic, auth_basic_user_file`

Configure switch: `--without-http_auth_basic_module` enables the module

Chapter 4, Limits and restrictions section

Autoindex

Autoindex enables automatic file listing for directories without an index file.

Key directive: `autoindex`

Configure switch: `--without-http_autoindex_module` disables the module

Chapter 4, Website access and logging section

Browser

Browser parses the User-Agent HTTP header and assigns variables in consequence.

Key directives: `modern_browser, ancient_browser`

Configure switch: `--without-http_browser_module` disables the module

Chapter 4, About your visitors section

Charset

Charset provides page content recoding functionality.

Key directives: `charset, override_charset`

Configure switch: `--without-http_charset_module` disables the module

Chapter 4, Content and encoding section

Core

Core provides core functionality such as daemonization and socket processing.

Key directives: `worker_processes, user`

Configure switch: this module is enabled by default and cannot be disabled

Chapter 2, Core module section

DAV*

DAV enables **WebDAV (Web-based Distributed Authoring and Versioning)** support.

Key directives: `dav_methods, dav_access`

Configure switch: `--with-http_dav_module` enables the module

Chapter 4, Other miscellaneous modules section

Degradation*

Degradation orders Nginx to serve a particular error page when low memory conditions are met.

Key directives: `degradation, degrade`

Configure switch: `--with-http_degradation_module` enables the module

Chapter 4, Other miscellaneous modules section

Empty GIF

Empty GIF allows serving an empty GIF file directly from memory.

Key directive: `empty_gif`

Configure switch: `--without-http_empty_gif_module` disables the module

Chapter 4, Content and encoding section

Events

Events allow you to select and configure the connection event model.

Key directive: `worker_connections`

Configure switch: this module is enabled by default and cannot be disabled

Chapter 2, Events module section

FastCGI

FastCGI enables FastCGI support.

Key directives: `fastcgi_pass, fastcgi_param`

Configure switch: `--without-http_fastcgi_module` disables the module

Chapter 5, FastCGI module section

FLV*

FLV enables seeking in FLV files.

Key directive: `flv`

Configure switch: `--with-http_flv_module` enables the module

Chapter 4, Content and encoding section

Geo

Geo affects a variable based on a map of values affected to IP addresses or address ranges.

Key directive: `geo`

Configure switch: `--without-http_geo_module` disables the module

Chapter 4, About your visitors section

Geo IP*

Geo IP enables support for MaxMind's GeoIP databases.

Key directives: `geoip_country`, `geoip_city`

Configure switch: `--with-http_geoip_module` enables the module

Chapter 4, About your visitors section

Google-perftools*

Google-perftools enables **Google Performance Tools** profiling support.

Key directive: `google_perftools_profiles`

Configure switch: `--with-google_perftools_module` enables the module

Chapter 4, Other miscellaneous modules section

Gzip

Gzip allows compression of the response body with the Gzip compression algorithm.

Key directives: `gzip`, `gzip_comp_level`

Configure switch: `--without-http_gzip_module` disables the module

Chapter 4, Content and encoding section

Gzip Static*

Gzip Static enables serving of pre-compressed response files.

Key directive: `gzip_static`

Configure switch: `--with-http_gzip_static_module` enables the module

Chapter 4, Content and encoding section

Headers

Headers allows defining arbitrary HTTP response headers.

Key directives: add_header, expires

Configure switch: This module is included by default and cannot be disabled

Chapter 4, Content and encoding section

HTTP Core

HTTP Core provides core HTTP functionality.

Key directives: listen, server_name, and so on

Configure switch: --without-http disables all HTTP-related functionality

Chapter 3, HTTP Core module section

Image Filter*

Image Filter provides image transforming functionality via GD Lib.

Key directive: image_filter

Configure switch: --with-http_image_filter_module enables the module

Chapter 4, Content and encoding section

Index

Index allows defining a file to be used as the folder index.

Key directive: index

Configure switch: this module is included by default and cannot be disabled

Chapter 5, Website access and logging section

Limit Conn

Limit Conn allows limiting of connections for a defined zone.

Key directives: `limit_conn_zone`, `limit_conn`

Configure switch: `--without-http_limit_conn_module` disables the module

Chapter 4, Limits and restrictions section

Limit Requests

Limit Requests allows limiting of requests for a defined zone.

Key directives: `limit_req`, `limit_req_zone`

Configure switch: `--without-http_limit_req_module` disables the module

Chapter 4, Limits and restrictions section

Log

Log provides access log customization functionality.

Key directives: `access_log`, `log_format`

Configure switch: this module is included by default and cannot be disabled

Chapter 4, Website access and logging section

Map

Map affects a variable based on a defined map of keys and values.

Key directive: `map`

Configure switch: `--without-http_map_module` disables the module

Chapter 4, About your visitors section

Memcached

Memcached provides directives for interacting with memcached (memory cache daemon).

Key directive: `memcached_pass`

Configure switch: `--without-http_memcached_module` disables the module

Chapter 4, Content and encoding section

MP4*

MP4 enables processing of MP4 files to allow visitors to seek within videos.

Key directive: `mp4`

Configure switch: `--with-http_mp4_module` enables the module

Chapter 4, Content and encoding section

Proxy

Proxy provides reverse proxying functionality.

Key directives: `proxy_pass`, `proxy_set_header`, and so on

Configure switch: `--without-http_proxy_module` disables the module

Chapter 6, Proxy module section

Random index*

Random index allows selecting a random file as the directory index.

Key directive: `random_index`

Configure switch: `--with-http_random_index_module` enables the module

Chapter 4, Website access and logging section

Real IP*

Real IP allows retrieving the real client IP from headers when using Nginx as the backend.

Key directives: `set_real_ip_from`, `real_ip_header`

Configure switch: `--with-http_realip_module` enables the module

Chapter 4, About your visitors section

Referer

Referer allows establishing a whitelist of HTTP referrers.

Key directive: `valid_referers`

Configure switch: `--without-http_referer_module` disables the module

Chapter 4, About your visitors section

Rewrite

Rewrite provides URL rewriting functionality.

Key directives: `rewrite`, `if`, `return`, `break`, and more

Configure switch: `--without-http_rewrite_module` disables the module

Chapter 4, Rewrite module section

SCGI

SCGI enables SCGI support.

Key directives: `scgi_pass`, `scgi_param`

Configure switch: `--without-http_scgi_module` disables the module

Chapter 5, FastCGI module section

Secure Link*

Secure Link provides link validation based on a hash to be located in the URL.

Key directive: `secure_link_secret`

Configure switch: `--with-http_secure_link_module` enables the module

Chapter 4, SSL and security section

Split Clients

Split Clients splits visitors into groups based on the variable(s) of your choice.

Key directives: `split_clients`

Configure switch: `--without-http_split_clients_module` disables the module

Chapter 4, About your visitors section

SSI

SSI provides Server-Side Includes functionality.

Key directives: `ssi, ssi_types`

Configure switch: `--without-http_ssi_module` disables the module

Chapter 4, SSI module section

SSL*

SSL enables HTTP over SSL support.

Key directives: `ssl, ssl_certificate,` and more

Configure switch: `--with-http_ssl_module` enables the module

Chapter 4, SSL and security section

Stub status*

Stub status provide server status information functionality.

Key directive: stub_status

Configure switch: --with-http_stub_status_module enables the module

Chapter 4, Other miscellaneous modules section

Substitution*

Substitution allows replacing content in a web page.

Key directives: sub_filter, sub_filter_once

Configure switch: --with-http_sub_module enables the module

Chapter 4, Content and encoding section

Upstream

Upstream allows setting up of load-balanced architecture.

Key directives: upstream, server

Configure switch: --without-http_upstream_ip_hash_module disables the ip_hash directive only. The upstream module itself is included by default and cannot be disabled.

Chapter 5, Upstream module section

User ID

User ID allows setting up cookies identifying visitors.

Key directives: userid, userid_domain

Configure switch: --without-http_userid_module disables the module

Chapter 4, About your visitors section

uWSGI

uWSGI enables uWSGI support.

Key directives: uwsgi_pass, uwsgi_param

Configure switch: --without-http_uwsgi_module disables the module

Chapter 5, FastCGI module section

XSLT*

XSLT allows applying XSLT templates on the response body.

Key directives: xslt_stylesheet, xml_entities

Configure switch: --with-http_xslt_module enables the module

Chapter 4, Content and encoding section

C
Troubleshooting

Even if you read every single word of this book with utmost attention, you are unfortunately not sheltered from all kinds of issues, ranging from simple configuration errors to the occasional unexpected behavior of one module or another. In this appendix, we attempt to provide solutions for some of the common problems encountered by administrators who are just getting started with Nginx.

The appendix covers the following topics:

- A basic guide containing general tips on Nginx troubleshooting
- How to solve some of the most common install issues
- Dealing with `403 Forbidden` and `400 Bad Request` HTTP errors
- Why your configuration does not apply correctly
- A few words about the `if` block behavior

General tips on troubleshooting

Before we begin, whenever you run into some kind of problem with Nginx, you should make sure to follow the recommendations given in the following sections, as they are generally a good source of solutions.

Checking access permissions

A lot of errors that Nginx administrators are faced with are caused by invalid access permissions. At two stages, you are offered to specify a user and group for the Nginx worker processes to run:

- When configuring the build with the `configure` command, you are allowed to specify a user and group that will be used by default (refer to *Chapter 1, Downloading and Installing Nginx*).

- In the configuration file, the `user` directive allows you to specify a user and group. This directive overrides the value that you may have defined during the `configure` step.

If Nginx is supposed to access files that do not have the correct permissions, in other words, which cannot be read (and by extension cannot be written, for directories that hold temporary files for example) by the specified user and group, Nginx will not be able to serve files correctly.

Testing your configuration

A common mistake is often made by administrators showing a little too much self-confidence. After having modified the configuration file (often without a backup), they reload Nginx to apply the new configuration. If the configuration file contains syntax or semantic errors, the application will refuse to reload. Even worse, if Nginx is stopped (for example, after a complete server reboot) it will refuse to start at all. In all of those cases, remember to follow these recommendations:

- Always keep a backup of your working configuration files in case something goes wrong

- Before reloading or restarting Nginx, test your configuration with a simple command—`nginx -t` to test your current configuration files or run `nginx -t -c /path/to/config/file.conf`

- Reload your server instead of restarting it—preferring `service nginx reload` over `service nginx restart` (`nginx -s reload` instead of `nginx -s stop && nginx`), as it will keep existing connections alive and thus won't interrupt ongoing file downloads

Have you reloaded the service?

You would be surprised to learn how often this happens: the most complicated situations have the simplest solutions. Before tearing your hair out, before rushing to the forums or IRC asking for help, start with the most simple of verifications.

You just spent two hours creating your virtual host configuration. You've saved the files properly and fired up your web browser to check the results. But did you remember that one additional step? Nginx, unlike Apache, does not support on-the-fly configuration changes in `.htaccess` files or similar. So take a moment to make sure you did reload Nginx with `service nginx reload`, `/etc/init.d/nginx reload` or `/usr/local/nginx/sbin/nginx -s reload` without forgetting to test your configuration beforehand!

Checking logs

There is usually no need to look for the answer to your problems on the Internet. Chances are the answer is already given to you by Nginx in the logfiles. There are two variations of log files you may want to check. First, check the access logs. These contain information about requests themselves: the request method and URI, the HTTP response code issued by Nginx, and more, depending on the log format you defined.

More importantly for troubleshooting, the error log is a goldmine of information. Depending on the level you defined (see `error_log` and `debug_connection` directives for more details), Nginx will provide details on its inner functioning. For example, you will be able to see request URI translated to actual file system path. This can be a great help for debugging rewrite rules. The error log should be located in the `/logs/` directory of your Nginx setup, by default `/usr/local/nginx/logs`.

Install issues

There are typically four sources of errors when attempting to install Nginx or to run it for the first time:

- Some of the prerequisites are missing or an invalid path to the source was specified. More details about prerequisites can be found in *Chapter 1, Downloading and Installing Nginx.*

- After having installed Nginx correctly, you cannot use the SSL-related directives to host a secure website. Have you made sure to include the SSL module correctly during the `configure` step? More details in *Chapter 1, Downloading and Installing Nginx.*

- Nginx refuses to start and outputs a message similar to `[emerg] bind() to 0.0.0.0:80 failed (98: Address already in use)`. This error signifies that another application is utilizing the network port 80. This could either mean that another web server such as Apache is already running on the machine, or that you don't have the proper permissions to open a server socket on this port. This can happen if you are running Nginx from an underprivileged system account.

- Nginx refuses to start and outputs a message similar to `[emerg] 3629#0: open() "/path/to/logs/access.log" failed (2: No such file or directory)`. In this case, one of the files that Nginx tries to open, such as logfiles, cannot be accessed. This could be caused by invalid access permissions or by an invalid directory path (for example, when specifying log files to be stored in a directory that does not exist on the system).

The 403 Forbidden custom error page

If you decide to use `allow` and `deny` directives to respectively allow or deny access to a resource on your server, clients who are being denied access will usually fall back on a `403 Forbidden` error page. You carefully set up a custom, user-friendly 403 error page for your clients to understand why they are denied access. Unfortunately, you cannot get that custom page to work and clients still get the default Nginx 403 error page:

```
server {
    [...]
    allow 192.168.0.0/16;
    deny all;
    error_page 403 /error403.html;
}
```

The problem is simple: Nginx also denies access to your custom 403 error page! In such a case, you need to override the access rules in a location block specifically matching your page. You can use the following code to allow access to your custom 403 error page only:

```
server {
    [...]
    location / {
        error_page 403 /error403.html;
        allow 192.168.0.0/16;
        deny all;
    }
    location = /error403.html {
        allow all;
    }
}
```

If you are going to have more than just one error page, you could specify a location block matching all error page filenames:

```
server {
    [...]
    location / {
        error_page 403 /error403.html;
        error_page 404 /error404.html;
        allow 192.168.0.0/16;
        deny all;
    }
```

```
location ~ "^/error[0-9]{3}\.html$" {
    allow all;
}
}
```

All your visitors are now allowed to view your custom error pages.

400 Bad Request

Occasionally, you may run into a recurring issue with some of your websites: Nginx returns `400 Bad Request` error pages to random visitors, and this only stops happening when visitors clear their cache and cookies. The error is caused by an overly large header field sent by the client. Most of the time this is when cookie data exceeds a certain size. In order to prevent further trouble, you may simply increase the value of the `large_client_header_buffers` directive in order to allow larger cookie data size:

```
large_client_header_buffers 4 16k;
```

Location block priorities

The problem frequently occurs when using multiple location blocks in the same server block: configuration does not apply as you thought it would.

As an example, say you want to define a behavior to be applied to all image files that are requested by clients:

```
location ~* \.(gif|jpg|jpeg|png)$ {
    # matches any request for GIF/JPG/JPEG/PNG files
    proxy_pass http://imageserver; # proxy pass to backend
}
```

Later on, you decide to enable automatic indexing of the /images/ directory. Therefore, you decide to create a new location block, matching all requests starting with /images/:

```
location ^~ /images/ {
    # matches any request that starts with /images/
    autoindex on;
}
```

With this configuration, when a client requests to download /images/square.gif, Nginx will apply the second location's block only. Why not the first one? The reason being that location blocks are processed in a specific order. For more information about location block priorities, refer to the *Location block* section *in Chapter 3, HTTP Configuration*.

If block issues

In some situations, if not most, you should avoid using if blocks. There are two main issues occurring, regardless of the Nginx build you are using.

Inefficient statements

There are some cases where if is used inappropriately, in a way that risks saturating your storage device with useless checks:

```
location / {
    # Redirect to index.php if the requested file is not found
    if (!-e $request_filename) {
        rewrite ^ index.php last;
    }
}
```

With such a configuration, every single request received by Nginx will trigger a complete verification of the directory tree for the requested filename, thus requiring multiple storage disk access system calls. If you test /usr/local/nginx/html/hello.html, Nginx will check /, /usr, /usr/local, /usr/local/nginx, and so on. In any case, you should avoid resorting to such a statement. For example, by filtering the file type beforehand (for instance, by making such a check, only if the requested file matches specific extensions):

```
location / {
    # Filter file extension first
    if ($request_filename !~ "\.(gif|jpg|jpeg|png)" {
        break;
    }
    if (!-f $request_filename) {
        rewrite ^ index.php last;
    }
}
```

Unexpected behavior

The if block should ideally be employed for simple situations, as its behavior might be surprising in some cases. Apart from the fact that if statements cannot be nested, the following situations may present issues:

```
# Two consecutive statements with the same condition:
location / {
    if ($uri = "/test.html") {
        add_header X-Test-1 1;
        expires 7;
    }
    if ($uri = "/test.html") {
        add_header X-Test-1 1;
    }
}
```

In this case, the first if block is ignored and only the second one is processed. However, if you insert a *Rewrite module* directive in the first block, such as rewrite, break, or return, the block will be processed and the second one will be ignored.

There are many other cases where the use of if causes problems:

- Having try_files and if statements in the same location block is not recommended as the try_files directive will, in most cases, be ignored.

- Some directives are theoretically allowed within the if block but can create serious issues, for instance, proxy_pass and fastcgi_pass. You should keep those within location blocks.

- You should avoid using if blocks within a location block that captures regular expression patterns from its modifier.

The origin of these problems comes from the fact that while the Nginx configuration is established in a declarative language, directives from the Rewrite module such as if, rewrite, return, or break make it look like actual scripting. In general, you should try to avoid using directives from other modules within if blocks as much as possible.

Index

Thank you for buying
Nginx HTTP Server
Second Edition

About Packt Publishing

Packt, pronounced 'packed', published its first book "*Mastering phpMyAdmin for Effective MySQL Management*" in April 2004 and subsequently continued to specialize in publishing highly focused books on specific technologies and solutions.

Our books and publications share the experiences of your fellow IT professionals in adapting and customizing today's systems, applications, and frameworks. Our solution based books give you the knowledge and power to customize the software and technologies you're using to get the job done. Packt books are more specific and less general than the IT books you have seen in the past. Our unique business model allows us to bring you more focused information, giving you more of what you need to know, and less of what you don't.

Packt is a modern, yet unique publishing company, which focuses on producing quality, cutting-edge books for communities of developers, administrators, and newbies alike. For more information, please visit our website: www.packtpub.com.

About Packt Open Source

In 2010, Packt launched two new brands, Packt Open Source and Packt Enterprise, in order to continue its focus on specialization. This book is part of the Packt Open Source brand, home to books published on software built around Open Source licences, and offering information to anybody from advanced developers to budding web designers. The Open Source brand also runs Packt's Open Source Royalty Scheme, by which Packt gives a royalty to each Open Source project about whose software a book is sold.

Writing for Packt

We welcome all inquiries from people who are interested in authoring. Book proposals should be sent to author@packtpub.com. If your book idea is still at an early stage and you would like to discuss it first before writing a formal book proposal, contact us; one of our commissioning editors will get in touch with you.

We're not just looking for published authors; if you have strong technical skills but no writing experience, our experienced editors can help you develop a writing career, or simply get some additional reward for your expertise.

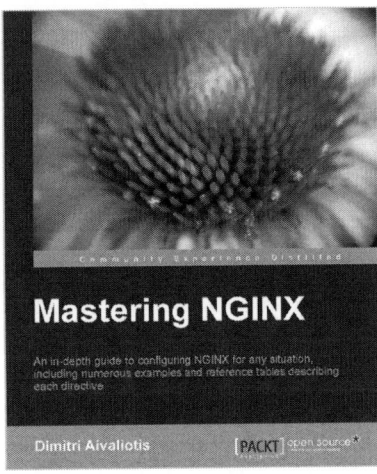

Mastering NGINX

An in-depth guide to configuring NGINX for any situation, including numerous examples and reference tables describing each directive

Dimitri Aivaliotis

Mastering Nginx

ISBN: 978-1-84951-744-7   Paperback: 322 pages

An in-depth guide to configuring NGINX for any situation, including numerous examples and reference tables describing each directive

1. An in-depth configuration guide to help you understand how to best configure NGINX for any situation

2. Includes useful code samples to help you integrate NGINX into your application architecture

3. Full of example configuration snippets, best-practice descriptions, and reference tables for each directive

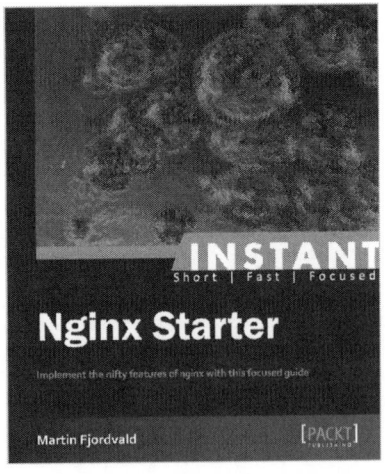

INSTANT
Short | Fast | Focused

Nginx Starter

Implement the nifty features of nginx with this focused guide

Martin Fjordvald

Instant Nginx Starter

ISBN: 978-1-78216-512-5   Paperback: 48 pages

Implement the nifty features of nginx with this focused guide

1. Learn something new in an Instant! A short, fast, focused guide delivering immediate results.

2. Understand Nginx and its relevance to the modern web

3. Install Nginx and explore the different methods of installation

4. Configure and customize Nginx

Please check **www.PacktPub.com** for information on our titles

Printed in Great Britain
by Amazon.co.uk, Ltd.,
Marston Gate.